Rolf and Christel Pistorius

Steiff

Sensational Teddy Bears, Animals & Dolls

Published by Hobby House Press™ Cumberland, Maryland 21502

Photography and arrangement of pictures by Rolf and Christel Pistorius.

Reproduction: reproteam gmbh, Weingarten
Printed in Germany

Translation: Marianne B. Brazee-Hägeli

ISBN: 0-87588-356-7

Table of Contents

For our playmates
Petsy
Zottynchen
Bambi

who "were born" in Giengen in 1954,
who accompanied us through our childhood,
and who, 30 years later, turned us into happy collectors.

Preface

The reproduction of people and animals for use by children in play may be as old as man himself. Excavations in the Lone Valley, not far from Giengen, revealed miniatures of ice-age mammals as well as carved bone pieces that had been used as children's toys. The main materials that were used initially for the production of toys were wood, paper, sheet metal, cardboard and papier-mâché. Margarete Steiff discovered that felt, in combination with sheep's wool (later excelsior), was perfect for the production of her first animals with a soft stuffing. They were first used as pincushions for housewives and later as toys for children.

The collecting of plush animals is nothing new. Those cuddly animals are very cute, and their soft coats beg to be petted. For most adults, the animals hold memories of their youth and are, therefore, dear to them. Very often these toys accompany people from the day of their birth to the end of their lives. Those who claim that these animals are nothing but lifeless pieces of material with excelsior personalities, obviously have never gazed into the eyes of a shaggy playmate, its coat worn off by hugs and the overwhelming affection bestowed on it through the years. Steiff animals and teddy bears are especially enchanting. It has always been something special to give or receive a Steiff animal. These highly-valued toys have been capturing the hearts of children for over one hundred years. But not only children, as adults throughout the world have been enchanted as well. Often the teddy bear that is now hugged by a grandchild used to be Grandma's dearest companion. Who would disagree? Steiff animals do have a soul!

With this book we would like, for the first time, to introduce to the connoisseurs and collectors of Steiff animals one of the most extensive collections of Steiff animals and Steiff teddy bears in Germany. We are introducing not only the unknown and rare, but also the popular animals, teddy bears and other toys produced between 1880 and 1980, exclusively from our own collection. This information is based on four years of research conducted on approximately 5000 items. All historical photographs are taken from our extensive archives, from our collection of Steiff anniversary publications, commemorative publications and old newspapers. These constitute the basis for this work. The collector will find the answers to many questions concerning the collection of Steiff animals in a special index, since we know very well from our own experience the specific concerns of the collector.

Unfortunately we were not granted access to the Steiff archives, despite excellent contacts within the Steiff company, because of its commitments to another publication. Without a doubt, the archives of the company would have presented an additional source for research. We have researched all the important points with the greatest care and to the satisfaction of serious collectors, basing our findings on our documents. However, this book does not claim to be complete. Keeping in mind that by 1913, thousands of different kinds of toys had already been produced and that by 1907, 1.7 million animals had been manufactured by Steiff, such a claim of perfection would be truly presumptuous. To have described this diversity completely and to the minutest detail and to have photographed all of it would have been simply impossible.

This book is essentially a work of reference for the collector. It contains an extensive cross-section of pictures presenting Steiff products stemming from over a century of Steiff manufacturing. This book is clearly arranged, organized by the characteristics of production and recognition and lists the animals by groups. This makes it easy to find the answers to specific questions very quickly. But even the general public, those not interested in collecting, will recognize playmates or dreams from childhood in the carefully arranged scenes.

Christel and Rolf Pistorius

Bambi in the Rain — How We Became Collectors of Steiff Animals and Teddy Bears

It is probably a part of human nature to rediscover things that we were fond of in our childhood. Therefore, it took but a small impulse from our memories to expand our collection from a few small animals and two teddy bears from the 1950s to a large number of Steiff toys within four years. Indeed, we have fond memories of the moment that triggered our great passion for this hobby. We had visited a flea market and discovered a small *Bambi* that was standing on one of the vendor's tables between kitchen utensils and other used junk, soaking wet from the rain. For the first time we were made aware of the fact that this *Bambi*, an animal which we ourselves had known and owned as a toy in the 1950s, was now a collector's item for adults. We dug out the plush animals of our own childhood, played with them and were happy that they had survived our previous efforts to throw away things from the past. Especially welcome as two dear friends were the two teddy bears *Zottynchen* (Steiff name: *Zotty*) and *Petzi* (Steiff name: *Original Teddy*). Our interest and sense of adventure was heightened further when a collector told us that old Steiff animals were practically impossible to find. We wanted to prove him wrong and began searching toy stores for older Steiff toys. Now and then we were successful, but we could hardly believe our luck when we found over 100 animals, dusty and forgotten in a drawer in one of the stores. Now we had a good foundation for a collection and through persistent and resourceful searches, we managed to build a collection of a thousand different Steiff animals in our first year.

Wedding of the Bears

Like most collectors of teddy bears and Steiff animals, we started collecting quietly and almost secretly, with little or no contact with other collectors. Friends and relatives made light of our unusual hobby and dismissed it as a mere diversion. However, this inspired us to celebrate our wedding in the spirit of our hobby, imitating the wedding of the bears in America at the beginning of this century. Legend has it that the wedding table in Theodore Roosevelt's house was decorated with a small plush bear from Giengen. The bear was given the name "Teddy," derived from the president's first name. Accordingly, we decorated the hood of our car with a large white teddy bear perched in the middle of a flower arrangement. Our childhood bears Petzi and Zottynchen were even allowed to come to church with us, wearing tuxedo and wedding gown with veil, of course. In fact, the tallest guest at our wedding was a Steiff *Petsy*, standing 8ft (2.4m) tall, who greeted the guests in front of the hotel entrance. Small teddy bears, dressed as bride and groom, held the name cards of the guests at the dinner table. The wedding cake was in the shape of a bear, decorated with a playful bunch of small

Christel and Rolf Pistorius with their tallest wedding guest, *Petsy*, vintage 1984.

brown bears made of marzipan. The wedding presents consisted almost exclusively of teddy bears for our collection. This somewhat unusual celebration was filmed by a team of the ZDF ("Zweites Deutsches Fernsehen," one of the German television stations) and later broadcast as part of the program "Teleillustrierte." Thus, even skeptics who had never before heard of our field of collecting were enthusiastic and our ideas were no longer considered "off-the-wall." By now, the collecting of Steiff toys is quite common and is becoming more and more popular.

Since not every collector has sufficient information available concerning the Steiff topic, we established the first Steiff animal consultancy at the International Collectors' Fair in 1987. Because of considerable response, it was repeated in 1988. We offered an opportunity to collectors, fans and friends of Steiff animals to come to us for advice and we exhibited parts of our collection.

We have systematically expanded our network and today offer consulting to collectors as well as expert opinions on Steiff toys all over Germany. We have been interviewed by the media and have exhibited parts of our collection. We have contributed to a TV production on teddy bears with our bears cast as the protagonists. Our teddy bears and animals had a truly unique experience when they were flown to Berlin with us (the large animals were transported by truck) in order to participate in the rather zany TV show "Hard to Believe." The host of the show, Pit Weyrich, introduced us and a part of our collection to the studio audience and viewers at home. All of these events have led to many more contacts with collectors and contributed to our reputation as experts on Steiff animals and teddy bears.

Zottynchen and *Petzi* as bride and groom, 1985.

Historical Overview

Margarete Steiff — Founder of a Global Company

Margarete Steiff, 1847-1909.

In the middle of the last century Giengen was a small town in the countryside of Wurttemberg, about 30 kilometers north of Ulm. Its inhabitants consisted mainly of farmers, weavers and other craftsmen. The little town had about 2000 inhabitants, and many of the families were related.

Apollonia Margarete Steiff grew up in Giengen. She was born on July 24, 1847. Her father was Friedrich Steiff, a construction foreman, and her mother was Marie Margarete Hähnle-Steiff. When she was 18 months old, Margarete fell ill. She suffered from a fever of unknown origin. Because of that illness, her legs lost all strength and her arms were left very weak. As she got older, the neighbors in the Ledergasse became used to seeing "Gretle," as Margarete was called, sitting in a small cart in front of the house. The little girl would have loved to run around with her two older sisters and her younger brother. Her mother became more and more worried about her. The money the children would inherit one day from their parents would not be sufficient to take care of the sick Margarete.

Margarete's father spent a lot of time traveling and he often talked to a great many people in an attempt to find a doctor who could heal his daughter once and for all. Finally, he heard about a famous doctor in Ulm. The adventurous trip by stagecoach to Ulm was the first exciting experience for the girl. After a long examination, the doctor determined that Margarete's mysterious illness was polio, a disease which, at that time, had no cure.

Unfortunately, an operation at a later date and several visits to spas in the Black Forest in 1856 and 1857 did not improve her condition. Margarete remained tied to her wheelchair.

Despite the odds, however, her mother decided that Margarete should at least go to school. Every morning her siblings pulled her to school in her little cart and a neighbor carried her into the classroom. Margarete was a good student, and soon her grades were above the average of the class.

After her confirmation, Margarete asked her father for permission to attend sewing classes. This endeavor proved to be much harder for her than it was for her sisters with their healthy arms. Her first attempts were extremely frustrating. The strength in her right arm was not sufficient to turn the wheel of the sewing machine. Being resourceful, Margarete tried to turn the machine around so that she could sew with her other, stronger arm. In this manner she learned everything in a short time: how to sew linens and clothes, how to knit and mend, how to embroider and how to work with felt.

In a few years she learned so much in the sewing lessons that she was a perfect seamstress. Her sister, Pauline, opened a store for ladies' apparel, and Margarete worked there with her. In 1865, the girls owned the only sewing machine in Giengen. In the following years Margarete sewed brides' outfits for friends and acquaintances in town and the surrounding areas.

In order to balance her daily sewing routine, she invested a lot of energy in learning to play the zither and became so proficient, she even ended up giving lessons.

In 1868, Margarete opened a ladies' apparel and clothing store in the house of her parents. Starting in 1877, she ran a small store on her own, selling ready-to-wear clothing made from felt. Her small shop soon became well-known. The first assistants had to be hired. Women's slips, coats for children and *Wandtaschen* were manufactured from a felt that was produced by an uncle in Giengen. The store's profit kept increasing, with the first larger shipments sent to Stuttgart, and soon a small factory was envisioned. In her first year, Margarete Steiff had purchased felt for 3,065 DM from Vereinigte Filzfabriken (United Felt Manufacturers), with whom she had close ties. Her brother, Fritz, started a family of his own and his six sons brought life and mischief into Aunt Margarete's shop. People liked to work there. The seamstresses were not merely brought on as hired help; people were poor here on the Schwabische Alb, and many married women had to work to supplement their husbands' income. In the Steiff home they found an open ear for their sorrows. Margarete helped everybody in her own way, just as she handled her own troubles. On November 30, 1880, and again on December 14th, a small ad appeared in the *Brenztalbote* advertising Margarete Steiff's business.

Kleiderfilz von 2 ℳ 20 ₰ pr. m an,
zugeschnittene Damenunterröcke
und Garniturstreifen,
fertige Damen- & Kinderunterröcke
in großer Auswahl,
Herrenschlafröcke, Knaben-
Ueberzieher,
Kinder-Mäntel und Jäckchen
empfiehlt und fertigt nach Maaß [96]
Margarethe Steiff.

Newspaper advertisement in *Der Brenztalbote*, November 30 and December 14, 1880.

Around 1880, Margarete happened upon a pattern for an elephant in a fashion magazine. She made the elephant out of felt, stuffed it with the best virgin wool and put a small blanket on its back. She gave those elephants to adults for Christmas and birthdays, to be used as pincushions. The children, however, loved the elephants as toys, and Margarete received more and more requests for the pincushions. On December 29, 1880, the first eight elephants were sold. Whenever time allowed it, a stock of the small animals was made in the shop. Margarete's brother, Fritz, had a great idea. He decided to take a bag full of elephants to the next Christmas market in Heidenheim to see if they would sell. He did not bring a single one back home.

For the children, who until now had known nothing but wooden horses, toys made of sheet metal and dolls with heads made of papier-mâché or porcelain, this soft and cuddly animal was something new. Even the smallest children were allowed to play with them. Margarete Steiff kept trying new patterns. She created animals made of velvet, such as a cat that had a ball hidden inside its body so that it made a purring noise when moved.

In 1886, the first patterns for riding and pull toys were created.

Her parents' house was now too small for the business. Her brother, Fritz, who was now attending a school for construction, encouraged her to build her own house. In 1889, a beautiful business building was erected in the Muhlstrasse. And Margarete's collection kept growing. She added dogs, a cute pink pig, monkeys, donkeys and camels. The use of felt increased dramatically, as did the sale of animals, from those first 8 elephants to 5480. The first catalog was published in 1892. Finally, on March 3, 1893, the company was registered and the first orders from Berlin and foreign countries arrived.

Margarete Steiff's first sewing room, re-created according to the original in 1957 in Giengen.

Partridge as paperweight, 9cm (4in), beige velvet. Beautifully painted, brush-painting. Wooden beak, lacquered, around 1898.

The first Steiff doll was manufactured in 1894. It had a body and clothes of felt and an unbreakable head. Margarete's paperweight animals were becoming more popular, as well. In 1894, the first traveling salesman was hired. At this time, the company manufactured colorful roosters made of felt and the animal toys received their voices. In 1895, the first toys were shipped to Great Britain. By 1897, Margarete Steiff had already employed ten workers in her shop and 30 more who were working in their homes. That same year, the Margarete Steiff Company participated in the fair in Leipzig for the first time. This was the starting point for extended contacts with companies abroad. Ever since, the fair in Leipzig has been visited without interruption. A large toy store in St. Gallen invited Margarete personally, and so she made the tiring trip.

Steiff animals gained in popularity both in Germany as well as abroad. Royal families discovered the Steiff toys were the perfect playmates for their children. Everyone realized that the animals had not been created for financial gain; the child was the most important aspect in the mind of the designer. The questions of how the child would carry the animal and how he would place the bird on the table determined posture and expression. Even the smallest children were not forgotten. "Only the best is good enough for our children," said Margarete Steiff, and it was more than just an empty slogan. It was her philosophy, and for an entire century it has remained the motto of the company.

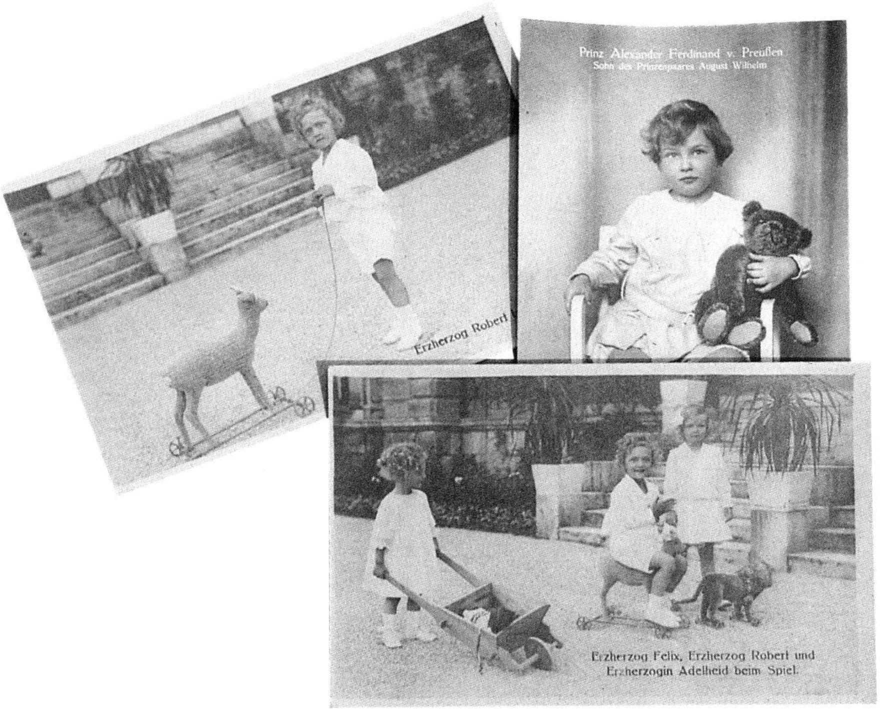

Prince Alexander Ferdinand of Prussia, Archduke Felix, Archduke Robert, Archduchess Adelheid, playing with Steiff animals.

The Nephews

Between 1897 and 1927, the six nephews of the founder entered the company, one after the other, but not without a thorough apprenticeship. Following the wishes of their father and their aunt, they all decided to enter professions that would serve the family business.

Richard Steiff was the first one to join the company in 1897. Ever since his youth he had worked for his Aunt Margarete. After his education at an arts and crafts school in Stuttgart and a business trip to England in 1898, he finally devoted his entire time to the design and production of toys with soft stuffing, contributing many new ideas.

He developed the plans for unusual production buildings made entirely of glass that would make history in the field of industrial architecture. The locals had a nickname for these glass constructions. They called them, only half-jokingly, "Virgin Fish Tanks," based on the fact that the outer walls were made entirely of glass and the majority of the employees were young women. These long and flat buildings of two or three floors let more than enough light into the work areas. The first glass building, the east building, measured 1,080 m2 and was erected in 1901. A second construction was built in 1904, the west building, adding 6,840 ms. The north building added 6,120 m2 in 1908, and finally the woodshop and several additional rooms were finished in 1910, measuring 1,080 m2. These additions brought the total work area to 15,120 m2.

It is Richard Steiff who was credited with the invention of the teddy bear. During his studies in Stuttgart he had seen the cute and playful brown bears at the zoo. He made drawings and clay models of the animals and finally had the idea to create a doll-like bear. As his aunt was looking for new items, he designed one of those bears in the toy animals department. He made it from mohair plush and gave it moving and flexible arms and legs. It so happened that the American President Theodore Roosevelt had a passion for bear hunting. It was during his time in the White House that the first patterns of the new bears were sent to America. In fact, the cute fellows became a national symbol for the president's hunting expedition with the bear eventually being named after the Roosevelt, immortalizing the familiar form of the name "Theodore." Thus, the "teddy bear" was born. Almost everyone wanted such a bear and in the first year of manufacture, 12,000 bears were shipped to America. The teddy bear became world-famous overnight and was to be the corner stone for the further development of the Steiff company.

The idyllic town Giengen on the river Brenz around 1905. The Steiff works (glass construction) in the background.

The Steiff Roloplan, a kite without tail, made of material and that could be folded up, is another one of Richard Steiff's creations from 1908. The kite created a stir at every air show and won many first prizes. The demand was so overwhelming that an entire kite department had to be created.

Together with the painter Schlopsnies, Richard Steiff designed and built large Schaustuecke (for details, see the chapter on Dolls). He had a knack for progressive technology and, therefore, saw to it that the company acquired the most modern and efficient equipment.

Another brother, Franz Steiff, dedicated his younger years to the art of weaving. He acquired valuable knowledge for the production of animals made of textiles and joined the company in 1898. His main responsibilities were the administrative organization of the factory, accounting, the purchase of materials and the increase of sales. He worked in England for several years and established caches of samples in Berlin, Hamburg, Milan, London and Amsterdam. In 1904, he represented the Steiff company at the World Expo in St. Louis. The company won the Grand Prize and Margarete Steiff, as well as Richard Steiff, received a gold medal.

Paul Steiff joined the company in 1899. He had finished an apprenticeship as draftsman and added to his knowledge by attending an arts and crafts school in Stuttgart as well as through an extended stay in the United States. He specialized in creating new shapes, characters and models within the department of design and experiments. In addition, his ongoing studies of animals and great talent led to an almost continual flow of designs for new and much admired animal toys. He took a special interest in the development of a wide variety of animal voices.

After graduating from business college in Cologne, Otto Steiff joined the company around 1900. He was responsible for distribution and spent a lot of time in England. He established the warehouse complex for the mail-order business. Later, he founded branches in New York and Paris and extended the network of sample caches worldwide. He also dealt with the area of advertising.

In 1906, a fifth brother, Hugo Steiff, came on board. He had attended a school of engineering. Purchase orders and quality control were his fields. His main contributions were the preparation of belt production for the widest variety of toy animals, riding animals and especially the sport vehicles. He also paid special attention to the construction of the glass buildings, their expansion and the improvement of productivity and efficiency. Hugo Steiff is also to be credited for preparing the factory for belt production and finally implementing it.

Advertising postcard for the Steiff Roloplan, around 1910

Steiff Zoo around 1910 (advertising postcard — Steiff Button in the Ear).

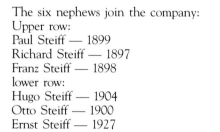

The six nephews join the company:
Upper row:
Paul Steiff — 1899
Richard Steiff — 1897
Franz Steiff — 1898
lower row:
Hugo Steiff — 1904
Otto Steiff — 1900
Ernst Steiff — 1927

On May 30, 1906, a family corporation was formed and Margarete Steiff promoted her nephews, Richard, Paul, Otto and Hugo, to managerial positions.

Her nephew, Ernst Steiff, did not join the company until 1927.

Original print of "Words at the Grave."

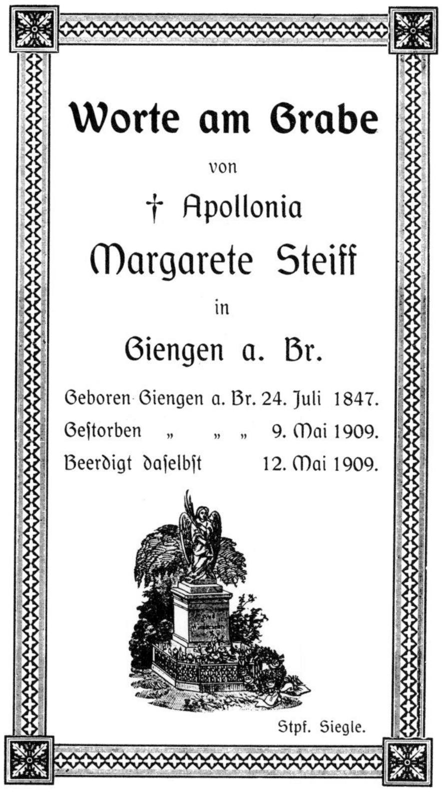

Worte am Grabe

von

† Apollonia

Margarete Steiff

in

Giengen a. Br.

Geboren Giengen a. Br. 24. Juli 1847.
Gestorben „ „ „ 9. Mai 1909.
Beerdigt daselbst 12. Mai 1909.

Stpf. Siegle.

Giengen in Mourning

On May 9, 1909, the flags in Giengen were flown at half-staff. All Steiff relatives and employees were stricken with grief. The founder, Margarete Steiff, the great inventor who handled her great task with such rare willpower, had closed her eyes forever. She had been a great benefactor of the poor and weak and provided income and bread to a large area. Her memory had been engraved in everyone's heart through her kind deeds and personality.

The town's pastor, Stadtpfarrer Siegle, gave this funeral address on May 12, 1909:

"My grace is sufficient for thee: for my strength is made perfect in weakness. Amen. (2 Cor. 12.9.) Dear mourners who have gathered here in the love of the Lord, Jesus. What can we say at this grave? I find it difficult to find the words that could express the effect that this hour has on us, that would do justice to the extent of our loss that we all have suffered. How much our dear **Entschlafene has meant to each and every one of us, without exception. First of all to the family, that has come so far in such a short time and that owes it all to her.

"Then there are a great many employees who are mourning not the loss of a boss, but the loss of a mother. There is a large group of workers whom she has provided with bread and work; and the work was not too much or too heavy, to be sure. And then there are many who are weak, crippled, poor and needy whom she helped with the greatest love, whom she helped build a life or, at least, helped lighten their burden. All those people are crying at this grave. And I tell you: Yes. cry; cry, indeed. It will be a long time before another 'Gretle Steiff' is born. [...]"

Yet, her work is still very much alive. It is continued in the manner in which she would have wanted it: by her nephews and a staff of trained employees, always adhering to her principles of quality.

Albert Schlopsnies on top of the show-piece "Noah's Ark," currently under construction.

Margarete's Life's Work is Continued

In the years following Margarete's death, the company experienced continual expansion. A considerable element in the success of the company were the untold talents and capabilities of the five nephews. They now used their education and practical training to the benefit of the corporation.

In 1908, the first teddy bears with an automatic rumbling bass voice were produced, as well as teddy bears with clothing and a line of coffeepot cozies. The *Purzelbaer* and the *Purzelaffe* with a strong clock mechanism followed in 1909. That same year, a considerable number of figures and caricatures like farmers, policemen, soldiers and the famous Graf Zeppelin were produced as well. The line of character dolls expanded drastically. The cute chimpanzees were also a great success. In 1910, pantom animals were produced for the first time. They were very similar to marionettes. Unmovable mannequins were arranged in a decorative way. They were the predecessors of the mechanical showpieces that were first manufactured in 1910. In autumn of that year, the Wertheim department store in Berlin became the talk of the town for its display of the Steiff circus. There were several arenas and Albert Schlopsnies had modeled it exactly after the Circus Sarrasani.

Between 1911 and 1913 Richard Steiff, together with Albert Schlopsnies, brought some rather funny and peculiar ideas to realization. They produced mainly caricature dolls and mechanical showpieces. The most famous showpieces were those of the fire fighters in 1912 and the "Staedtle" (small town) in 1922.

A new innovation, the Steiff tripod, was introduced in 1911. Together with the Roloplan kite, the tripod made for wonderful aerial pictures.

In 1912, uniform pricing was introduced. The collection grew, and so did profits. Innovative ideas in advertising led to the distribution of small advertising stamps in toy stores, much to the children's delight.

In 1913, the first animals with automatic steering were produced, the collection of dolls and caricatures was expanded considerably, as were the species of animals.

Advertising postcards around 1910, dressed bears and chimpanzees:
Babad: Bear in bathing suit
Babo: Bear in boy's suit
Bagi: Bear in girl's dress
Basa: Bear in sailor's suit
Basi: Bear as female sailor
Baho: Bear wearing pants made of felt
Batro: Bear in a jersey
Baru: Bear in Russian dress
Schiru: Chimpanzee in Russian dress

As it happened, the collection included almost all the animals in Noah's Ark. This was most likely the time when the idea to build Noah's Ark was conceived. It was shown at the "Bauausstellung" in Leipzig and the "Hygieneaustellung" in Stuttgart and was a great success.

In 1913, another feature of flexibility and natural appearance was marketed: *Record Peter.* Wheeled animals were improved considerably.

At the beginning of World War I in 1914, three of the managers were drafted immediately. However, a shortage of production materials was not felt until the period between 1917 and 1921. That period produced Steiff animals made of substitutes: lower quality cloth as well as materials resembling paper. In order to use the many machines and avoid the closing of the company, production for the army started in 1915. Thousands of garrison caps, canteen covers and gas masks were delivered. Later, large numbers of igniter screws were produced in shifts.

The wood shop, too, was busy with the delivery of hand grenade handles. The toys themselves which were produced allowed the children to play war.

"Gala Performance at the Circus Sarrasani": Design by Albert Schlopsnies from the *Illustrierte Zeitung* No. 3561, September 28, 1911.

Fire fighters, designed by Albert Schlopsnies in 1912, introduced in the *Illustrierte Rundschau*: "[...] the main purpose of the presentation of the fire fighters here is to demonstrate the things that Albert Schlopsnies and Margarete Steiff can accomplish when they team up. These are the great artists that made the small town in Suebia, Giengen on the river Brenz, world famous as well as the biggest competitors of Sonneberg and Nuremberg. Whoever is interested in the wonderful dolls of cloth and all the other cute items manufactured by Margarete Steiff, Inc. should request the company's price lists. It is worth the trouble."

STEIFF
KNOPF IM OHR
Unsere Stoffpuppen sind bekannt durch ihre Dauerhaftigkeit, ihre gediegene originelle Wiedergabe, sie sind weichgestopft und gegliedert. — Jedes Stück trägt als Schutzmarke einen Knopf im Ohr.
Junghelden.
(Der kleine Haudegen mit seiner Kriegerschar.)
Größe 28 cm. Figur 3 Ofiz. 28 (Offizier). Figur 1 Fan. 28 (Fahnenträger) 2) Trom. 28 4) Gew. 28 (Gewehrträger). 5) Säb. 28. 6) Käppi 28. 7) Fez 28.
Detailpreis das Stück Mk. 3.60 (nur in Deutschland gültig).
Spielwarenfabrik
Margarete Steiff, G. m. b. H.,
Giengen-Brenz (Württemberg).
Katalog No. 20 kostenfrei.

"The Little Trooper and His Band of Warriors." Advertisement from the *Illustrierte Zeitung* No. 3778.

Dolls in uniform were sold as young heroes, together with soldiers in national and international uniforms.

After the war, the production was rebuilt and reorganized, making best use of the scarce materials available and the remaining personnel. The high pre-war quality of materials and accessories had to be reached again, and slowly but surely this was achieved. But the years until 1920 were hard. Much of the toy production was taken up by toys made of wood such as animals, toy chests and children's furniture. Then, on February 24, 1920, Richard Steiff was elected a member of the Trade Association.

In 1921, the first scooters were produced. First, the Steiff Skiro, then the Steiff Skirit.

The year 1922 produced the Steiff Schlopsnies doll. In 1923, when currency depreciation was at its height, Richard Steiff moved his family to America. He took along his showpiece *Staedtle* which he was convinced would be a success. Albert Schlopsnies and Johannes Schaufelberger (general manager) traveled with him. A very rare and historical memento, a postcard, has been preserved from this trip. Richard Steiff wrote this farewell message shortly before his departure on March 7, 1923, aboard the ship S.S. President Arthur to a colleague and friend in Giengen.

On September 4, 1923, Schlopsnies and Schaufelberger sent their regards from Atlantic City to Giengen. They had visited the Elephant Hotel in Margate City and were overwhelmed by its size. Albert Schlopsnies wrote "[kind regards from this beast of an elephant! Yours, Schlopsnies."

left: Backside of the postcard of March 7, 1923. S.S. President Arthur of U.S. Lines with the signatures of Richard Steiff and Albert Schlopsnies.
right: Postcard of September 4, 1923, Elephant Hotel, Atlantic City, New Jersey. (Remarks on the side by Albert Schlopsnies.)

From left to right:
Popular dogs: *Charly*, 1928, *Treff*, 1928, *Rattler*, 1931, *Bully*, 1927, *Molly*, 1925.
far right: *Fluffy, the cat*, 1926.

Anniversary elephants
From left to right:
Elephant, woolen miniature, 2in (5cm), red cover made of felt, certificate, in transparent box, 100 years Steiff 1980, with anniversary publication 1880-1980, "Past and Present of a Brand."
Elephant, mohair, 2¾in (7cm), No. 6307.00, with red rubberized cover. Inscription: "1880-1955, 75 Years Steiff."
Small brochure: "The First Elephant" and anniversary publication celebrating 75 years Steiff: "The Cradle of the Teddy Bear."
Elephant, felt, with red felt cover and golden paper plaque, imprinted with: "50, 1880 - 1930" with laurel leaves and anniversary publication: "50 Years Steiff Button in the Ear - From the Sewing Machine to the Toy Factory."

Advertisement postcard for toy dealers: An invitation to visit the fall fair in Leipzig, August 30 to September 3, 1931.

In 1923, the factory was expanded once again. This time, several concrete buildings were added.

Beginning in 1925, cats and dogs became the preferred animals. The first one to be presented was the Steiff *Molly*. After 1927, *Bully the Dog* was the biggest sales hit. He was available in many sizes and shapes. *Fluffy the Cat* (1926) was very popular, as well. Plush animals were now preferred to animals made of felt.

Soon the first toy cars were made. Colorful animals became more and more popular, including rabbits, ducks, bears and dogs. *Bully* was even sold in blue.

In 1927, Ernst Steiff, the youngest of the family, returned from America to Giengen after 14 years. He was then given the position of executive secretary in the company.

The new favorites in 1928 were the dogs *Treff* and *Charly*.

In 1929, the driving animals were given a new steering system which was now led through their heads.

In November 1930, the Steiff company and the town of Giengen celebrated the 50th anniversary of the toy factory Margarete Steiff, Inc., with a splendid party. As an anniversary special, a small elephant was produced. This tradition was repeated at the 75th and 100th anniversaries.

In the early 1930s, the small bear *Teddy Baby* was issued in 12 different sizes, and this time made of mohair.

The benefits that the Steiff company offered its married employees should also be mentioned since they were very progressive for their time. Over 20 apartments were set aside in several buildings. These were rented to employees at a special low rent. The employees were also given the opportunity to grow and harvest their own vegetables in nearby gardens. Employees who wanted to build their own homes were given low interest loans in order to encourage such ventures. Furthermore, the company offered a large, well-equipped cafeteria that provided good and inexpensive meals for the many workers. For the people working in serial production, the company offered a break in the morning and the afternoon. At those times, the cafeteria delivered milk and fresh bread. The workers made good use of this benefit.

Towards the end of the 1920s and early in the 1930s, the Steiff company felt the crunch. Production decreased and people were let go. Better materials such as mohair, velvet and felt were replaced in part by substitutes like woolen plush and rougher materials. Although from the mid 1930s to the end of the decade, the portion of mohair increased again, after the end of the decade mohair was replaced increasingly by artificial silk plush.

A major impact on the company and, indeed, on the entire German economy was the beginning of World War II. In 1943, mohair materials were no longer available. Caps were produced in 1944. The majority of the employees had been drafted, which left but a small group to do the work. Finally, the company had to close down due to a lack of raw materials.

Production started up again after the war with much care and effort, using the scarcest resources. Carts, which were often the only means of transportation for the people, were manufactured. They could be paid for with wood coupons, just like folding sports cars for children. At the fair in Leipzig in 1946, the Steiff company at last presented ten items again, all made from artificial silk plush.

After the currency reform of 1948 and the first deliveries of mohair plush, pre-war quality was reached once again. Moreover, the repertoire was extended and improved. In part, the old patterns and cuts were still used, but new patterns were added constantly. Large numbers of plush miniatures were manufactured for collecting purposes. The beginnings of a new economic upswing could be felt. Beginning in 1949, the company was represented at the toy fair in Nuremberg every year.

In 1950, the Office of Pattern Development designed a curled up hedgehog called *Mecki*. From 1951-on, he was part of the official program. *Mecki's* head was made of poured rubber. The Diehl brothers granted Steiff the license for this process. *Mecki* became the symbol of the magazine *HOR ZU* and, together with his wife, *Micki,* he charmed audiences. Just as the early years of the 20th century were known as "Years of the Bear," these years were now called the "Mecki Years."

Also since 1950, a unique zoo has been in the making, with constantly-added new species of animals, known and unknown. From the teddy bear and the raccoon to the tiniest woolen bird, from animal babies to the life-size St. Bernard, almost everything can be found. These new patterns, once again, managed to capture the foreign markets.

In 1953, teddy's 50th anniversary was celebrated with the creation of a new pattern. *Jackie*, as the birthday teddy was called, was sold together with a small brochure.

The "Cozy animals," made of Dralon and used for washing, appear in the catalog for the first time in 1955.

The 100th anniversary of Theodore Roosevelt, whose name the teddy bears carry, led the Steiff company to organize a big "Teddy Festival" in 1958, in conjunction with American instituties and celebrities. A big parade attracted some 25,000 spectators, children's ballets as well as ballets of teddy bears and animals, a German-American children's party, the unveiling of a bust of Roosevelt, the placement of a commemorative plaque at the house of Margarete Steiff and a traveling exhibit of Roosevelt memorabilia were other events that gave the media plenty of occasion and opportunity to make the name "Steiff" and the teddy bear even more popular.

The creative years between 1960 and 1964 produced many new creations such as the lobster, spiders and the bat, all of which are interesting and much sought-after rare toys for today's collectors.

During the 1960s and the 1970s, new shapes and materials were discovered and were incorporated into the manufacturing process. However, in the early 1970s, sales were sluggish because the toy market was flooded with cheap imports. As a result, Steiff attempted to compete with the production of inexpensive items, but the company was not able to gain a significant market share this way. Only at the beginning of the 1980s did business begin to pick up again. The boom of collecting Steiff animals spilled over from America to Europe and the name "Steiff" was now heard everywhere. A special program for collectors was established which added replica and museum items.

Over the span of 100 years, many hands have contributed to the expansion of a small idea into a large factory. Margarete Steiff's work was continued and expanded in the face of every possible obstacle of time, thanks to tenacity, stamina, a willingness to make sacrifices, imagination and faith. The history of the Steiff company is linked to the life story of Margarete Steiff.

Proposal for advertisement in a store window for the occasion of Theodore (Teddy) Roosevelt's 100th birthday. Horse with figure measures 1m (3ft).

Teddy Festival in Giengen to celebrate Theodore Roosevelt's 100th birthday in 1958.

Steiff-Animals as Collectors' Items

Where Can Old Steiff Animals Still Be Found Today?

Years ago we were told by professional collectors that it was hopeless to hunt for old Steiff animals; there simply were not any to be found. It is becoming increasingly difficult to find old animals from the time before the world wars. Should a collector decide to start a collection dating back to before 1940, he must be aware that his collection will grow ever so slowly. Collectors' items that were manufactured after 1949 are much easier to find, of course. Animals from the 1950s and 1960s are still fairly easy to find, especially if they were part of the regular sales program of the Steiff company. They appear in flea markets, toy exchanges and auctions. It is important that the collector keep in touch either with other collectors, with whom he may exchange items, or with dealers who have the opportunity now and then to buy Steiff animals. It is also important to read toy magazines. Steiff products are sometimes offered for sale in the classified ads, as well. Sometimes old animals can be found in toy stores where they were forgotten in storage rooms. These, however, are extremely rare and lucky finds.

If one keeps in mind the great numbers of Steiff items produced in the 1950s and 1960s, one can easily say that, even with a small investment, the variety of animals makes for a beautiful collection. This does not apply to teddy bears and older animals. Unfortunately, many of those were destroyed or thrown away during the wars. But there is, nevertheless, the possibility some teddy bears are still sleeping quietly in attics and cellars.

Steiff Animals: Yesterday's Toys — Today's Antiques

Many a visitor to antique stores is surprised to find, placed in a china cabinet from the 17th century between rare porcelain, glasses or paintings, a totally love-worn teddy bear, sitting between antique jewelry and miniatures. Whether they have been eaten by moths, worn down by the affection bestowed on them or simply weakened by age, Steiff animals are a hit in every condition. In the mid 1970s, the United States was swept by a wave of collectors' enthusiasm for Steiff animals, and European (especially German) toy stores literally sold out time and again.

Especially in demand were items of the 1950s and 1960s that were hidden away in the old caches and warehouses. Today, teddy bears and plush animals appear in the catalogs of famous auctioneers. In Germany, however, the classic collector of Steiff animals did not become known until the beginning of the 1980s. By "classic Steiff collector," we mean a person who chose this hobby out of his love for detail and expression, for the special charm and rareness of a toy. We

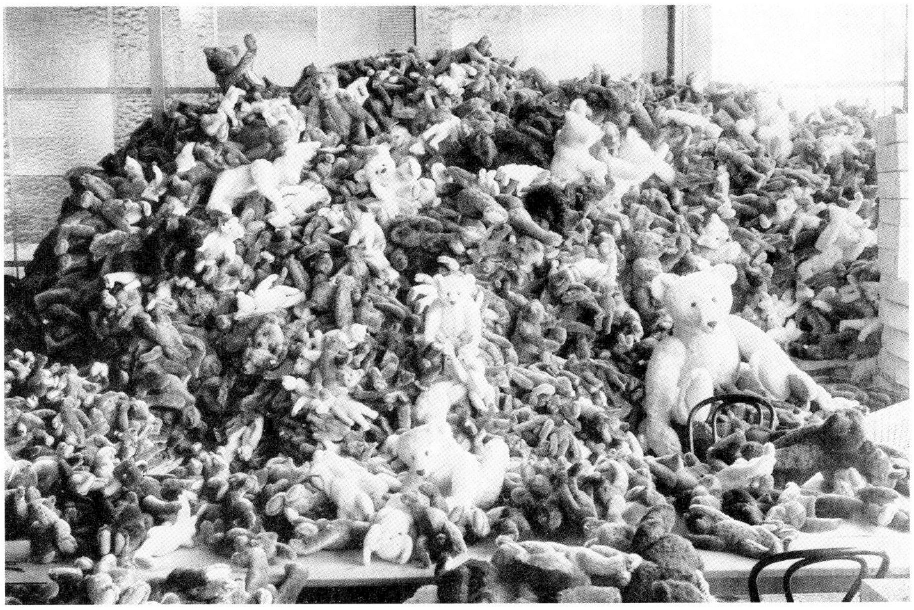

The daily pile of bears at the Steiff factory in 1907.

are not talking about children, teenagers or adults who have collected 10 or 20 animals over a long period of time, which are later sitting on a shelf or in the attic. A collection of old Steiff animals, with their own special development and production story, is a piece of cultural and industrial history. These comforting soul mates of children have turned into an investment that is now much sought-after by interested people in Europe, as well. Although plush is not traded on any stock market, with prices published in exchange reports, the serious collector usually knows quite well how much a collection is worth. Pieces that are 50 years old or older are considered antiques in the toy market and particularly valuable. The older plush animals appeal mainly to adults, who like to remember the companions of their childhood. Often, they have held onto the small animals for decades and are happy to find out that the value of their old toy is much higher today than the sales price at the time of purchase. Many adults have dug out their animals of old and get appraisals to find out the toy's collector's value. The owners have no intention to sell the animal; they simply would like to know the value. This enthusiasm about appreciation is often the first step towards a serious collection. There are collectors who are so taken by their passion that they sink a small fortune into their collection of Steiff animals. Children, on the other hand, prefer current toys. They do not see the past or the memories in old toys and appreciation is not a consideration.

Many years ago the slogan "an animal for life" was created. Had today's Steiff boom been expected back then, the slogan probably would have read: "an animal for four generations."

To Collect Bears, Animals or the Entire Steiff Repertoire?

A new collector often faces the question of the entire repertoire or whether he should concentrate and specialize on one section. Of those interested in the hobby, the percentage of teddy bear collectors in the U.S.A. is about 80 percent, while only 20 percent collect Steiff animals. During the last few years, a growing trend towards collecting Steiff animals was noted in Europe. Each individual collector discovers quickly which area is most attractive to him. The longer a collection is in existence, the more clearly an area of speciality can be discerned. Usually, this is the area that the collector enjoys most. The Steiff repertoire is so extensive that there is something for every taste. Teddy bears that are displayed together with Steiff animals or articles are especially cute and look playful and alive. Collectors of dolls were often introduced to collecting Steiff dolls by the toys' accessories.

It is also very pleasing to collect a certain group of animals. There are dog, cat or rabbit collections, collections of exclusively fairy-tale characters, advertisements or miniatures measuring up to 18cm (7in). No matter how extensive such a selection may be, there will always be surprises in the search and discovery. Certainly, this hobby is a hobby without end. For instance, the main catalog of 1911/1912 already featured 1700 different Steiff animals. A special variety that can be used to establish a collection, known since 1980, are replicas.

Unused or Love-worn?

The opinions about the condition of a collector's item vary greatly. Many collectors do not mind if a teddy bear or animal has been freshly stuffed, repaired or worn out. On the contrary, they see in each "wound" of the teddy bear his special character. They imagine the many small hands that squeezed and petted the beloved teddy.

Others, however, collect only animals that still have the button, the tag and the collar label. This is especially the case in the U.S.A. Of course, every collector is delighted to find a piece that is in mint condition. However, the animals themselves should be the priority, not the tags and buttons. Perfectionism should not be taken to the point where an animal is not bought because it is missing the button or the tag, even though it has been established that it is an extremely rare piece and can probably not be found anywhere else. An experienced collector does not necessarily require these features to recognize a Steiff animal. For the beginner, it might be a little more difficult. It is possible every once in a while he buys the wrong animal and finds out only later that he bought a product by Hermann, Schuco or a plush animal without any brand name. Every new collector has to pay his dues, but the most important thing is that he likes the animal. The brand becomes secondary; the expression is the main point. Whether "mint condition" means the presence of button, tag or collar label, the actual condition of the plush animal, the stuffing, the original eyes, and so forth is what is relevant, is largely a matter that depends on the collector's individual interpretation. Those who have never held a completely unused teddy bear from 1920 in their hands can hardly imagine that such a thing actually still exists. Therefore, they will consider a teddy bear, all worn-out by the love and affection bestowed on him, to be in excellent condition because of his advanced age. It is a question of individual feeling and the experience and knowledge of a collector which plays an important role in his estimate of an animal's condition. When speaking of Steiff animals, one talks often about love-worn veterans. Experience shows, of course, that it is easier to find an animal from 1960 in mint condition than one from 1920 or earlier. A connoisseur who appreciates very old rarities will hardly be bothered by a less than perfect condition. He recognizes the age and possible uniqueness behind it. A teddy's patina may express the deep love of his previous owner. This often awakens memories in the collector which, as a matter of fact, are responsible for his hobby.

Which Factors Determine Rarity?

Which is the rarest Steiff animal? How does one recognize rareness? These questions are asked over and over again and are very difficult to answer. The rarity depends on several factors:

Age Of a Steiff Animal:

The age of a Steiff animal can be determined or, at least estimated by using catalogs, looking at the cut (the placement or shape of the seams), the materials used and, if still present, the markings (button, tag and collar label). The statement "the older, the rarer" usually holds true. But the age is not the only thing that must be considered, since popular animals that were produced from the end of the 1920s until late in the 1930s (e.g. the dogs *Bully* or *Molly*) are certainly more common than, for example, the wolf that was in the sales program in 1964. Age, therefore, is not the only factor. The central question remains: for how long was the respective Steiff animal part of the sales program and in what numbers were they produced?

Two original teddy bears from the 1920s looking at each other; 5in (13cm), yellow/brass, no voice box.
Bear on the left extremely love-worn and robbed of his hair by moths.
Same model on the right, mint condition. They both have a special appeal.

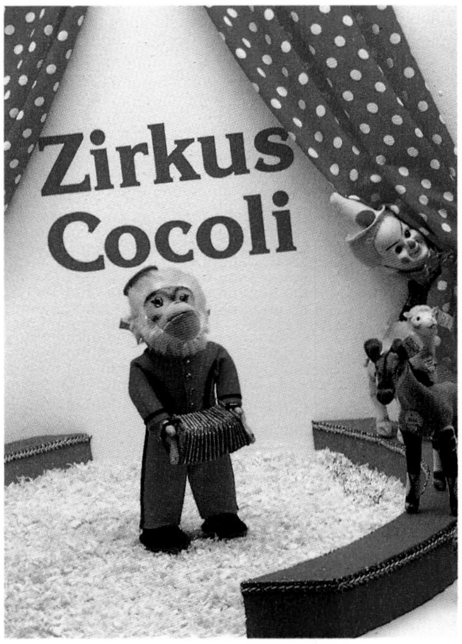

Cocoli, the baboon, 11in (28cm), 1952-1958, section of the Pistorius exhibit "Teddy's Dreamworld," 1988.

Production — Time Span in Sales Program

Exact information about the number of manufactured articles of old Steiff animals is available only in a few cases today. The only method to determine when an animal was added to and removed from the program is the careful review of old catalogs. However, how can a collector who does not possess a complete archive of old catalogs determine whether an animal is rare or common?

There are some very distinct examples, e.g. *Coco*, the gray baboon. He was part of the program for 12 years, but he was not a cute toy for children. On the contrary, his well-defined features and wide open, grinning mouth probably elicited fear or, at least, an uneasy feeling in every child. Furthermore, the intricate pattern and the size of the animal made it relatively expensive. For these reasons it is very difficult to find the gray baboon in mint condition today. Also part of *Coco's* family is *Cocoli*, a well-dressed baboon. He was manufactured for seven years, but in very small numbers. He is rarely found fully dressed and in good condition.

The collector should remember that smaller numbers of animals were produced in the early 1950s than in the 1960s and 1970s. That means that animals from the 1950s are more difficult to find.

How long an animal remained part of the sales program depended, quite naturally, on demand. Therefore, it was obvious that children asked for cute animals, be they pets or animals from the farm or the forest. These were the animals they wished for so they could pet and love them, and these were the animals they were given.

Among them are cats (e.g. *Susi*), dachshunds (e.g. *Waldi*), poodles (e.g. *Snobby*, with customary poodle trim, jointed legs), squirrels (e.g. *Perry*), fish (*Flossy*), turtles (*Slo*), deer and white lambs (*Lamby*). All of them were part of the menagerie for more than 15 years. Since they were very popular, they were produced in large numbers. Therefore, they are also very common.

Uncommon and much sought-after rarities are the advertising articles. These are animals that were produced explicitly for companies, institutions, businesses, and so forth and were not sold in toy stores, nor were they produced in large numbers. Since they were not listed in sales catalogs, they are almost completely unknown and very rare.

Animals with an ambiguous aura are rare, as well. These included skunks, wild boars, donkeys and storks, for example, or exotic animals that were not well-known in the 1960s, such as the okapi, the Indian panda or the gazelle. Also, to this group belong animals that elicit disgust in children, e.g. lobsters, snails, lizards, spiders and snakes.

Most animals that are legendary or larger-than-life are also rare. Among them are *Sigi*, the seahorse, produced only in 1959, and the dinosaurs that were produced in small numbers only in 1958 and sold primarily in the U.S.A. One show piece dinosaur, measuring 4m (13ft), was produced. Certainly, this was an animal that would not fit into many children's rooms. It is, therefore, safe to assume that only very few of those monsters were produced.

Larger animals, those over (25cm) 10in, and show animals, measuring from approximately (50cm) 19½in, were not only less popular for reasons of size, but also because of their cost. Small animals were bought much more frequently. For this reason, the smaller versions of most species were kept in the program much longer than the larger animals.

We can, therefore, generalize that the larger an animal is, the rarer it must be.

Dinosaur No. 635/1299,90, showpiece, length 4m (13ft), circa 1960.

Slim chances for survival for the early Steiff figures made of old rubber.
left: Flawed head of a gnome of the 1950s. The old rubber is deteriorating; the neck has already dissolved and has fallen off the body.
right: It is obvious that the head was attached with a disk (cardboard disk, metal washer and bent-over metal pin). This gnome was not part of the regular program and is, therefore, very rare.

Chances for Survival

The chances of survival for each Steiff animal depends greatly on the degree with which it was played. Much favored animals that were cuddly and petted and squeezed for generations have much less of a chance of survival. Teddy bears take first rank in this category and many a much-loved veteran has ended up in the trash can.

The rubber quality of old, such as that used in the production of the head and body of *Mecki*, dwarves and clowns and so forth in the early 1950s is were very sensitive to direct sunlight and bright light. The figures of this old rubber are, therefore, a very rare find in good condition.

During the creative 1960s, an abundance of new animals from a fantasy world were added to the menagerie. There was the spider with its legs of sensitive chenille and the bat with its thin cape made of synthetic materials. These were all fairly fragile creatures that were not meant for rough play. The use of these more fragile materials corresponds directly to the life expectancy of a plush animal.

Age, production quantities and play value determine the rareness of a Steiff animal. There are many more rare items that could be listed here according to the variety of this area of collection. However, the collector should rely on his own feeling and intuition.

To Recognize and Identify Steiff Animals

Presentation of an advertisement piece for the introduction of the teddy bear, *Dolly*, in 1913. Very ingenious is the oversized left ear which emphasizes the button.

Buttons

"Button in Ear" is a trademark that has made its way as an almost household name and has been an effective advertising slogan from its introduction decades ago until today. The button, always in the animal's left ear, has become an important means of identification and a sign of quality for the collector of plush animals. Unfortunately, many of the buttons have been removed by parents or were lost during some game so that recognition and determination of age have become rather difficult.

Based on research and examples from our own collection, we have determined the following time frames for the different buttons:

The elephant button has been in existence since November 1, 1904. Margarete Steiff informed her clients at that time that her animals would from then on feature in their left ears a button made of nickel embossed with an elephant with an upraised curved trunk. This trademark was in use until 1905.

Between 1905 and 1909 blank buttons were used, measuring 4 or 6mm (.15 or .23in) in diameter. We believe that these animals were not of lesser quality, as were the animals with blank buttons made after 1984.

In 1905/06, the Steiff button was introduced. The name "Steiff" is embossed in block letters, the last F underscored to the E. This button was made through the pre-war years. It was used with hardly any change and few interruptions until 1950 and was attached with prongs. The sizes vary between 4, 5, 6 and 8mm (.15, .19, .23 and .31in) in diameter. An interesting item is the dog, *Bazi*, first produced in 1950, who features an 8mm (.31in) button with the Steiff logo described above and a US flag. The buttons measuring 4 and 6mm (.15 and .23in) in diameter that were made from the end of the 1930s until 1950 show the final F underscored only to the previous F or to the I. Buttons measuring 5mm (.19in) date from after 1926 are not known to us.

left:
Elephant button, from November 1, 1904, until 1905.

right:
Blank button without embossment, 1905-1909.

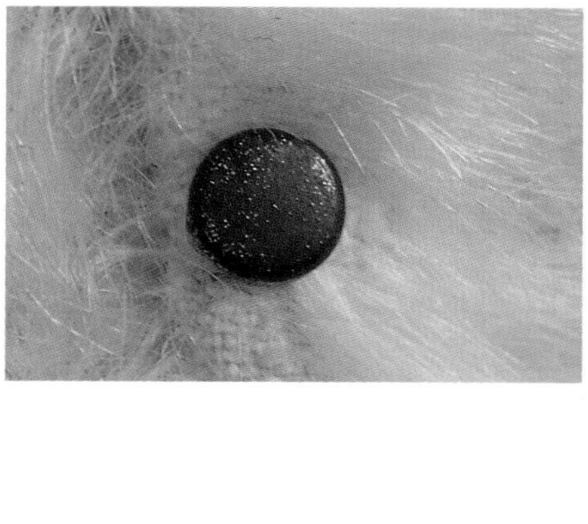

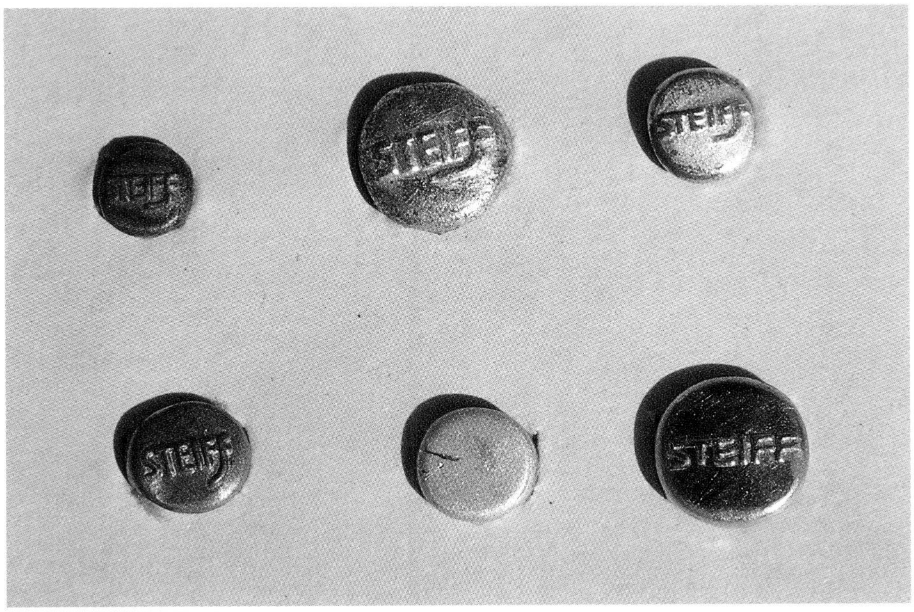

Overview of Buttons, I:
top:
left: pre-war button from 1905/06 until the mid 1920s. Sometimes found to be shiny, of silver color.
middle and right: pre-war buttons as used between the early 1920s and 1950.
bottom:
left to right: pre-war button resembling the color of brass, as used in late 1930s (F not underscored quite as far).
Blank button without imprint, 1946-1948.
Steiff button with block letters without underscored F, 1950-1952.

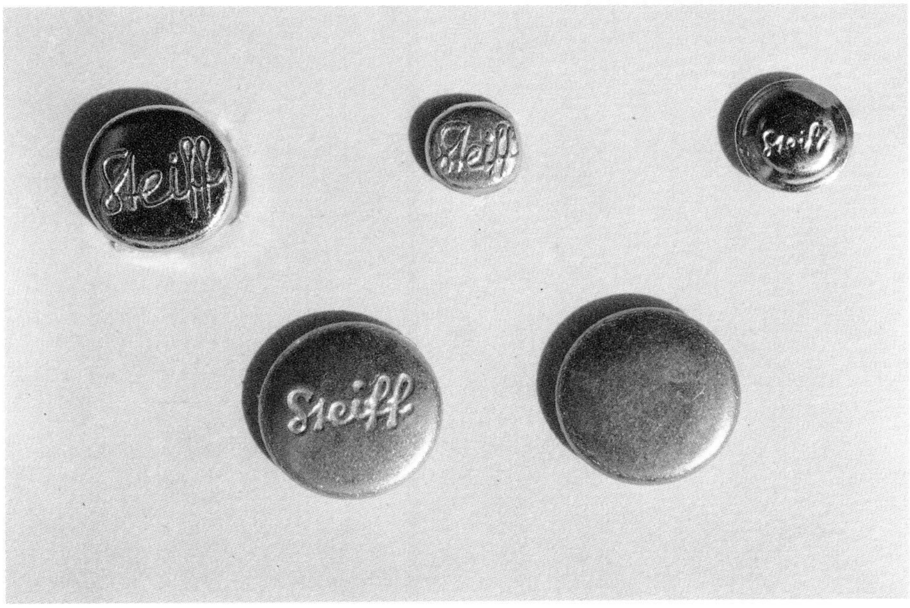

Overview of Buttons, II:
top:
left to right:
post-war button, 1950-1969/70.
post-war button, 1950-1969/70, used in woolen miniatures until the mid 1970s.
lentil button, 1969/70-1978/79.
bottom:
left: Golden brass button in two parts, from 1979.
right: Same button as above, but without Steiff imprint for animals of second quality, from 1984.

The following are some indicators regarding the year of the pre-war buttons. From 1905/06 until the middle of the 1920s, the buttons were originally silver and shiny. With time, however, most buttons turned dark gray. This change was caused by oxidation and peeling of the silver surface and often damaged by pests. Animals manufactured between the early 1920s and 1940 usually featured a button of shiny silver color. Toward the end of the 1930s, pre-war buttons resembling the color of brass were used at various times. Between 1948 and 1950, dull pre-war buttons of a color resembling aluminum were used.

During the 1920s and 1930s the first issue of a production series was given an additional button in its right ear, mostly 6 or 8mm (.23 or .31in), with the imprint "sample." Some of these samples were set aside for fairs or stores, but they were also used by the seamstresses as patterns. In the mid 1930s, a button in the shape of a bear's head appeared for a short time. Between 1946 and 1948 blank buttons, without the Steiff logo, were put into the ears of most animals.

Around 1949, a new Steiff button with closely set block letters and without the underscored F was used. It was of silver color, sometimes dark gray, and measured 6mm (.23in) in diameter. Around 1950, yet another button with drawn-out block letters appeared, also without the underscored F, measuring 8mm (.31in) in diameter and was of a shiny silver color, although this patina sometimes changed due to oxidation. Examples from our collection seem to indicate that they were used as a transition until 1952, both with and without the American flag.

After 1950, the post-war button was introduced. It was shiny and of silver color, flat with embossed writing. Depending on the size of the animals, it measured 4, 5, 6 or 8mm (.15, .19, .23 and .31in). The earlier examples of those buttons sometimes show spots of rust. These post-war buttons were used until 1969-70. However, these buttons were used in woolen miniatures until the late 1970s. The buttons used up to this point were held in place by two prongs.

After 1969/70, silver buttons in the shape of lentils were used (called lentil buttons from here on). The name Steiff was embossed in cursive writing. The lentil button measured either 5 or 6mm (.19 or .23in) in diameter and the backside was made hollow like rivet. It was used until 1978/79. After this period the two-part golden brass button of 9mm (.35in) diameter was used. It was slightly rounded and featured the Steiff name in cursive writing.

After 1984, the same button was used without writing, known as a blank button, for animals of second quality. These are animals which were taken out of the batch because they showed some imperfection at final inspection (e.g. seam not properly aligned, eyes not on the same level, snout features skewed, and so forth). The buyer would often hardly recognize these tiny imperfections. The expression of the animals is almost always flawless.

During the transition period from the lentil button to the two-part brass button between 1977 and 1979, a golden brass button was used for a short time, measuring 5mm (.19in) diameter with an embossed cursive logo, comparable to the post-war button.

The years indicated are meant as general guidelines, since the old buttons were used up even after new buttons were created. It is, therefore, possible that the change in buttons can vary depending on the size of the button. Since small buttons were used for small animals and, since these toys were more common, it can be assumed that small buttons were used up much faster.

In addition, the production of a special stamp, known as an embossing tool, was necessary for the writing. This special effort was not made after World War II, however, which explains the blank buttons in that period. The life span of such button stamps was limited so that they were only replaced by new ones after the old ones were completely worn down. It is, therefore, highly unlikely that there was one set day on which the buttons change from one kind to another.

Flags

The so-called "protection labels" that were attached with the button in the ear are called "flags" in collectors' jargon. The materials used were paper, a special paper laced with fibers in a crisscross pattern, coated linen or woven material. Our guess is that flags were not used until after 1908-1910. Their colors differed according to their age and included white, red and yellow. They also featured different script written mostly in black. Until 1925, the flags were white. Some were made exclusively from paper, others from the laced paper, and still others from paper reinforced by a lattice pattern of threads on the reverse side.

After the time between 1926 and 1934, red flags made from coated linen, similar to wax cloth, were used. If they were faded or exposed to moisture at some time, they will often appear in a shade of orange. We have also found red paper flags on woolen animals. Between 1934 and 1980, the flags were yellow and made from the same material. However, from 1940-1951 light yellow or beige flags were used as a result of the scarcity of materials. They are often mistaken for white flags which, of course, leads to an incorrect age estimate. After 1980, some of the flags were made of woven material and were white and folded. They were used mainly for replicas and special editions. In general, a yellow flag of the same material with red writing was used after 1981. All the other flags mentioned above usually had black writing printed on them.

The imprint on the earlier white flags was limited to the listing of the item number, usually four digits, with the warning "Protected" (geschutzt). We found "Steiff Original 28" on a felt doll measuring 11in (28cm). On early flags there is also the possibility of a two-digit serial number, the item number and the remark "Steiff Original Germany." Unfortunately, the serial numbers are only rarely printed onto the flags. The serial number constitutes the only certain way to distinguish toys among the variety of Steiff animals. The usual wording after World War II reads "Steiff Original geschutzt — Artikelnummer — Made in Germany" (Steiff Original protected — item number — Made in Germany). The reverse side was blank until 1950. Only after that year was it used to indicate the materials used, (e.g. "51% wool-49% cotton").

left:
White flag 1908-10 until 1925. Interesting is the fact that the serial number (86 = pincushion) is printed on the flag as well.

middle:
Red flag 1926-1934

Overview of Flags
left to right:
top:
Red paper flag as used with woolen miniatures between 1931 and 1934.
Yellow flag 1934-1940. For small series, the numbers were sometimes written by hand. Reverse side blank.
Light yellow or cream-colored paper flag between 1940 and 1951. middle:
US flag, 1949-1953/54.
Yellow flags made of coated linen were used between 1950 and 1980. The flag shown below existed until the mid 1950s, then was lengthened by about 1/5in (.5cm) with the words "Preis - Price" added (free space for awards). The item number with the comma was used until 1967.
bottom:
Copyrighted bracelet (used for dolls starting in 1922). In connection with flag and button starting in 1937. The picture shows the version used in rubber figures from the 1950s and 1960s. Yellow flag with space for awards. From the 1950s until 1980. Lentil button 1969/70 until 1978/1979. The item number with a slash was introduced in 1968.
Woven flag made of cloth, folded, from 1981.

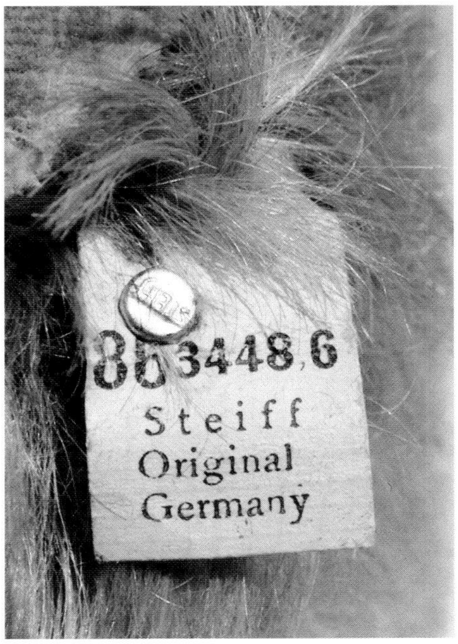

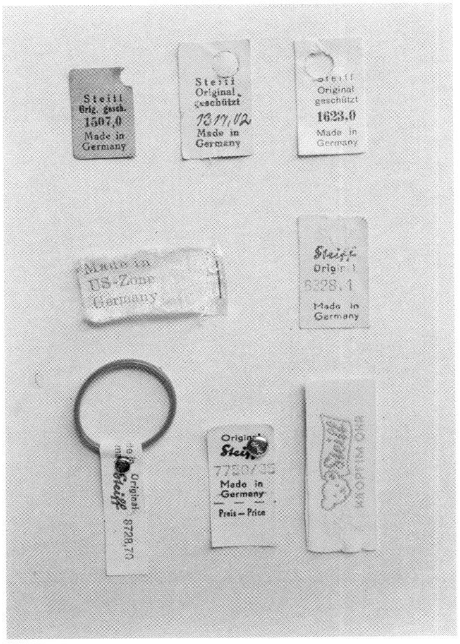

From the mid 1950s, the flags were lengthened by about 5cm (1/5in). They now carry the additional words "Preis/Price" with open space for awards. Felt dolls with pressed faces, *Meckis, Clownies* and many other rubber figures were given a copyrighted bracelet onto which the flag together with the button were attached.

Old animals with the button still in the ear are often lacking the flag. By carefully lifting the button, pieces of the old flag can sometimes be found so that one can determine the age of the animal. Special care is required if the buttons are rusty, however! White or yellow pieces of flags often appear orange or red when touched by rust.

US Flags

A further means of identification are the so-called US flags. This marking had to be attached to every item manufactured after World War II in the US sector of occupied Germany according to US directive. Giengen was located in the US sector and the Steiff company was, therefore, subject to the order. The company solved the problem by attaching a piece of linen or a silk ribbon with the imprint: "Made in US Zone Germany." The tags were sewn into a particular seam of the Steiff animal. The width of the tag measured approximately 1-2cm (.39-.78in), the length 2-3cm (.78-1.18in).

Depending on the shape of the animal, the US flags were more or less visible. In most cases, it was sewn into the seam of the right front leg. This flag frequently in the way when the animal was played with so that it was often cut off. Therefore, only remainders of the flags can be found when the seam is pulled apart in the right spot. The US flags are very helpful in determining the age of an animal since they were only attached between 1949 and 1953. Steiff animals and Steiff teddy bears with a US flag are considered extremely interesting by collectors.

Collar Tags, Information Tags and Trademarks

Collar Tags

The mainly round cardboard signs hanging from the chest, neck or collar of the animals are called collar tags. They are found in a variety of forms and can often be an important factor in determining the age of a toy, if in fact they are still present.

As early as 1898, some of the animals were given tags. In those days, the tag consisted of a round cardboard sign which featured an elephant on metal wheels. It was used until 1902/03. The button was then introduced and the elephant tags were no longer needed. The collar tags were forgotten until 1926. Now they were made of white cardboard with a silver metal edge and resemble the ones used by the company of the Gebrüder Süssenguth in Neustadt, which were used as early as 1925 for *Peter Bär* (*Peter Bear*). The names of the animals are printed in black (e.g. *Molly, Bully, Fluffy*, and so forth) as well as "Steiff Original." In certain cases the item number is added (e.g. 3310) together with an indication that a patent is pending. The white collar tags with metallic edges and diameters of 20 and 30mm (.78 and 1.18in) were only used until 1928 and are now considered rare.

Starting in 1928 the tags had a red edge and the print read "Steiff Original Marke." The head of a yellow bear with square cheeks peeks out of the bottom of the round cardboard tag. His features, the eyes, head and smiling mouth were painted on with fine lines in blue. The inner area of the tag was of beige color with the name of the animal in brown, sometimes even with information such as the date of the patent. This collar tag was not changed until 1950, but we can assume that during the war and the post-war years it was sometimes omitted. These tags appear in diameters of 18 and 30mm (.7 and 1.18in).

The shape of the bear's head changed after 1951. It remained angular, but the blue lines were now thicker. The snout changed quite notably. The cheeks showed indentations where they joined the tag at the bottom of the ears; however, in every other respect the tag remained the same until 1953/54. After 1953, the bear's cheeks become round. Then the tags measured 18, 30 or 50mm (.7, 1.18 or 1.97in). The new tag was first introduced with *Jackie, the Bear,* the first with brown writing which, shortly afterwards, changed to blue. Within the inner circle was printed the animal's name or simply "Original Steiff." This tag did not change until 1971.

After 1972, the collar tag was colored yellow and red and measured 20, 30 or 50mm (.78, 1.18 or 1.97in). It remains unchanged until today on animals which are part of the regular children's program. Only replicas sometimes show a white tag with black writing or a collar tag with the round or angular bear. In general, animals with collar tags are considered more valuable by collectors than animals without tags. This is especially true if the tag features a special animal name and not just "Original Steiff."

left to right:
top:
Elephant mark 1989-1902/03.
Tag with metal edge 1926-1928.
middle:
Bear head collar tag with angular bear head with indentations 1951-1953/54.
Bear head collar tag, bear with round cheeks, 1953-1971, imprint of animal name.
bottom:
Bear head collar tag, bear with round cheeks, 1953-1971, imprint: "Original Steiff" for animals without names.
Yellow and red collar tag since 1972.

Information Tags

Red or blue tags in the shape of a bear's head were used for Schlopsnies dolls in the early 1920s. Other tags can be found on animals with mechanisms in their necks. A cardboard sign explains in three languages the function of the mechanism (see the chapter on dogs, picture on page 87). Musical animals were delivered in the 1920s together with a scroll that provided the buyer with information regarding the musical work. Various tags included information about certain materials (e.g. Dralon) and washing instructions were also attached to the animals from the 1950s through 1970s.

Trademarks

Besides collar tags and information tags, there were a number of other trademarks that appeared in advertising and catalogs. For example, the first catalog, published in 1892, featured a camel being treated very roughly by two boys. This was to demonstrate the sturdiness and durability of the Steiff animals. In those days there were steel frames installed in the animals. In 1898, the elephant replaced the camel as the trademark.

After 1905, the slogan "Button in Ear" sported different characteristics, with various bear head forms following after the mid 1920s. Since these trademarks were hardly ever used as a labeling or marking of plush animals, but rather in catalogs and advertisements, we will not give a detailed description at this point.

Posture and Moving Mechanisms

The popular animals of the Steiff company featured such an abundance of postures that it is necessary to read the original catalogs cover-to-cover in order to be able to collect every pattern. To list all of those for each animal would go too far. For this reason, we would simply like to give some examples of each variety, knowing full well that not every animal was featured in every posture, on wheels or with neck mechanisms.

For each new model a typical posture was designed and the reaction of the customers awaited. Only after the animal had been accepted by the consumers were new postures developed and produced for the same species. The tiger of the 1950s, for example, was available in the following versions:
— sleeping, as a "floppy-animal,"
— lying (curled up),
— sitting with mouth opened and closed,
— standing on all four feet (leaping),
— jointed,
— on wheels.

from left to right:
Tiger standing on all four feet, 1959.
Tiger lying (in half circle), 1953.
Tiger sitting, open mouth, 1959.
below:
Floppy tiger, 1956.
Tiger, jointed 1952.

As a rule, collectors do not appreciate animals in lying and sleeping positions. They are too strongly geared to babies and often have closed eyes of simple stitching which makes them appear lifeless and without expression. They are also very common. Standing animals are very common as well, with third in scarcity the various sitting animals. Jointed animals are considered rare. Due to the intricate manufacturing (each body part had to be sewn separately), they were the most expensive toys and were not bought very often, even though their play value for the children was definitely the highest.

The body parts were jointed with cardboard disks. One disk lies in the body, a second one in the arm, the leg or the head, so that for a fully-jointed teddy bear, ten cardboard disks are required. The disks are secured by a bent metal pin. Since the beginning of the 1980s, washer-safe animals have been equipped with new synthetic joints (*Teddy Petsy*, 1984). The original cardboard disks would not be able to stand the rough treatment of a washing machine for an extended period of time.

The rarest animals are by far those who stand upright, with the exception of *Waldili* who was manufactured for 38 years. They were sold in smaller numbers since they were rather expensive, due to their detailed wardrobe. When these animals are found today, they are often missing the original clothing. It was usually lost during play at some time.

Wheeled animals are considered rare, as well, because of their higher sales price when compared to the animals measuring 10cm (4in) and 20cm (8in). The early wheeled animals were always equipped with a wooden frame. Later, the frames were made of metal. These animals were stable enough to even carry adults. The early iron wheels of the riding animals with pedals were made of metal strips with a cast hub and riveted spokes. Until the turn of the century, cast iron wheels with four or six spokes were used (even in smaller animals up to 12cm [5in]). There were also wheels with round patterns resembling church windows.

After 1905, animals up to 43cm (17in) had wheels with four spokes, while the wheels of larger animals had six. The axles did not penetrate the early animals' feet or hooves. Later, the metal frame protruded in the form of loops from the bottom of the animals' feet through which the axles were guided. Wheeled animals over 43cm (17in) were reinforced by iron bars running the length of the animal. These connecting bars were welded to the ends of the metal frame after 1905-1908. After the mid 1920s, all frames, even those of the smaller animals, were welded.

In the 1924 catalog an even greater number of wheeled animals were shown. The individual descriptions do not say, however, whether the animals were delivered with iron or wooden wheels. We have found contradictory information. In the general description of the 1924 catalog we read "[b]y using our carefully constructed wooden wheel with the metal hub we have achieved a surprisingly effortless, elegant and almost silent ride. The wheel is lighter but just as durable as the iron wheel." In the 1930 anniversary publication, we found a statement claiming that wooden wheels were used exclusively after 1914 since they could be manufactured in the wood shop of the factory. It is also possible that all the new wheeled animals could not be photographed during the difficult years after World War I; therefore, the old pictures showing animals with iron wheels were shown. We assume that the wooden wheels were introduced gradually between 1914 and 1926 and that the catalogs and pictures were not updated until later. The wooden wheels were at first varnished to preserve their natural color, with some of them displaying the Steiff signature. After 1922-2925, they were lacquered with red, blue or green.

Towards the end of the 1920s, a bronze hub was used for the smaller animals. To achieve greater stability and a smoother ride, disk wheels with lightly colored rubber tires were introduced gradually after 1926/27 in most animals larger than 43cm (17in). The advantage of the tire was the possibility to ride on almost any surface without a problem, such as in an apartment, on a floor or on asphalt. Between the early 1930s and 1952, black tires were used, but after 1952 only white ones. The rubber tires carried the Steiff signature. Over the years, various accessories were added to the riding animals, such as saddles.

Wooden eccentric wheels have been around since 1913. If the rumors are true, they were invented by a careless worker who did not drill the hole in the exact center of the wheel. This caused the wheel to run unevenly, but it also made the sequence of movements of the animals more beautiful and natural.

"In this way the natural movement of the animal — leaping, running or waddling — are copied in the most ingenious way." This was the description in the 1924 catalog. The entire Steiff repertoire was enriched considerably by the addition of animals on eccentric wheels, with the animals that could be pulled increasing in play value. For decades, animals on eccentric wheels remained a sales hit.

In 1913, together with animals on eccentric wheels, animals on the so-called "Hollander" were added to the menagerie. When they were pulled, they made funny rowing movements and were also called Record animals. At first there was only *Record Peter*, the chimpanzee, measuring 20, 25 and 30cm (8, 10 and 12in) and *Record Teddy*, available in a 25cm (10in) size. In the early 1920s, they were followed by riding Record felt dolls, such as *Max* and *Moritz* (the Katzenjammer Kids), *August*, *Struwwelpeter*, and *Puck the Dwarf*. In 1925, the white chimpanzee was added and in 1926 came *Felix the Cat*. Towards the end of the decade, *Rabbit*

Record Teddy, 1913. The sequence of movements is clearly visible. Advertisement in the *Illustrierte Zeitung*, August 7, 1913.

and *Petsy* joined the group and in the early 1920s *Teddy Baby* and *Orangu*. After 1945, only the rabbit *Record Hansi* (until 1962) and *Record Peter* (until the beginning of the 1970s) were produced. After 1926, vehicles with clockworks to wind up were taken into the program. These four wheeled animals included the white chimpanzee, *Urpeter* and the teddy bear, *Urteddy*. On three wheels were the brown chimpanzee, *Urfips* and the felt boy, *Urboy*. They are considered extremely rare. Jointed animals and figures with clockworks were available as early as 1909. They were chimpanzees, Eskimos and bears. They could be wound up by turning their right arm and do somersaults as a result. A special feature was their weight, with toys such as *Purzelbär*, 23cm (9in), weighing 530gm (19oz). This far outweighed the average teddy bear of that time, which stood 22cm (9in), but weighed only 280gm (10oz). By 1916, the *Purzelschimpanse* (chimpanzee) is the only one left in the program, and even his days were numbered. Production stopped completely after World War I. In 1934/35 another *Purzelbär*, this one blonde and measuring 18 or 23cm (7 or 9in), was made available once again. His success was rather modest and in 1936, it was taken out of the program. A third attempt was made with *Turbo Teddy* in 1951. His legs were not jointed but rather, fixed at an angle so that he was in a sitting position. We were only able to find him in an American novelty catalog of 1951 without his felt vest. There was no mention of him in German catalogs so that we assumed that he was produced exclusively for sale in America. However, we do know of single items in Germany that feature a red felt vest. *Turbo Teddy* was caramel-colored and had glass eyes. All of the somersault animals and figures are considered very rare.

Animals with neck mechanisms from the 1931 catalog listing addenda to the main catalog of 1929.

Nodding animals on eccentric wheels were first available in the main 1929 catalog. The head was connected to the eccentric axle which caused the animal to nod its head. Available were a polar bear 22cm (9in), an elephant 22cm (9in), a lamb 25cm (10in), and a goat 28cm (11in). They were part of the program for a very short time and are very rare.

In the addenda catalog published in 1931, the first animals with new head movements through a copyrighted neck mechanism were introduced. The mechanism was described as follows "[t]he simplicity of the handling is remarkable. The mechanism is unbreakable and allows play in many positions and with various expressions typical for the animal by simply turning the patented spring hidden in the tail. If the animal is held in the left arm and the right hand turns the tail in a manner invisible to the spectators, it is possible to perform entire pieces for handpuppets. For example the monkey Fips is moving happily and full of mischief, the elephant is playing with his trunk, Molly, Bully and Rattler beg, lie in wait or are angry. Kitty the Cat is cuddling, etc."

Using a mechanism in the neck of plush animals was nothing new. The Schuco company had invented a few years before the well-known Yes/No-mechanism and had introduced it successfully into the market. The Schuco mechanism allowed for a flawless Yes/No movement of the head by moving the tail of an animal. The Steiff mechanism, however, allowed a circular movement of the head by turning the tail. Even today we have not found a defective mechanism in a Steiff animal, even if it had been played with extensively. In fact, even if the animal had gotten damp, the movement mechanism still worked perfectly although grinding noises could be heard when turning the tail. Animals with neck mechanisms are considered rare because they were not bought very often due to their relatively high price in the 1930s. They were about 20 percent more expensive than a comparable animal without a mechanism. Although in 1931, 31 models were available in a total of 152 sizes and colors, by 1939/40 only *Rattler the Dog, Kitty the Cat*, and the polar bear, which was only produced in 1939/40 were still sold in a total of 13 different sizes.

In the mid 1930s, animals and dolls with snap joints entered the program. They were capable of amazing metamorphoses. A hinge-like construction in the upper leg made it possible to stretch the leg completely to the front and to stay in place. A slight tap brought them back into the initial position so that the animal or the doll could stand upright. Best known are the circus elephant (insertion of hinge allows opening of mouth) and the circus bear, both of which also feature neck mechanisms. The heads of Steiff dolls were made of celluloid and their bodies of felt, but they did not have the mechanism. They were only in the program for a short time, while the elephant and the bear were included until 1938. They are all considered to be very rare.

The fact that the Steiff company manufactured marionettes is hardly known. In 1910, chimpanzees in sizes of 25, 28 and 35cm (10, 11 and 14in) and bears measuring 25 and 28cm (10 and 11in) were available as so-called "Pantom animals." Further interesting creations in the same context were:

— Animals with ball-joint neck, e.g. polar bear and pig from 1909,
— rabbits with jointed ears from 1911, gallop animals: two animals or an animal and a figure are attached to a riding frame (on wooden wheels) and when pulled go through funny galloping movements; novelty 1925,
— Charleston animals ("floppy animals" made of colorful velvet) from 1927,
— drinking cat with dish "squeeze her body and she will drink" (text taken from catalog in 1934),
— musical animals with trigger work from the end of the 1920s and in the 1950s (only part of the program for a few years),
— riding animals, whose front axle was usually rigid, featured a number of different steering mechanisms, e.g. steering through the animal's head (from 1929).

The variety of postures and moving mechanisms was incredibly wide and probably unmatched in the history of plush animals.

Circus bear, 1936, item No. 12/8332H with snap joints and mechanism in neck.

Expression, Decorations, Painting, Marking

Decoration is the expression used for the method of sewing the nose, mouth and claws onto the animal using yarn or thread of various colors. Also part of the process is the painting of animals, the attachment of eyes and sewing of the ears. Each reader should try to imagine a Steiff animal or a Steiff teddy without any decoration, painting or eyes. The animal would seem to be naked and empty, devoid of all life. Only these additions determine, to a great extent, the animals' expression. The strength of the yarn depended on the size of the animals or the quality of the materials. In earlier years, when the animals were made from velvet and felt, thin cotton threads were used for the decorations. The decorations influenced an animal's facial expression considerably. If the thread pulled too far down to the side of the mouth, teddy bear looked sad and the dog appeared mean. If the thread pulled up higher and more to the side, they would smile and have a friendly look on their faces.

For the modeling and decoration of the first snouts for the initial bears, and as a prototype for the seamstresses, a substance was used that was easy to form, similar to sealing wax. For the first time, the term "gutta-percha" appeared, which was a thickened milky juice from a tree in Malaysia, similar to caoutchouc. Individual teddy bears with leftovers of this material are still around today. They are probably samples. The bears with embroidered noses, however, went into serial production. Pieces of felt were placed underneath the embroidered noses of teddy bears of 40cm (16in) or more (standing) until the end of the 1920s.

The yarns were primarily black and brown, although on white teddy bears they were sometimes light brown, or even beige/pink. *Petsy's* nose was pink embroidered, reinforced by a piece of pink felt underneath the yarn. *Jackie Bear's* snout was embroidered lengthwise with dark brown yarn and a pink stitch running across his nose, as is customary with deer and reindeer. Since the snout decorations of the teddy bears were primarily done by hand, they can differ considerably. Whether they have been sewn lengthwise or from side to side depends on the size and age of the teddy bear.

Manner of nose embroidery:
Until about 1950: up to 35cm (14in) side to side, from 40cm (16in) lengthwise,
1950s/1960s: up to 15cm (6in) side to side, from 18cm (7in) lengthwise,
1970s: 11cm (4in) bending bear side to side, all others lengthwise,
Zottys: always lengthwise,
Teddy Babies: up to 15cm (6in) side to side, from 18cm (7in) lengthwise, (sizes refer to standing animals).

Jointed bears received five claws on their paws and feet until 1905/06, after which they were given only four. Bears who were standing on four feet were given four claws on each foot, *Record Teddies*, three claws and early bears on wheels, five claws on each foot. Other animals like dogs, cats and rabbits usually have three claws, embroidered with bead yarn or painted or sprayed onto the feet. House and wild cats have mainly red or pink noses, while dogs' snouts are usually black and, in a few cases, dark brown.

The painting or marking of an animal was an important factor in the overall expression. Sometimes all it took was a touch of dark brown color or a shadow around the eyes and the belly button (see *Jackie Bear*). The marking of the dromedary of the 1950s and 1960s was very interesting. Only the brown shadows on its legs and feet gave it the true-to-life expression.

top:
Typical nose decoration by Steiff in the 1920s and 1930s.
left: embroidered lengthwise.
right: embroidered from side to side.

bottom:
Typical for Steiff teddy bears before 1905/06 are the five sewn-on claws (teddy, see page 39).

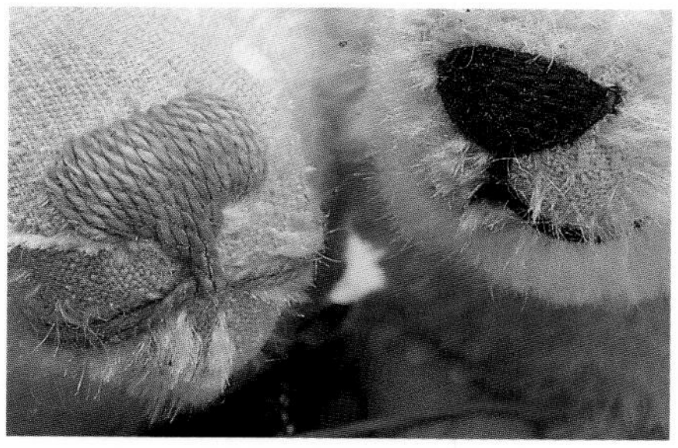

Steiff teddy bear 1905/06, 40cm (16in) (measured standing up), with shoe-button eyes. Stuffed with wool excelsior, no voice, five claws. Very light — 335 grams (12oz) (soles of feet, see page 50, left).

Very old felt and velvet animals were colored by hand with a paintbrush, a technique that is unimaginable today. Furthermore, animals, teddy bears and dolls used to have very strong painted-on features. Therefore, if they have been exposed to very little light, they appear to be almost too strongly painted which gives them an unnatural look. But the fashion trends of those days were responsible for the coloring and the old animals merely retained their original character. Today, some of the cut-out sections of the colorful animals are colored under steam, using water resistant, non-toxic colors. For the final decorations, only small additions are necessary which are done with a spray gun. Whenever the same pattern is needed for large numbers of animals, it is woven directly into the plush.

Since the final look is determined mainly by the fact that the animals are mostly hand-crafted, no animal looks exactly like the other, and teddy bears of the same age and size can vary greatly. Each has his own face. The seamstresses were given a warm-up period of 10 to 12 months. They were paid by the number of finished pieces and did not all work with the same precision. This does not imply that their work was any less than careful but simply means that each seamstress expressed her individual sewing style. A difference of 1-2mm (.04 to .08in) when sewing a seam and an animal stuffed with more or less material made the animal either pudgy or skinny. Deeply seated and tightly sewn eyes, partially covered with plush, make them seem smaller than eyes that were sewn less tightly. If the eyes are placed closely together, the animal has a mischievous look on its face.

Velvet cat as a child's rattle, 1905/09, brush painted, shiny button.

If the ears are far apart, they make the teddy bear into a thinker. Ears can influence the teddy bear's individual appearance quite considerably, too. Whether they are placed closely together on the head or far apart on the sides of the head and whether they are big or small influences teddy's looks distinctively.

However, the final character of the animal or teddy bear is not determined until children have played with it. The teddy bear is touched and petted in the same spots over and over. This leads to bald patches, and mothers fix the worn-out paws with multi-colored material.

Keeping in mind the many factors contributing to the teddy bear's character, it is understandable that it can be rather difficult to determine the exact age of a bear. Much practice and exact observation skills are required to date Steiff teddy bears accurately. It is very helpful to have objects available in one's own collection to compare with so that the collector may study the differing characteristics carefully.

Numbering System and Sizes

NUMMERN-ERKLÄRUNG

Jede Ziffer hat ihre Bedeutung. Die Nummer bezeichnet genau das Aussehen des Tieres nach Serie, Stellung, Stoffart, Höhe in cm und Ausstattung.

Die Zahl vor dem Strich bedeutet die Serie (Tiername) **26**/1328,02 = Foxterrier

Die Ziffern nach dem Strich:
Tausender = Stellung

1 - - -	stehend	**1**343,2
2 - - -	liegend	**2**312
3 - - -	sitzend	**3**317
4 - - -	aufwartend	**4**322
5 - - -	gegliedert	**5**325
6 - - -	jung	**6**522
7 - - -	karikiert	**7**314
9 - - -	Mechanik	**9**335,3

Hunderter = Stoffart

- 1 - -	Filz	**1**17
- 3 - -	Mohairplüsch	3**3**17
- 4 - -	Samt	6**4**12,0
- 5 - -	Wollplüsch	6**5**22
- 6 - -	DRALON-Plüsch	6**6**20
- 8 - -	Holz	**8**95
- 9 - -	Stahl	3**9**80

Zehner und Einer = Höhe in cm

- - 22	22 cm Kopfhöhe	13**22**,0

Die Ziffern nach dem Komma = Ausstattung

- - - -,**0**	ohne Räder	1328,**0**2
- - - -,**1**	Druckbalgstimme	6328,**1**
- - - -,**2**	starke Druckstimme oder Zugstimme	1328,0**2**
- - - ,**3**	Musikwerk	
- - -,**ST**	Steuerung	
- - -,**ex**	Exzenter-Räder	1310**ex**

Wichtig! Da sich die Hauptnummern wiederholen, bei Bestellung stets angeben Tiername oder Serie

Foxy 1328,02 oder **26**/1328,02

cm = inches
03= 1¼
04= 1½
06= 2½
07= 3
08= 3¼
09= 3½
10= 4
12= 5
14= 5½
15= 6
17= 6½
18= 6½
19= 6½
22= 8½
23= 8½
25=10
28=11
35=13½
40=16
43=17
50=20
60=24
65=25½
75=29½
80=31½
100=40

Numbering system from 1957/58 main catalog

In 1905, Steiff introduced a new numbering system that indicated posture, material, size and additional information like voice, musical work, eccentric wheels, mechanisms in neck, and so forth. This numbering system remained the same until 1967, with the exception of a few changes. We will take a closer look at the system taken from the main catalog of 1957/58. We did not choose an earlier catalog on purpose since chances are much better to find animals from the 1950s that still have legible numbers on their ear tags than to find pre-war animals in the same condition.

We took the fox terrier, No. 2671328,02, as an example. The first two digits before the slash indicate series or species, i.e. 26 stands for fox terrier. After 1959, a third digit was added before the slash to allow for more numbers. Now, the serial number for the fox terrier was 260. After 1965, the number was changed again, this time to 422. The serial number was not printed onto the ear tag. It was only indicated in the sales catalog. The tag only showed the four to six digits following the serial number. The first one identifies the posture. The numbers 1 to 7 have had the same meaning throughout the years. In 1957, 8 was not in use. But back in 1911, 8 meant ball-joint neck, in 1924 it meant figure with wheels and in 1961, dolls and figures. The second digit identifies the material. Here, the meaning of the single digits changed over the years and new numbers have been added, e.g. for Dralon. The third and fourth digits indicate the size measured to the head. In lying animals this digit indicates the full length in centimeters. The digits after the comma (one or two digits) refer to the animal's features. The 1911 catalog, for example, uses ...., 6 for tuxedo and ...., 7 for muzzle or backpack. In our example, the number 2671328, 02, therefore, stands for: fox terrier (26), standing (1), mohair (3), size 28cm [11in] (28), no wheels (0), strong squeeze voice or pull voice (2).

Since 1968, special serial numbers are no longer used according to the catalog. They are now integrated into the new numbering system. Material and posture are no longer indicated.

The new number for the fox terrier is now: 4220/28. The two digits after the slash indicate the size in centimeters. The size listed in the catalogs may differ from the actual measurements of the animals by 1cm to 3cm (.39 to 1.18in). This is due to the fact that they are handmade and certain deviations simply cannot be avoided. Furthermore, if the animal has been used in play, its legs may be bent out of shape to the extent that the original size is considerably larger. It is important to know when measuring teddy bears that until 1933, they were measured in a sitting position. Most catalogs, however, list the full length as well. After 1934, they were only measured completely stretched out or in standing position.

An exception was made in the case of the jointed *Niki* rabbits from the 1950s and 1960s. They were measured in a sitting position, including their long, stretched out ears.

Materials

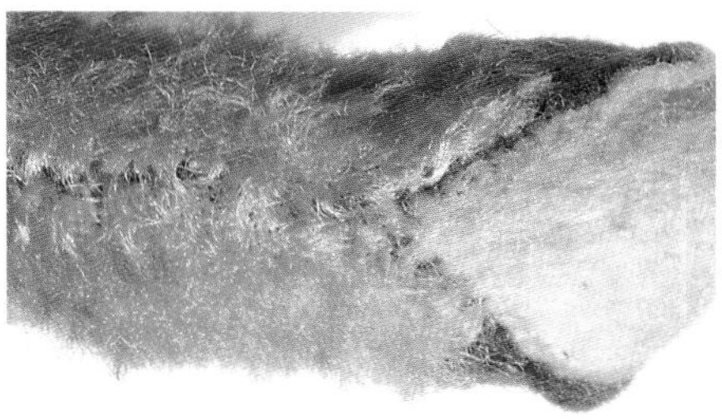

left: silk plush
right: felt

Were we to compare the textiles used in 1880 to those of the 1980s, we would find hardly any similarities. When Margarete Steiff finished her first elephant as a pincushion over 100 years ago, felt was the perfect material. Felt is elastic and easy to sew, stuff and shape. The fact that large amounts of flax were grown in the area around Giengen was another lucky coincidence. Besides agriculture, which was not enough to sustain the entire population, the growing of flax led to the development of another occupation. First, flax was processed to into yarn, later even linen. The craft of weaving followed soon after. There were dyers in town who dyed the weavers' products according to the clients' wishes. Margarete Steiff's uncle, Hans Haehnle, was trained by a dyer. Hans showed great interest in the profession and he realized that the production of felt was very simple and inexpensive. In 1858, he founded the wool-felt manufacturing company of Württemberg in Giengen (Württembergische Wollfilzmanufaktur). It is self-evident that Margarete received felt at low prices for the production of her ladies' clothes from her uncle. Only woolen felt of the best quality was used and clothes made of felt were in high fashion in those days. Felt is a textile product made of hair (mostly from animals) that is intertwined in no orderly fashion. The hairs' scales interlock when they are milled under damp heat. The cover page of the first catalog in 1892 reads: "Felt via mail-order, felt-toy factory." The catalog indicates that beside the toy production, a mail-order business for felt had been running very successfully for several years. Especially recommended were large pieces of felt of all types and colors, felt cloth and felt decorations. Felt is described as follows: "Felt has the quality of a lint-free material without a so-called 'thread-line,' it is usable on either side, is especially well-suited for decorating entire rooms. Beautiful work made of felt can be finished with little effort by cutting it jaggedly and placing it on top of felt of contrasting color." The catalog offered finished and half-finished articles such as game rugs, mosaics, sofa cushions, thread baskets, window protectors to keep out drafts, cart covers, tablecloths, household bags, newspaper holders and much more. This was a large selection that increased the order of felt tremendously. Large riding animals in connection with cast iron wheels, carts, sleighs, baskets and **carrier chairs and the first dolls with a body made of felt and multi-colored rags appeared soon. The 1901 catalog described the legally protected construction of the animals and their covering materials as felt, especially manufactured and of the highest quality. However. plush (wool, cotton) and velvet were already listed as well, and all the materials were treated against moths as best they could be.

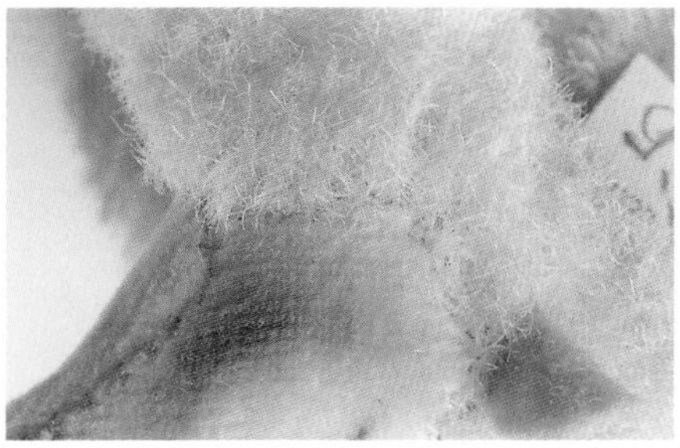

upper picture:
top: wool plush
bottom: velvet

lower picture:
top: Dralon
bottom: mohair

Wool or cotton plush is a warp pile fabric. Plush is less closely woven than other fabrics which leads to a special system of threads. It differs from velvet in that it features a considerably higher pile and it feels dull to the touch. The legs, faces and ears of lambs are made of felt, their bodies of thick wool plush. Even here the structures differ greatly, from the finest curly wool plush to thorough and thick, burly wool plush.

Velvet is a very fine and soft material with a short pile that stands straight up. It was used for the production of small toy animals and children's rattles and, in 1903, the first dolls with velvet faces, hands and clothes were offered for sale.

When the first teddy bear was "born" in 1903, a material was needed that would reflect the characteristics of his fur in the most natural manner. At the Leipzig Fair at Easter, March 2-14, 1903, Steiff introduced a jointed bear, similar to a doll made of silky plush, identified by the number 55PB. "Silky plush" must be mohair which surpasses the earlier wool plush because of its shiny quality. Mohair plush was first mentioned in a catalog in 1906. Mohair is not an artificial product, but rather the most noble fiber, taken from the mohair goat or Angora goat. The goat was discovered in 1550 by a Dutchman in Angora (today: Ankara). But mohair was not shipped to Europe until after 1820. The goats, however, could not possibly survive in Germany. They require the climates of Turkey or South Africa. The Steiff company imported mohair from England where the mohair wool was processed to yarn. German weavers then processed it further into mohair by giving it a cotton base. The mohair fiber lacks natural crimp, is shiny, thicker than wool and very durable. It can also be dyed very easily. While teddy bears and animals were made of mohair, riding animals with and without wheels were still made of felt. Besides mohair plush (very shiny) and especially long-haired mohair, there is the short-haired sealskin. Whenever appropriate for a certain species, this cotton based cloth that shows the characteristics of sealskin was used instead. Animals made of sealskin were sold as cheaper items.

A further type of plush is burlap. Its texture resembles that of sack cloth with prickly hair. It was used as early as 1897/98 for bears standing on four feet or in upright position. After 1905, it was used for bulldogs, rabbits and deer, among others. Burlap is a lot cheaper than mohair. In the 1911/12 catalog, velveteen and lamb plush (white) were listed as well.

The production of felt dolls led to the use of a variety of materials for clothes, and the shoes were made of the finest leather. Teddy bears wore knitted sweaters and cloth caps.

During the last year of World War II in 1918, Steiff was forced to use substitute materials for the toy production. The catalog listed a mohair substitute without giving details about its characteristics.

During the first post-war year, 1919, Steiff did not publish a catalog. If needed, descriptions of single animals were **mimeographed. These descriptions read as follows: "Due to the lack of genuine plush substitutes are used. We use only highly refined substitutes in terms of quality and finish. Forms and accessories remain identical with the genuine cloth toys. Other so-called substitute cloth toys are not comparable to our brand." The papers reported in 1920 that the price of wool had risen again considerably after its price seemed to decrease at first. Therefore, further price increases for all products of the wool industry were to be expected. A lowering of prices was nowhere in sight. Teddy bears were still made of mohair substitute and offered for sale. Substitute materials such as cellulose and nettle fiber appear, as do for the first time terms like "cellulose plush" or "cellulose wool fur." The text of an advertisement from those days reads: "The new working materials have been used more and more, even for toys. It is for example everyday practice that our dolls are not dressed in wool or silk, but rather in rayon and 'cellulose wool.' Neither the teddy bear nor the plush lion have a wool or cotton plush coat any longer, but rather a very nice cellulose skin that has found many friends, especially abroad." The wood of firs and pine trees was the main raw material for the production of cellulose. Cellulose is an important half material in the production of paper. It was also used to make rayon, cellulose wool and gun cotton. This yellowish-white material was invented in 1846. The fibers used in cellulose wool are short-trimmed, very loose chemical fibers with a natural curl.

Nettles made for a cotton cloth not unlike linen with a varying density of thread. This cloth was on the market both as raw nettle or bleached nettle and was sold earlier under the name "Kattun." Nettle was a very inexpensive material.

With the introduction of the Schlopsnies doll in the early 1920s, a variety of materials were used. The dolls were wearing wool hats, socks, shoes, pants and caps made of linen, lederhosen, hats, embroidered linen dresses, pants and dresses made of velvet, skirts made of silk crepe and voile, lamb plush jackets, blouses and bonnets made of batiste, print dresses with lace, flannel nightgowns and pajamas and felt slippers. This wide variety of doll clothing required a well-stocked store of textiles, ribbons, cords and threads. Leather was needed for saddles, collars, leashes and horns. In 1924, the same model rabbit in sitting position was sold in four different materials: felt, mohair, long pile silk plush (white, very soft, light) and in white velvet, sprayed brown. For teddy bears, a single colored or brown (sprayed) plush with especially long pile was used.

Towards the end of the 1920s and in the early 1930s, good materials such as felt, velvet and mohair became scarce. Substitutes such as flannel, cotton plush, rayon and Alpaca plush were used.

Flannel was used as a substitute for felt and resembled the material used for sheets. A cotton or linen cloth was slightly roughed up so that the structures of the single threads were barely recognizable. The surface formed a slight fuzz or a dense cover of lint, but it was not as soft and cuddly as mohair. Cut and model of a flannel animal compared to a high quality mohair version are just as intricate.

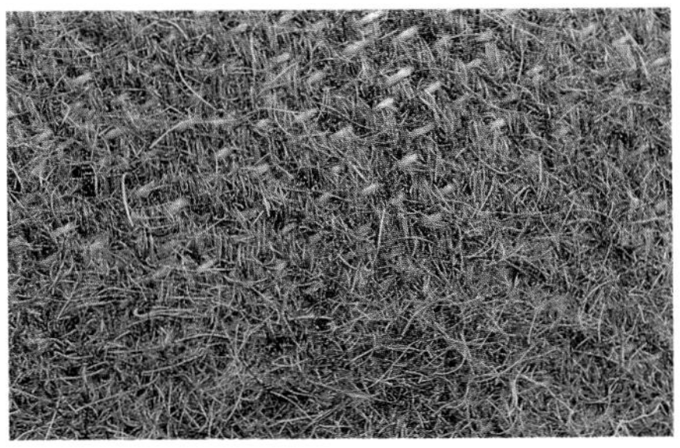

top:
burlap

bottom:
nettle fiber

The fur-like character of mohair plush could not be duplicated by the even surface of flannel. Much of the character and expression of the animal was lost. Flannel animals, however, were an inexpensive alternative to the costly mohair or wool plush animals. A small financial advantage was gained during production because flannel is easier to sew. But most of the savings were due to the considerably lower cost of flannel as compared to the expensive mohair plush. For example, while a mohair rabbit cost 3 Reichsmark, the cheap edition of the same model cost only 1 Reichsmark. The 1933 catalog offered three sizes of cheap rabbits made of orange flannel for sale.

Alpaca plush is a fabric woven of cotton thread and the shiny and soft white Alpaca wool, the wool of a species of Llama from South America.

By 1930, there were 12 sizes of *Teddy Babies* in mohair and nine sizes in wool plush. Wool miniatures were made of moth-proof wool (Nomotta).

In 1934, the company considered the production of a gray elephant made of soft leather under item No. 20/1717. The elephant, however, was never mentioned in a catalog. The so-called "wash-animals" (soft baby animals that can be wiped off and that were made especially for infants), produced between 1937 and 1940 and made of colorful wax cloth with a soft stuffing must have been the inexpensive alternative. In 1940, the teddy bear program was comprised of six sizes. The smallest teddy bear, 10cm (4in), was made of mohair plush; all the others were made of rayon. It was thanks to mohair plush that the teddy bear production did not come to a grinding halt during World War II (in 1943, mohair was unavailable) and it helped re-start production around 1947.

Artificial silk plush (rayon) was the generally accepted name for the synthetic fiber in the form of endless threads until 1953. "Rayon" is the artificial name for artificial silk. Rayon was the first artificial spinning thread used for the production of textiles. The thread is even and thin and as shiny as silk, but has never replaced silk. Instead, it found its own independent spot among textiles. Finally, in 1948, the new salary treaty with Switzerland offered an opportunity to once again gain access to mohair. Animals made of rayon sold very poorly abroad and the customers were requesting quite urgently the well-known pre-war quality.

After 1948, mohair plush is once again available but silk plush was still used until 1950/51. During this time, silk plush teddy bears with paws made of linen or tweed were produced, as well. Still there were some animals that were made of wool plush (burly wool plush). Animals from the time after 1950 had differing pieces of information concerning their production materials printed on the backsides of their tags.

For mohair: 51% wool, 41% (sic!) cotton, or 59% wool, 41% cotton, or 70% wool, 30% cotton. For wool plush: 80% wool, 20% cotton.

For mohair with a higher wool content: 68% wool, 32% cotton.

For velvet animals: 100% cotton.

For felt animals: 100% wool or 95% wool, 5% rayon.

For synthetics: "All new Material."

Animals that were produced before 1950 did not have any information concerning their production materials printed on their ear tags.

An inexpensive substitute for the best mohair is Dralon plush. In 1955, the Cosy wash animals entered the program. They were made of thick and indestructible Dralon plush. They are soft and comfortable and can stand to be soaked and washed completely as long as they do not end up in the "hot" cycle. Dralon is a poly-acrylic fiber. There are two kinds of this fiber. Firstly, the finer and more solid one and secondly, the dull and fluffy, woolly one that exceeds the durability of wool, by far. Dralon animals are, therefore, very durable and they dry very fast after laundring. Their fur feels light, soft and warm. Some of them were made partially (20%-40%) of wool or cotton.

In the 1960s and 1970s, further synthetic materials were used such as Crylor, Perlon velours, Dralon fur (imitation fur) and Orlon (synthetic material) and velours like polyester. Today, every client wants the highest quality but is not always prepared to pay a high price. Animals made of woven plush, knitted plush and two-pole plush are, depending on their finish (interior, decorations) washable or can only be wiped off. As a special attraction, machine washable toys were produced in 1981 (*Dorma Bear, Knöpfchen Bear and Molly Panda*) and 1982 brought *Toldi Bear*, made from woven fur and machine washable, as well.

Woven plush is about half as expensive as mohair of the finest quality. It is an even fabric made on looms and durability is one of its features.

Even less expensive is knitted plush. Its quality, however, is considerably lower. The demand for animals made from knitted plush is not that great. The stitches form V-shapes and are made with knitting machines. It is reinforced on the backside to make it more durable.

The so-called two-pole plush is used quite frequently. It consists of hairs that differ in length. With its thick lower pelt and the long covering hair, it gives the impression of genuine fur with all the characteristics of an extremely soft and beautiful pelt. Designers regret the fact that these old materials are no longer in use. The fluffier the material, the more difficult it is to retain the natural look. Modern woven plush is unable to reflect details. For a series of replicas and a repertoire of miniatures (from 1989) woven mohair pelt (can be wiped off) is used. Wool felt is still around but sometimes it is replaced by synthetic velvet or the washable Niki fabric (1982, *Niki Teddy*).

Animals made from synthetic plushes hardly belong to the collectors' items today. Some of the exceptions are *Cosy Sigi* (sea horse), *Little Green Man* and *Electrola Fox*. We are sure that in a few years, even animals made of Dralon and other synthetic materials will be collected.

Stuffing Materials

The term "stuffing" was still unknown around 1890. The first catalog of 1892 mentioned the use of fine, soft "stuffing material" as well as the use of flexible metal frames to preserve the form. In the beginning, wool was used and the term "re-processed wool" was introduced. Re-processed wool is also called "tired" wool, due to the fact that it has lost its elasticity. Around 1890 excelsior was already used, sometimes mixed with silk cotton, also known as kapok. In 1911, stuffing material was described as light, soft and pure (i.e. no wood shavings. animal hair, and so forth).

from left to right:
above:
Sheared wool, Kapok stuffing.
below:
Raw long fiber, fine wooden wool.

Excelsior consists of wood shavings of 1 to 4mm width and 0.03 to 0.4mm thickness. It is gained by using a machine to shave the strips off a wooden roll. Steiff never manufactured any teddy bears stuffed with straw, contrary to common but mistaken descriptions. They were always stuffed with excelsior. Depending on the size of the animals, the stuffing can only be performed by men since it requires a tremendous amount of strength. The animal must be tightly stuffed and the stuffing may not show any holes. Specialists were trained within the factory explicitly for this hard and difficult work. The competition was aware of that fact and in 1920, ads like the following appeared in the local paper, *Der Brenztalbote*: "First class manufacturer of woolen toys in Thüringen is looking for stuffers for large plush animals. Expenses paid. Detailed applications to be sent to this paper."

Silk cotton or kapok is similar to wool. It grows on the seed of the West African cotton or kapok tree and the Indian silk cotton tree. Kapok is water-repellent and not attractive to vermin. The K series (kapok series) was introduced in 1925 among the novelties. A teddy bear was described as especially soft and light, stuffed with kapok and featuring a blonde mohair coat and squeeze voice. He was available in seven sizes ranging from 25cm to 50cm (10 to 20in), measured standing upright. Furthermore, there were colorful bears with long-haired plush coats, kapok stuffing and squeeze voice. They were available in pink (*Teddy Rose*) and yellow, measuring 33, 36 or 40cm (13, 14 or 16in). Dogs such as *Molly* and *Flock* and cats were also featuring kapok stuffing. "K" was added to the item number to indicate the stuffing material. In 1926, the teddy clown made of mohair plush sprayed with brown color was introduced into the program. He, too, was stuffed with kapok and was, therefore, soft and light.

In 1929, the stuffing material was described as consisting "...of long fiber, light, soft and pure. It will not wad up in balls and preserves the animal's distinct and beautiful shape." After this, no further details were printed in catalogs about the interior of the animals. We can assume, however, that excelsior remained as the main stuffing material until the end of the 1960s. Later, softer materials were used. During the transition period, a mixture of excelsior and natural fibers similar to cotton were used. An exception was made in the production of the *Cosy* and *Floppy* line in the mid 1950s. They were given a foam rubber filling. In the early 1960s, the animals were stuffed with synthetic fibers or foam rubber. In the mid 1960s, the stuffing was described as foam rubber and after the late 1960s, synthetic fiber was used because it does not rot (e.g. 1967/68: *Cosy Teddy*, Dralon plush, synthetic fiber). The switch from natural to synthetic fiber was explained as follows: Natural fibers present a hygiene problem after they have been exposed to dampness for an extended period. The animals were no longer stuffed with a random amount of stuffing material. The amounts needed for each animal were carefully calculated. The amount of fire-resistant foam rubber necessary was blown with a pneumatic jet directly into the limp arms and legs. Bodies shaped with foam were especially easy to cover. Pre-shaped foam animals by Steiff feature a specially prepared foam body that is extremely soft, but always regains its original shape. The coat of fur was simply pulled over the foam starting with the ears (e.g. 1969: *Minky Zotty*, 1971: *Toddel Bear* from the *Eltern* magazine — super soft, 1976: *Zotty* with foam body).

For especially firm shaping of the animals, excelsior treated with a water-repellent was still in use (also treated to decrease flammability and against vermin). Excelsior was also used in some replica whose stuffing should resemble as closely as possible that of the original. However, today's stuffing materials are generally synthetics.

Eyes

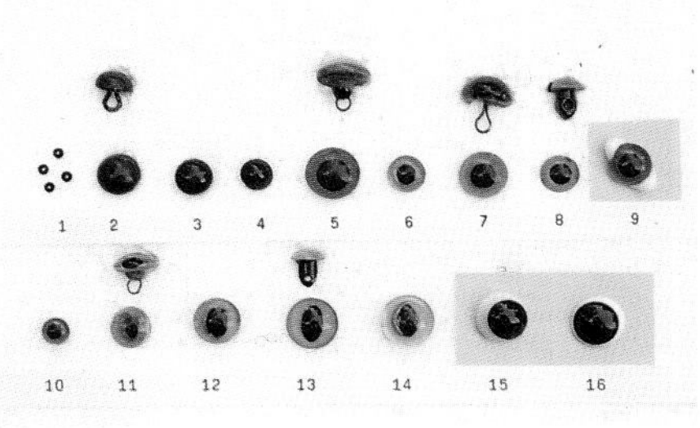

Eyes are an important element in determining the facial expression of a plush animal. Steiff has always placed great value on the use of eyes of high quality and expression. It is, however, rather difficult to determine the exact time of use for the various types of eyes since the transition was often drawn out over a period of a decade or even more. During years of crisis or war, old stock was used up and old production methods were re-activated due to lack of materials or the drying up of foreign sources.

Black pearl eyes were used between 1880 and 1900-1905. In some cases, e.g. in rabbits, red pearl eyes were used. But as early as 1892, the customer was able to obtain animals with glass eyes for an additional charge. These eyes gave the animals a much more lifelike expression. It should be noted that between the turn of the century and 1910, shoe-button eyes were the most common type. Glass eyes were not used until after 1910 for teddy bears, dolls and animals.

Shoe-button eyes were used during and in some cases, even after World War II, since glass eyes were not available. Shoe-button eyes are made of a pressed substance whose slightly uneven surface is varnished with a dull black.

Glass eyes are available in the following variations: completely black, brown or blue with round, black pupil or yellowish-green with black slit pupil. The glass eyes of Steiff animals and teddy bears are usually made of clear glass with a black pupil. Then they were painted on the backside either light or dark brown (for the so-called teddy eyes), or green (for the so-called cat eyes). The colored backside shines through the eye which gives it a natural look. This effect is only present in those painted glass eyes as they were used by Steiff, primarily. They are, therefore, another important means of recognition, even though other manufacturers have used the same eyes at times, as well. One also has to keep in mind that the eyes of older animals may have been replaced by other, unpainted eyes, and the color on glass eyes from the 1940s may have peeled off.

During the periods around 1919/20 and 1932/34, Steiff animals were made without painted eyes. Samples from those times show original eyes consisting of glass that was colored brown, the backside unpainted, and with black pupils. These eyes were often used in teddy bears of the Teddy Hermann company and other manufacturers of plush animals.

Black and white squinting glass eyes were used in dolls as early as 1911, but they were used especially for dogs until the early 1960s. Plastic versions can be found at times even later than that.

Glass eyes with backsides painted in light or dark brown, with black pupils that show a small white corner on either side were not used until the 1930s. They are called corner or poodle eyes since they were used very frequently in poodles after 1950.

The glass eyes used by Steiff are very easily recognizable by their protruding loop bridge and the poured wire loop used to attach the eyes. Steiff often placed colored felt underneath shoe-button or glass eyes in order to emphasize the eyes of various species or to give them a more expressive look (even in the early *Zottys*).

1. Pearl eyes, 1880-1900/05
2. Shoe-button eyes made of pressed substance, with metal loop, dull black varnish, 1895-1910 (above: side view)
3. Black glass eye, in teddy bears after 1910, until early 1920s, in animals after 1910, until early 1960s
4. Black plastic eye, after early 1960s
5. Brown painted glass eye with black pupil. Typical eye for teddy bears, animals and dolls from 1910 until early 1960s (above: side view with loop bridge typical for Steiff eyes)
6. Brown and black glass eyes as above, lighter brown
7. Not a Steiff eye, brown-colored glass, so-called "Hermann Eye," used by Steiff for a very short period between 1919/20 and 1932/34 (above: side view, clearly revealing absence of loop bridge)
8. Plastic eye, backside painted brown, black pupil, early 1960s (above: clearly visible sharp edge typical for plastic eyes)
9. Brown painted glass eye with white corners, used primarily between 1930 and early 1960s in dogs and rubber figures
10. Blue painted glass eye with black pupil, from 1910 until early 1960s, typical in dolls after 1910 and polar bears of the 1950s
11. Blue and green painted glass eye with black slit pupil, after early 1920s until approximately 1940. Typical in cats and predators of those days (above: side view)
12. Green painted glass eye with black slit pupil. 1947 until early 1960s (mainly in cats)
13. Green painted plastic eye with black pupil, after early 1960s in cats (above: side view)
14. Not a Steiff eye, green, colored glass
15. Black and white glass eye (squinting eye), from 1910 until early 1960s
16. Black and white plastic eye, from early 1960s, mainly in dogs

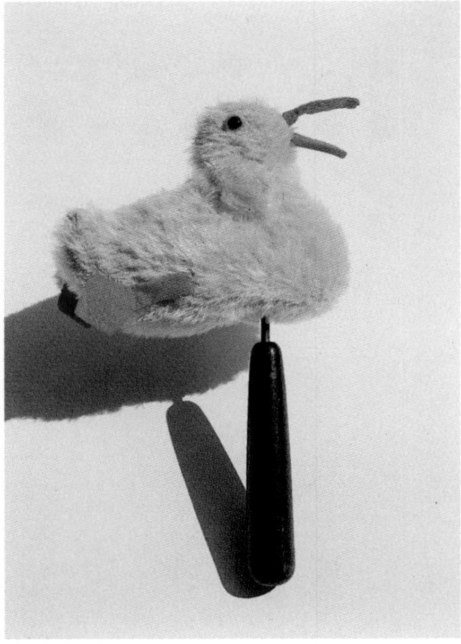

Swinging duck with chirping voice that sounds when duck swings from side to side.

Plastic eyes were introduced from the 1960s-on and, by the end of the 1960s, replaced glass eyes completely (except in display animals.)

If a collector picks up an animal, he often performs a typical test. He checks behind the eyes with his fingernail to find out whether he is dealing with a glass or a plastic eye. If the edge of the eye feels even and rounded, it must be a glass eye. If the edge sharp and pointed, the eye is made of plastic. Glass eyes are cooler to the touch than plastic eyes. A trained collector can also recognize a glass eye because of the optical power of expression.

A cord that ends in a knot at the backside of an animal's head is often reason for surprise and the significance of the cord is unknown. If the knot is removed, the surprise is even greater to see the eyes fall off! The knots were the ends of the eye attachments. The eyes were individually sewn on with double (sometimes quadruple) thread and a special needle. They were sewn onto the front and the threads were pulled straight to the backside of the head, then pulled inside again. The size of the eyes determined the thickness of the thread.

Today, there is a special method for the attachment of eyes in compliance with the most recent tough laws on child safety for toys.

Voices

Animals with voices appeared in the first Steiff catalog of 1892. Available were dogs, rabbits, cats, bears and sheep with voice boxes. They were described more closely in the catalog of 1901. They were made of "leather, without mechanisms and extremely sturdy. They can be heard upon squeezing the animal's body, etc. and are present in almost all items (by now). In the smallest, however, for reasons of space, they are replaced by rattling balls." Such animals are known as rabbit or cat rattles. The information about voices that is published in Steiff catalogs is rather sketchy. It is known that teddy bears with automatic growling voices were available starting in 1908. This voice was the predecessor to today's tilt or cuddly voice, activated by tilting the bear.

This voice was installed around 1911 in bears measuring 32cm (13in) or more (standing), during the 1920s in bears measuring 40cm (16in) and in the 1950s in bears measuring 43cm (17in). Two voices could be found in large teddy bears, 75cm (30in). The voice boxes were installed opposite each other so that the growling could be heard when tilting the bears forward and backward. Even chimpanzees larger than 43cm (17in) featured an automatic tilt voice in 1911. Paul Steiff was trying constantly to perfect the various voices. Very soon a separate voice production was established.

In a special report of the *Illustrierte Zeitung* No. 3561 of September 28, 1911, on the "Cradle of the Teddy Bear," the following could be read: "Even success leads to invention. Why not put a voice inside the bears' bodies? Tiny bellows with voice plates were invented. Teddy learned how to growl happily. But since tests with the bellows revealed voices from God's entire world, the beasts to match these funny sounds of nature had to be created. The ox was made to match the "moo." To match the screeching, the monkey was made, and to match the barking, a dog was created.

from left to right:
in back:
Automatic voice saying "Mommy," in dolls after 1911. This very interesting mechanism resembles a mixture of bellows and mousetrap.
Pull voice for riding animals, in this case a riding bear measuring 50cm (20in). Inscription: "Bär 50."
Two plastic voices of the 1960s/1970s. Black voice: tilt voice for larger teddy bears, white voice: squeaking squeeze voice for animals and small teddy bears.
front:
Squeeze voice (bellows) in predators, 28cm (11in), (tiger, young lion, leopard) 1950s and 1960s. Inscription: "Raub 28."
Simple squeaking bellows for ducks with eccentric wheels and Record animals, after 1913.
Elements of double-tone squeeze voice: rubberized linen used as connection between the two oval cardboard pieces. Spring, two small metal openings, two cardboard covers to protect against dust of excelsior (1920-1965).

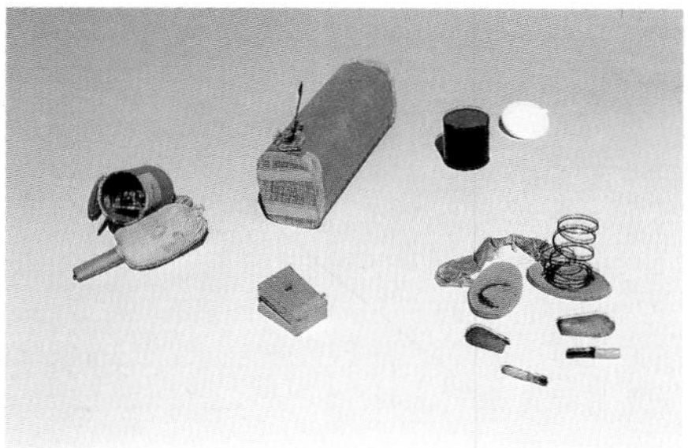

"A donkey came to match a donkey's cry, and a lion to match the roar. How the children rejoiced! They pulled the ear of the little plush pig from Giengen, and — lo and behold! — they heard it oink!" In this manner, Giengen captured the market again, this time with the most various and imaginative animal voices.

Dolls were given automatic voices that said "Mommy," and riding animals were given pull voices. The voice boxes were made of rubberized linen and leather in those days. In 1916/17, teddy bears of 30cm (12in) or more (standing) were available with either squeeze voices or automatic growling voices. Besides, some teddy bears were given double tone squeeze voices, i.e. the growling sound when the bear is pressed as well as when the pressure is released. In the mid 1920s, four especially soft teddy bears were available, measuring 28, 32, 35 and 43cm (11, 13. 14 and 17in), sitting, in the following colors: white, blonde or dark brown. They are equipped with a special squeeze voice that could be activated by pressure from any side.

Pull voices were most common in riding animals and animals on wheels. They are activated by pulling a string on the backside of the animals. The voice can be heard either when pulling or after releasing the ring.

Squeeze voices consist mainly of bellows with openings for intake and release of air. A small elastic metal band is placed in the air-release opening. It begins to swing when the air escapes and covers the opening shortly, generating squeaking or growling voices. Steiff created a whole repertoire of interesting voices, some of them with highly complex mechanisms that copy the appropriate animal voices as closely as possible. This is true especially in old voices. But, unfortunately, these old voice boxes are often defective for various reasons. The rubberized linen of the bellows often hardens, depending on age and storage. It becomes brittle and holes appear. The air that is to be released through the small opening escapes through the side. In automatic tilt voices, a lead weight is attached to the bellows, causing them to move when tilted. Often this weight has fallen off due to insufficient glue or because the teddy bear has been thrown around too much. When the bear is tilted, the weight merely causes a rattling sound.

Even though it is very difficult for an amateur to repair voices, the attempts are worthwhile. The joy is especially great if, after all the trouble, the voice made especially for each species is sounding once again. In this way, the collector becomes familiar with the entire spectrum of animal voices and the wealth of ideas and inventions of voice production at the Steiff factory. This is especially true for voices from the time between 1910 and the mid 1930s. We found an especially interesting voice in a swinging duck. It has a wooden handle and if it is swung back and forth using this handle, it makes a quacking noise that very closely resembles the strong voice of a young duck.

From the mid 1960s-on, the rubberized linen and the cardboard pieces were replaced for reasons of high cost and in order to make them washer-safe. Now, plastic voices were used. The typical uniqueness of each voice, however, was lost. They all sound very similar.

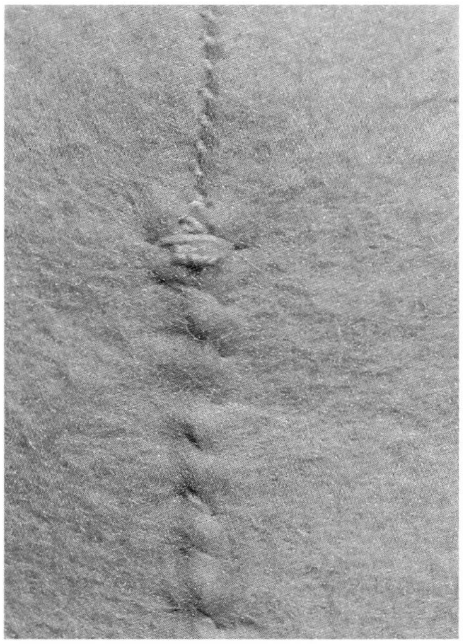

top: machine-sewn seam
bottom: hand-sewn seam

Further Characteristics Determined by Production Methods

Besides eyes, decorations and coloring, there are further characteristics of Steiff teddy bears and animals that are closely linked to production methods.

Let us begin with the cut. Mohair is stored in large bales. The required amount is laid out and stencils with small holes are placed on the backside. These stencils are designed to leave as little leftover material as possible and to use the material in the most efficient way. A mixture of colors is pressed through the holes in the stencils onto the material, but not enough to show on the front. This is how the cutting edges of the individual parts are indicated. These have to be cut out very carefully between the pile, work that has to be done by hand. A machine would cut the long hair at the edge much too short, leading to ugly seams. The punching out of several layers placed on top of each other is only possible if the material is "flat", e.g. with felt or short-haired plush used for small animals.

The cut-out parts are sewn together, inside out, in the sewing department according to pre-determined plans (depending on the model) using the most modern sewing machines. The empty plush body is then turned around and the head, arms and legs are attached with cardboard disks and splints (see picture, page 27). The body is stuffed and the voice is added. Now the teddy bear is sewn up completely, usually at the stomach. This hand-sewn seam on the stomach is especially typical for the following Steiff teddy bears:

— *Original Teddy Bears* 1905-1965
— Panda bears
— *Teddy Babies*
— *Petsy Bears*
— *Orsi Bears*

For the following teddy bears, this rule does not apply. Here, the hand-sewn seams run down the backs of the teddy bears.

— Koala bears
— *Jackie Bears*
— Zoo Bear, *Zooby*
— shaved *Original Teddy Bears* after 1966.

Zotty, due to the cut, has a seam on each the right and left side of the stomach; the one on the left side is hand-sewn. Bears from around 1903/04 have a seam running from side to side across the head (from ear to ear). These bears have no hand-sewn seams on their bodies since they were stuffed through the throat.

Cardboard disks were sometimes worked into the soles of their feet. These were wrapped in dark felt in very early models. And above those, the real outer felt for the soles was sewn. *Teddy Babies* and panda bears feature flat, thick cardboard disks in their soles in order to increase their ability to stand upright. Standing animals without wheels, animals in sitting or lying positions or other jointed animals have a hand-sewn seam on their stomach. Due to the placement of the metal frame, animals on wheels have the seams on their backs. In dolls, the seam is either in the front or the back in the middle of their bodies.

A further important characteristic in Steiff animals and teddy bears may be the way in which the ears have been attached. Ears are usually sewn onto the finished and stuffed head and not, as was the case with the products of many competitors, pulled or stuck into the head or sewn into the seams.

left: Soles of a teddy bear from 1905/06. A cardboard insert covered with dark blue felt and a fold (lengthwise) is placed underneath the outer layer of felt.
right: Soles of rough material in *Teddy Babies* of 1930 with flat, stable cardboard insert to increase ability to stand upright. Rough material was used frequently during times of war or crisis instead of felt.

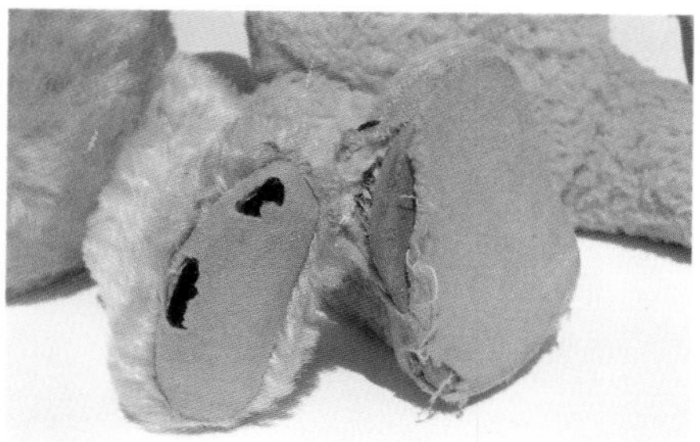

Dicky Bear replica, 1985
left: replica in original condition
right: forgery — replica made to look old (contributed by a collector who wishes to remain anonymous)

A typical characteristic of Steiff teddy bears is the hand-sewn seams found at the upper ends of the arms. The arms were sewn up on the back side and the paws were set in on the back side, as well. Then the arms were turned inside out and stuffed through the small opening. It is through those small openings that the metal washers and splints are inserted, as well. The washer made sure that the head of the loop could not slip through the cardboard disk. The arms were now sewn shut by hand on the upper end. The same technique was used for the legs.

Be careful when coming across a plush animal or a teddy bear that is offered for sale as a Steiff animal but does not have the above-mentioned characteristics!

Forgeries

Old Steiff teddy bears are considered something special among bear collectors. They fetch enormous prices. Therefore, forgers began to copy them in order to make money illegally. An Englishman had the idea to attach the famous button to cheap toy bears. Even auction houses suffered from this practice since they were often offered forgeries. Collectors should, therefore, obtain expert opinions for their protection in case they consider buying highly valuable objects. Even at flea markets, the most amazing things can be seen. An animal that has never even been near the factory in Giengen is given one of the unmistakable characteristics, such as the button, the flag or the collar tag. The most imaginative displays can be found and every connoisseur will have to smile or loose his cool when he finds the button in the right ear of an animal, the ear tag sewn to the chest, or a cut-out catalog picture glued to the animal's coat — and all this on a Japanese product made in 1987!

One group of especially cunning forgers were caught after selling their forgeries at flea markets in Germany in 1987. A teddy bear appeared at the markets that, according to the vendor, was supposed to be a Steiff bear from around 1930. He had the characteristics of a seemingly old bear: large hump, pointed snout, long bent arms and tightly stuffed with excelsior. Since several collectors were interested in the bear, there was no time for long consideration and it was sold for a large sum of money. The joy was great since such a rare real bear would not be easy to find ever again, especially since it was in mint condition and had such a beautiful melancholy look in his old glass eyes. The grin on his face identified him as a rare *Dicky* from the early 1930s. The collector was surprised to find out, however, that a friend of his (a collector, himself) found another old bear only a week later. They looked at their bears carefully and had them evaluated. When the paws were looked at more closely, colored synthetic fabric of the 1980s appeared underneath the old material. The evaluation determined that the collectors had purchased forgeries that had been prepared systematically and with incredible impertinence. The original bear (of whom not much remained) had been the *Dicky* replica of 1985.

The form must have been what inspired the forgers to make an old teddy bear out of this new one. The interior had been removed and the bear was stuffed with excelsior. The plastic eyes had been replaced by glass eyes and all four paws had been covered with old material. The nose and claw decorations had been scraped off, the mohair coat had been shaven shortly and in some spots, even worn off to show the material below, and the bear had been treated with grease and dragged through the dirt. In other words, even if the artificial signs of age look real, a bear with a hump and long arms is not necessarily old and great care is warranted. The only authentic thing about this bear were the sad eyes after all that he had been through, as every collector and fan of old bears can imagine. One consolation for the collectors was that the forgeries became known very rapidly and the fake teddy bears disappeared fast. Unfortunately, the prices that collectors are willing to pay have risen to heights that make forgeries appear very lucrative. Therefore, fake animals keep appearing on the scene. The financial loss can even out, but the collector's humiliation to have been fooled by a forger remains.

Maintenance and Storage of Steiff Animals

Correct maintenance and storage of a Steiff collection are essential. Not everybody has the means to keep his collection in glass chests. As the collection grows, space problems become imminent. True, plush animals are unbreakable and can be stacked if need be, but in old and sensitive materials like felt, velvet, rayon and rubber, pressure spots can show up that are difficult to eliminate. In any case, the collection should be kept protected from light and dust and in as even temperature as best possible. Animals made of mohair are not quite as delicate. They may get covered with dust with time, but can be vacuumed without a problem, or the dust can be removed from the surface with soft brushes. However, exposure to cigarette smoke and grease (kitchen vapors) over the years lead to deposits that can only be washed off.

It is not difficult to keep and take care of a Steiff collection and even to carry out smaller repairs at home, if only a few ground rules are known and observed.

Much nonsense has been written about the first cleaning of a newly purchased dirty or defective animal and many new collectors are surprised to hear what adventurous procedures some animals have to put up with. Rule number one is the careful check for vermin (moths and their nests, larvae, wood worms, and so forth). Even if the animal's origin is known and the previous household was clean, it is never certain whether the animal has not spent the past decades quietly in some attic until shortly before it was sold. The areas most favored by vermin are deep seams and folds on the ears, between disk joints, underneath the eyes and in the nose embroidery. These places have to be inspected most carefully, perhaps even with a magnifying glass. This same goes for bald spots in the plush coat. Most common are the discoveries of tiny black crumbs, transparent scales or white gauze-like fabric. These are dried up eggs, nests or larvae of the moth. Even though they cannot do any harm any longer, they must be removed. Depending on the kind of animal, brushes of different sizes and hardness (in tight spots toothbrushes may be used) will do the job. If the material underneath is very thin and the excelsior is shining through, a very soft brush must be used in order not to break the fabric. Even vacuuming has proven to be useful if a fine nozzle is used. But please be careful when vacuuming porous paws or paws with holes. Use a vacuum only if a firm underlying material is present.

"...I hope they will not repair me!"

Felt animals and dolls sometimes have small holes, about the size of pins. They may be the result of wood worms. One controversial method suggests to expose those things to the shock of placement in the freezer for 50 hours. But be careful: If the dolls are not packed airtight, humidity may build up which will lead to spots on the thin and worn-out felt. An alternative is the purchase of chemicals that produce toxic fumes. However, these chemicals can be hazardous to your health, so extreme care is necessary. Before even applying these drastic measures, make sure that wood worms are indeed working on the inside of the doll. Place the part you want to examine on a dark surface and let it sit for two weeks or so. Then knock slightly with your hand against the doll. If fine dust falls out of the holes, wood worms are the likely cause.

As early as 1911, "Guma Detergent" was advertised in the catalog. We have realized that rubbing the items down with soapy lather is very effective for cleaning surfaces. We recommend you use pure soap flakes. Make a lather with soap and warm water (the concentration depends on how dirty the item is) and rub down the plush that has previously been brushed, using mostly lather, with as little water as possible. Repeat this procedure until the item is sufficiently clean. Remains of the lather are removed with a sponge and clear water. Dry the item with a soft and clean towel. The pile of the plush should be brushed out again while it is still damp, using an appropriate brush, to return the hair to its original state. In addition, very long mohair has to be combed.

Fresh air but no sunlight, hair dryer or heater should be used to dry the item. If the coat feels hard after cleaning and drying, that means that not all the soap has been rinsed off. It will disappear easily when brushed once again. Since the excelsior may stain the color of old and thin felt paws, be careful with the use of soap and of humidity. Rayon and velvet require very careful cleaning with a very mild detergent. Velvet that has been soaked will always be hard and firm. Even if treated with strong steam, it will rarely return to its original quality. Dirty animals made of rayon clean nicely with a mild detergent, but the coat remains slightly curly and loses its original shine.

The cleaning of old felt animals and of faces and bodies of dolls is very problematic. There are different gasoline solutions available and experiments with solutions of ash and vinegar have supposedly proven useful. However, one needs to consider whether those items will not lose a lot of their historical character in the restoration process. If the felt is only slightly dirty, often the brushing off of dust with a soft brush will work wonders. The felt is stirred again and its original color will appear once more. Do not brush for too long a time. The felt may become thin and transparent. Small "wounds" do not subtract any value from the teddy bear, but a badly repaired flaw will not increase it in value, either. Each individual collector has to evaluate each case in question. He knows best whether he can handle thread and needle. A teddy bear with a complete emergency operation will gain neither in expression nor in value.

Heads made of rubber and PVC (*Mecki*, dwarves, neanderthals, and so forth) can be cleaned with soap and water, using cotton swabs for the cleaning. We recommend that they be treated with baby oil afterwards. If the rubber is very brittle, treat it only with oil. Do not use powder since it will be almost impossible to remove it from the porous material later.

Clothes of the animals should only be rinsed in a mild detergent or shampoo in tepid water. Never wring or stretch. When washed, felt may lose its form, can be bleached or lose its texture. Parts made of leather (reins, leashes, saddles, collars) can be treated sparsely with silicon paste.

Animals from the 1950s and 1960s that are stuffed with excelsior are often put through a complete wash cycle in a washer, then tumbled dry. In many cases this may work just fine, but in some animals wire has been used to strengthen the structure that is invisible on the outside. This wire may punch through to the outside and cause great damage. The excelsior may get lumpy and may start to rot. Totally crippled animals with broken glass eyes and soggy cardboard disks have appeared at times. And we will not even mention the sad look in the eyes of a washer-tortured teddy bear. Today's Steiff animals have plastic joints. They are low-maintenance toys and washer safe.

A wonderful white bear (judging from the expression, probably female!). Never played with, white long-haired mohair, body stuffed softly with virgin wool. Measuring 28cm (11in) sitting, 39cm (15in) standing. Nose decoration of light brown thread, underlying black felt. Shoe-button eyes, four embroidered claws (light brown) on each paw, no voice. Blank button, 1905/07. Very rare.

MARGARETE STEIFF

Bears and Teddy Bears

Steiff teddy bears were discovered by photographers early on as models. The picture shows a beautiful white bear from around 1908. The verses indicate the close friendship between man and teddy bear.

Note: Unless indicated otherwise, all bears feature the following main characteristics:
— jointed, i.e. full movement of arms and legs,
— with swivel head,
— mohair,
— paws and soles made of felt,
— excelsior stuffing,
— brown eyes with black pupil,
— snout black or dark brown embroidered,
— tilt or squeeze voice (dependent on size),
— "cm" indicates full size (measured standing upright).

The invention of the teddy bear has to be recognized as a milestone in the history of toy production. But a few years of the production of plush animals had to pass before the teddy bear came along. Everything started with the felt elephant of 1880. The production of bears did not commence until 12 years later. In 1892, bears were made as parts of the game of skittles. Tumblers and bears standing on all fours (sometimes on iron wheels) followed later. Towards the end of the 19th century, a large number of different riding bears and bears on wheels were offered. Bears, however, were not as popular as household pets taken from everyday life. Bears were only known from the zoo or the circus, and they were known to be dangerous animals that children were afraid of. Only the dancing bears in the circus were funny to watch and seemed to be less dangerous.

Richard Steiff is credited with the invention of the teddy bear. Inspired by his drawings of bears made in the zoo and the jointed porcelain doll, he designed a fully-jointed bear. But not until after 1913 was this bear advertised in the catalogs as a teddy bear. At first, he was standing upright and did not look especially cute. He was made of mohair plush which looked like fairly authentic bear skin. The toy, however, was not very huggable due to its hard excelsior stuffing. These early bears were too heavy for children. A metal frame inside the bear's body was used to suspend the arms and legs and to grant full movement. The models were improved over the years, i.e. they became cuddlier, softer and lighter. In the novelty list of 1903/04, the first jointed bear was shown, item No. 55PB.

Illustration on page 56:
A true dream teddy bear: Never played with, golden long-haired mohair, 50cm (20in). Squeeze voice (unusual for this size), ears round. Described as a novelty item in the 1925 catalog, item No. 12/5335,1K, soft kapok stuffing, partial use of small amounts of excelsior to strengthen the form. Very rare. The book *Margarete Steiff und der Teddybär-Die Geschichte eines Lebens* (*Margarete Steiff and the Teddy Bear - The History of One Life*) which the teddy bear is reading was published in 1947 to celebrate Margarete Steiff's 100th birthday.

Bear 35 PB, 1903/04

He was introduced at the fair in Leipzig in spring 1903, but did not receive a lot of attention. Only towards the end of the fair, after everybody had already given up hope of the bear's success, did an American buyer order 3000 pieces on the spot. In 1904, 12,000 jointed bears were sold, among them one with item No. 35 PB. In the following years, a tremendous development of the company history could be witnessed.

In 1906, Steiff produced as many as 400,000 bears and in 1907, 975,000. These so-called "Years of the Bear" and the explosive development of the Steiff company were aided by the great popularity of President Roosevelt. Every child in America wanted a "teddy."

The development from the metal frame to the bears with disk joints was the first step towards weight reduction. A further step was the almost complete replacement of excelsior by light virgin wool. Only in places crucial to the stability and shape of the bear was excelsior added. The typical characteristics around 1905-1907 were:
— black shoe-button eyes,
— arms, legs and head jointed with disks,
— hand-sewn seam on stomach,
— stuffing sometimes excelsior only, sometimes virgin wool with little excelsior, therefore very light,
— felt underlying nose decorations in bears over 40cm (16in),
— cardboard disks, covered with dark felt, bent lengthwise, inserted into soles,
— ears sewn on far apart on the head,
— no tilt voice,
— arms bent.

Typical bears from before World War I and the early 1920s. Brass-colored mohair with black glass eyes. The bear measuring 13cm (5in) has no claws, no voice and a very pointed nose sticking up into the air; ears are sewn on far apart. The larger bears, 22 and 32cm (9 and 13in), have four claws each on paws and feet, embroidered in black. Side-squeeze voice. The bear measuring 22cm (9in) has very long, straight arms, angular, without the felt paws that are usual for a bear this size.

After 1908, Steiff bears were given automatic growling voices. After 1910, or thereabouts, the shoe-button eyes were slowly replaced by black or black and brown glass eyes. Teddy bears are available in the following sizes (standing): 10, 15, 18, 22, 25, 30, 32, 35, 40, 46, 50, 60, 70 and 115cm (6, 7, 9, 10, 12, 13, 14, 16, 18, 20, 24, 28 and 45in). The miniature bears measuring 10cm (14in) are especially sought-after by collectors. Their development and change of form between 1910 and 1968 is shown on page 61.

left: Teddy bear made of brass-colored short-haired plush, 46cm (18in), black glass eyes, 1910-1914.
right: Teddy bear, dark brown, 34cm (13in), with partially replaced paws/soles, 1910-1914.

Typical *Original Teddy* as manufactured between 1930-1950.
left: 27cm (11in), yellow. The paint behind the glass eyes has peeled off, blank button, around 1948.
right: 27cm (11in), dark brown, 1935-1950.

Teddy bear around 1908/10. Ears far apart, loyal expression of shoe-button eyes and typical snout decoration.

Riding bears and bears on wheels have been available since the turn of the century in a large variety. They are either made of short-haired plush (inexpensive series) or of mohair plush. Children are very fond of them and they are very sturdy.

The jointed polar bear with ball-joint neck was an interesting new development in 1909. Furthermore, there were available:

- Teddy bears with muzzle and leash,
- teddy bears in knitted bathing suits, boy's outfit, and so forth,
- bear with hot water bottle,
- *Pantom Bear* (marionette),
- bear with clockwork.

The repertoire of teddy bears remained unchanged until the late years of World War I. After the war, teddy bears were made of cellulose plush and nettle fiber. The partial use of shoe-button eyes and black glass eyes was back until brown glass eyes were available once again. Until the late 1920s, *Original Teddy* barely changed.

left:
Bear, 74cm (29in), dark brown, shoe-button eyes. Black felt underlying nose decoration. Very large feet, soles of felt, underlying a strong insert of cardboard. Ears very far apart. Tilt voice in stomach. Very pleasant and friendly expression, vintage 1905-1908.

right:
Side view of bear. Obvious is the typical original form of the old bear with large hump, long and bent arms and pointed nose. The hump is only more visible in animals measuring 50cm (20in) or more. It is not quite as noticeable in smaller animals.

from left to right:
Fully-jointed polar bear with ball-joint neck (patented by Steiff), 13cm (5in) high, 24cm (9in) long. White mohair, some hair lost, black glass eyes, after 1909. Newly produced as replica in 1988. Very rare.
Later edition of polar bear, 7cm (3in), for hanging from rubber string (missing) above crib. Black glass eyes, green collar of mohair, heavy bell, after 1926, only in the program for a short time.
Polar bear, 17cm (7in), blue and black plastic eyes, head fixed, leather collar with bell. This polar bear was made around 1966, but the model was available as early as 1950. Further versions are sizes 12cm (5in) with black eyes and 25cm (10in) with blue and black eyes. All from after 1950.

After 1925, novelties were developed once more after the decade of war and crisis. Production had been stifled and Steiff had hardly taken up any new ideas. "Steiff Teddy Bears, especially soft and light, with kapok stuffing, blonde mohair plush, squeeze voice." This is how the bears of the kapok series were advertised in the novelty catalog of 1925. They are available in seven sizes ranging from 25cm (10in) to 50cm (20in), standing, and the bear seems to be pudgier than the *Original Teddy* from the same time. Further novelties from those days were the white, blonde or dark brown bears wearing colorful vests (*Teddybu*). These, however, were merely the *Original Teddy Bears* measuring 22, 25, 30 or 32cm (9, 10, 12 or 13in), standing, wearing felt vests. A bear on a bicycle, made as a talisman for cyclists (*Tali Bär*) was introduced in 1925. It carried a small flag and could be attached with a clamp. Colorful bears made of long-haired plush were also introduced in 1925. They were stuffed with kapok, had squeeze voices and were available in pink and yellow. Unusual were their sizes of 33, 36 and 40cm (13, 14 and 16in), standing, and later even 48cm (19in). The pink bear has been available as a replica since 1987/88 (*Replik Teddy Rose*), but this time with excelsior stuffing and tilt voice.

In 1926, the *Teddy Clown* followed. He was made of yellow mohair or mohair with brown tips and wore a clown's hat and a ruff.

left:
Original Teddy, 35cm (14in), yellow, after 1935.

right:
Side view of teddy bear on page 56. Hump is relatively small, flat forehead, arms are long and bent. Leftovers of the white flag still visible under the button.

bottom:
The ages of the smallest teddy bears around the size of 10cm (4in) are often difficult to determine. The six *Original Teddy Bears* shown here were made between 1910 and 1968. They have no claw decorations and no voices. The five on the left are fully jointed and have small black glass eyes.
From left to right:
White bear with light brown nose decoration, ears far apart, around 1910.
Brass-colored bear, early 1920s, black nose decoration. Ears close together.
Yellowish bear, mid 1920s. Head is not shaped as flatly as previous bears, ears still placed even more closely together.
Yellow bear with US flag on right arm, 1951-1953, noticeably skinnier than *Dickerle* (*Little Fatso*, fifth bear from left) from the 1960s. This model was around until 1964.
He is followed after 1965 by *Biegebär*. Caramel-colored, swivel head, bendable arms and legs, black plastic eyes and soft stuffing. The simplified cut was less expensive to produce than the cut of the jointed bears. We recommend very carefully comparing the shapes of the head as well as the ear positions.

Petsy, 40cm 16in), much sought-after, very rare in mint condition, blue glass eyes with black pupil. Mohair: formerly with brown tips, now faded, almost white. Claws are pink/red, as is the snout (felt underlying). Seam in middle running vertically from forehead across snout, 1928.

In 1928, it was followed by *Petsy*, again made of brown-tipped mohair with movable ears (due to a wire insert). He features the characteristic blue glass eyes with black pupil and a red/pink nose decoration. The *Teddy Clown* as well as *Petsy* were in the program for but a short period of time and are considered extremely rare in their original condition. Two musical bears appeared during the same year, featuring a pressure-activated musical work. They were called *Musik Petsy* and *Musik Teddy*. *Petsy* was also available in the *Record* version, mounted on an automatic vehicle. For a short time, *Record Teddy* was produced in 20 and 25cm (8 and 10in) sizes in golden (orange-yellow tips) color. Since the mid 1920s, the well-liked pulling vehicles, *Roly Droly*, were available. When pulled, two bears move in opposite directions.

After 1930/31, a new type of bear became the big hit with children. He is described as follows in the catalog: "Teddy Baby, jointed. Maize-colored, white or dark brown mohair plush. Model or a true-life talking young bear, friendly face, standing or sitting, as desired." *Teddy Baby* was first available in sizes 8, 10, 13, 15, 18, 20, 25, 29, 32, 35, 42 and 45cm (3, 4, 5, 6, 7, 8, 10, 11, 13, 14, 17 and 18in), standing. In the catalog of 1957/58, *Teddy Baby* is advertised for the last time, but only in the sizes 9, 22, 28 and 40cm (4, 9, 11 and 16in), and only maize-colored or dark brown. The smaller sizes with their cute velvet feet are especially popular with collectors.

from left to right:
Petsy, 25cm (10in), tipped mohair, blue glass eyes with black pupil, red/pink embroidered snout, mid seam, 1928.
Yellow teddy, 33cm (13in), same model as *Teddy Rose*, after 1925.
Original Teddy, 35cm (14in), white, typical model for late 1920s.
Original Teddy as before, but blonde (brass-colored).
Teddy Clown, 25cm (10in), tipped mohair (also available in yellow), clown's hat and ruff, after 1926.
Teddy Rose, after 1925.
Original Teddy as above, dark brown.
Illustration from Steiff's main catalog, 1929.

Riding bears and bears on wheels offered by Steiff around 1910. *Illustrierte Zeitung*, July 31, 1913.

The typical characteristics of the *Teddy Baby* are:
— in-set snout made of short mohair (in smaller sizes, made of velvet),
— open mouth in sizes 20 and over,
— little paws point to the back,
— flat feet made of short beige mohair with inserted cardboard disks to improve standing ability (in small sizes, feet made of velvet),
— paws and soles made of burlap instead of felt. After the mid *1950s*, made of rubber material similar to suede.

Teddy Babies were made of wool plush for a short time after 1930/31 (white, maize or dark brown), available in eight sizes, 18-45cm (7-18in), standing, with closed mouths. But as early as 1933, they were taken out of the program, as were the white mohair *Teddy Babies*. Those two are, therefore, considered extremely rare. *Teddy Babies* made of wool plush or rayon plush, with open mouths, were made during and after World War II. In the early 1930s, a *Record Teddy Baby* was available for a short time.

Roly Droly vehicles to pull.
Illustration from main catalog, 1929.

below:
from left to right:
Teddy, 13cm (5in), white, no claw decorations, bell inside body. Originally, the bear had been hanging on a string, to be suspended above a crib, 1922-1925. Typical shape of teddy bear as produced between 1910 and 1929.
Teddy, 19cm (7in), white, pointed snout, ears far apart, 1922-1925.
Teddy, 19cm (7in), white, head and snout more rounded, ears closed together, snout embroidery larger. Typical teddy bear 1935-1950.
Teddy bear as described previously, yellow.

Proud bear, brass-colored, never played with, original condition, relatively small shoe-button eyes. Mohair around snout has been shaved (original). Snout embroidery is horizontal. Long bent arms, ears far apart. Around 1910. Very rare in this untouched condition.
His favorite toy: felt duck, gray, green and orange, decorative seam in blue, varnished (natural color) eccentric wheels. Black eyes, glass pearls. One link of an *Entkett* (duck chain) from the 1920s.

Record Teddy mounted on automatic vehicle, 18cm (7in), 23cm (9in) if vehicle included, green wooden wheels, item No. 12E/320. Three black claws on each paw. Highly unusual color "golden" (the description "orange and yellow tipped" would be more accurate).
White ruff made of linen with blue buttonhole stitches around the collar, 1928. Very rare in this color.

Teddy, brass-colored, 36cm (14in). Very pointed snout. Felt paws and soles have been replaced. 1922-1925. Holding *Schlenkerteddyli*, 25cm (10in), rayon plush with knitted material, open mouth, made of felt, head attached with disk. Also available as *Werf Teddy* (*Throw Teddy*) with various clothes, 1946-1948.

From left to right:
Teddy Baby, 28cm (11in), maize-colored mixture of wool plush and alpaca plush, mouth closed, 1930/31.
Teddy Baby, 40cm (16in), dark brown, curly mohair, paws and soles made of beige burlap, production 1939-1941 and 1948/49. In-set snout and large feet made of beige low-pile mohair. Open mouth made of felt. Large *Teddy Babies* often do not look very friendly, but appear to be dangerous.
Teddy Baby, 28cm (11in), maize-colored rayon plush, open mouth made of felt, around 1948. Blank button. Playing with St. Bernhard, 10cm (4in), wool plush, 1929.

The "Star" of *Teddy Babies* of 1934, 8.5cm (3in), no voice. In-set snout, velvet, closed mouth, feet made of maize-colored velvet (look like slippers) with brown painted claws. This model available from 1930/31 until 1958.

left:
Schnappglieder Teddy (snapping joint teddy bear) with mechanism in neck, 25cm (10in), maize-colored, arms attached with disks, snapping joint legs, paws and soles made of velvet. Mouth can be opened, made of felt. Flat feet with wire reinforcement to improve ability to stand. Probably a prototype. Early 1930s.

right:
Schnappglieder Teddy, in sitting position.

Teddy Dicky, the grinning bear, was introduced in the 1930s, as well. He was available in 12 sizes between 10 and 70cm (4 and 28in), standing, in the colors blonde and white. The claws, colorfully painted onto the velvet paws and soles and the laughing mouth are typical for *Dicky*. The grinning expression is created by painting a long mouth, pointing way up towards the eyes, onto the snout. However, *Dicky* did not seem to have been too much of a success since he was cut from the program in 1936.

It is remarkable how much the teddy bear repertoire was cut in the 1930s. However, an addition to the program was the *Circus Bear*, 32cm (13in), with snapping joints and swivel head. His resemblance in cut to the *Teddy Baby* is obvious. He features a beige in-set snout (mouth closed, however), felt paws that are pointing to the back and flat feet with inserted cardboard disks. Since his cost was about twice as much as any other teddy bear of comparable size, it is safe to say that only a few bears were sold.

During this time, in the early and mid 1930s, another beige *Schnappglieder Teddy* with swivel head, 25cm (10in), was produced. His paws and soles were made of velvet. A very unusual feature are the separately added thumbs and toes. His mouth was made of felt and could be opened. The shape of his head was similar to that of the *Teddy Babies* or the small *Teddylis*. Since we have found no reference to this bear in any catalog, he might be a prototype.

The typical riding bear manufactured in the 1930s was made of dark brown mohair and had a beige in-set snout. He was available in five sizes, up to 50cm (20in), was mounted on red wooden wheels, and in sizes of 60 and 80cm (24 and 31in) on red metal wheels with black rubber tires. He was produced until 1958. Post-war versions were available in sizes 43, 50, 60, 80 and 100cm (17, 20, 24, 31 and 39in), all equipped with disk wheels. This brown bear differs from the young bear of the 1950s in the following ways: He features a darker mohair, a more pointed and lighter colored nose and a larger hump. In addition, the brown bear had a little tail. The first versions of the young bear were available after 1939.

In 1938, the first black and white jointed panda bear was introduced. Before World War II, he was available only in 30cm (12in). After the war, the bear was produced in six sizes, ranging from 15 to 50cm (6 to 20in). Production stopped in 1961/62. From the mid 1950s, the felt used to cover paws and soles was replaced by a gray rubber material that resembles suede.

Jackie, the anniversary bear, made for the 50th anniversary of teddy bears in 1953.
left: 1987 replica.
right: Original, in the program 1953-1955, rare.
Each measures 25cm (10in), carrying original booklet that accompanied them.

left: standing bear (No. 12/1343,2) on red wooden wheels, 43cm (17in), dark brown, light brown, in-set snout, four embroidered claws, light brown, on each paw. A favorite riding animal for children, from the early 1930s until 1958. Fairly rare in good condition.
right: *Young Bear* with red disk wheels and white rubber tires, also measuring 43cm (17in), caramel-colored. First versions available as early as 1939. During the early 1950s with fixed frame, after 1957 additional version with steering mechanism offered. After 1967, offered with so-called "pull-steering." The animal automatically follows the direction in which it is pulled. Frequent riding animal.

School of bears with 13cm (5in) teddy bears from the years between 1910 and 1940.
Teddy Teacher, 22cm (9in), 1910-1923.

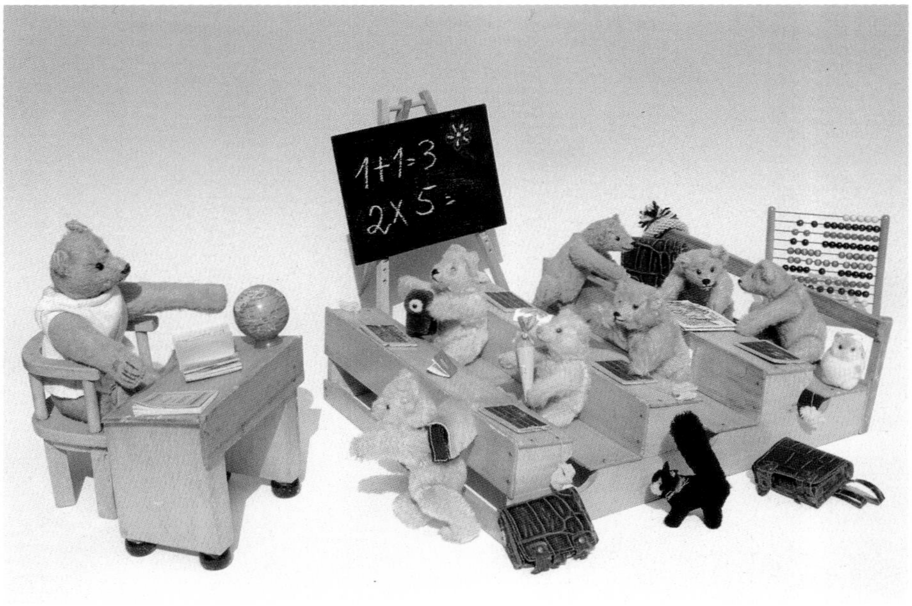

Typical white bear family of the 1930s, sizes 10, 13, 20 and 32cm (4, 5, 8 and 13in), light brown decorations. The 10 and 13cm (4 and 5in) bears have no voice. Among the colors offered at that time, white, blonde and dark brown, white bears are the rarest.
Woolen bird, 7cm (3in), gray and white mixed, yellow wire feet. This bird was available in five more colors. He was one of the first woolen miniatures produced by Steiff after 1931.

Two *Original Teddy Bears* of 1946/47. Typical form for bears in the 1930s and 1940s, 30cm (12in). Rayon plush, paws and soles of the yellow teddy bear are made of beige linen (replacement for felt.) The dark brown bear has as replacements light brown material, similar to tweed.
They are playing with a rare yellow, green and blue mohair play ring from the early 1930s, 30cm (12in) in diameter. Three woolen birds are sewn onto the ring.

Illustration on page 69:
Panda bear, looking for berries, 35cm (24in), strong squeeze voice with double tone. Gray rubber material resembling suede covering paws and soles, 1956-1962. Panda bears of the 1930s and early 1950s have paws of felt. The panda bear was offered in catalogs after 1938 and is rare, regardless of its size.

Special postal stamp of Giengen.

What are the differences in design of the Steiff *Original Teddy Bears* from the year 1905 to 1950? It is interesting that Steiff hardly changed the few illustrations in the catalogs up to 1933. After 1934, the bears were measured standing up and are given a little more special attention. Rough points of reference are the following characteristics and years: 1905-1910, shoe-button eyes, ears far apart. After 1910, black and brown and black glass eyes. After the early 1920s, brown and black glass eyes, exclusively. The ears remain far apart until the end of the 1920s and are only moved closer together during the 1930s. The illustrations on pages 59, 61 and 68 show typical *Original Teddy Bears* from 1930-1950. During this time, there were no major changes in cut. A new generation came into play in 1951. *Original Teddy* is given a new cut (see pages 70 and 72). The following chart gives an overview of the different sizes and colors combined with the years:

Height cm	in	caramel-colored (light brown)	golden (yellow)	dark brown	white
10	4	1951-1964	1951-1964	1951-1964	1951-1964
15	6	1951-1967	1951-1967	1951-1964	1951-1964
18	7	1954-1967	1954-1965	1954-1964	1954-1964
22	9	1951-1967	1951-1965	1951-1964	1951-1964
25	10	1951-1967	1951-1967	1951-1964	1951-1964
28	11	1951-1967	1951-1965	1951-1964	1951-1964
35	14	1951-1967	1951-1967	1951-1964	1951-1964
40	16	1956-1967	1956-1967	1956-1964	1956-1964
43	17	1951-1967	1951-1967	1951-1964	1951-1964
50	20	1951-1967	1951-1967	1951-1964	1951-1964
65	26	1951-1967	1951-1965	1951-1964	1951-1964
75	30	1951-1967	1951-1965	1951-1964	1951-1964

The bear measuring 10cm (4in) was replaced after 1965 by *Biegebär*, the bendable bear. In the 1950s and 1960s, teddy bears measuring 10 and 15cm (4 and 6in) did not have a voice, bears measuring 18-40cm (7-16in) had a squeeze voice and bears between 43 and 75cm (17 and 30in) had an automatic tilt voice.

Original Teddy Bears
Comparison 1930-1965.
from left to right:
Original Teddy as produced between 1930 and 1950. Nose embroidered with black thread, horizontally.
Original Teddy from between 1951 and 1953 with US flag. This model was available between 1951 and the late 1950s. Nose embroidered with black thread, vertically.
Original Teddy of the early 1960s, up to 1967; nose also embroidered vertically.

Dark brown *Teddyli* (girl), 25cm (10in), head made of mohair, open mouth of felt, beige in-set snout, the backs of hands and feet are made of dark brown mohair. Arms hanging down and made of burlap, as are the body and legs. Clothes made of felt and linen. The flag "Made in US Zone Germany" is attached to the right leg. Very rare in this condition (never played with). Item No. 91/12/325M, 1950-1958.
The maize-colored *Teddyli* (girl) was in the catalog for only five years and is, therefore, even more rare. Body, same as above, but wool plush was used instead of mohair. White in-set snout and hands and feet. Clothes made of linen with white collar made of felt. Flag "Made in US Zone Germany." There were models of boys to match each girl. Dark brown *Teddy Baby*, 10cm (4in) made of mohair/velvet, leftovers of US flag in the seam of the right arm.

middle, left:
After 1951, there was a new model of the *Original Teddy*.
left: 35cm (14in), yellow, with flag "Made in US Zone Germany," 1951-1953.
right: 30cm (12in), caramel-colored, produced between 1955 and 1963.

middle, right:
Zottelbär (*Shaggy Bear*) *Zotty* was very popular.

from left to right:
Floppy Zotty, 17cm (7in), very soft sleeping animal, after 1953, common.
White *Zotty*, 28cm (11in), made only in 1961/62, very rare.
Late model of a *Zotty*, 22cm (9in), plastic eyes and lentil button, produced between 1969/70 and 1978.
Early model of *Zotty*, 28cm (11in). Felt underlying the black and brown glass eyes, flag "Made in US Zone Germany." 1951-1953. *Zotty* bears were made of mohair until 1978.

bottom:
Wedding of bears. Two *Original Teddy Bears*, measuring 10cm (4in), white, 1960s and yellow, 1950s. Black glass eyes. Woolen birds with wire feet, 1930s.

The Brown Bear Family on an outing. Bear types as offered between 1951 and 1964 in the Steiff repertoire, in 12 sizes, from 10 to 75cm (4 to 30in).

bottom, left:
Original Teddy (1950s type), 52cm (20in), caramel-colored, silver button with block letters without drawn out F, letters very far apart. Leftovers of a beige paper flag, no US flag, 1951. He is playing with the dressed rabbit (female) *Hansili*, 25cm (10in), swivel head made of wool plush, blue and red dress made of felt and linen, squeeze voice, burlap body, 1951-1955, rare.

bottom, middle:
Original Teddy, 35cm (14in), just caught *Tulla*, the goose, on the farm and also has to take care of the little pink velvet piglet (*Tulla* and piglet from the 1960s). The classical teddy bear of the 1950s, common caramel coloring, slender body and pointed snout. 1955-1963, easy to find.

bottom, right:
Original Teddy, No. 5341,01, 39cm (15in), honey-colored. A difference in cut is clearly visible compared to the bear of the 1960s. Typical is the shaved snout. No claw decoration, after 1966.

The bears measuring 10 and 15cm (4 and 6in) do not yet have paws and soles made of felt. The bear measuring 18cm (7in) features beige soles made of felt. The paws of teddy bears from 22cm (9in) are also made of felt. Teddy bears from 18cm (7in) have four embroidered claws on each paw. Bears measuring 10 and 15cm (4 and 6in) do not have claw decorations. Up to 15cm (6in), snouts were embroidered horizontally, in larger *Original Teddy Bears* are embroidered vertically. This decoration is dark brown in caramel-colored and white bears, black in yellow and dark brown bears. Glass eyes were used up to 1963; then they were replaced by plastic eyes. The only exception were bears measuring 10cm (4in). Black plastic eyes were pulled into the head. *Original Teddy Bears* of the 1950s and 1960s were basically stuffed with excelsior. Between 1951 and 1953, a US flag was sewn into the seam of their right arm.

In order to distinguish more easily the bear type of the 1930s from the type of the 1950s or 1960s, we have listed the characteristics once more on page 70. While the position of the ears remained almost unchanged, the shape of the head and body have changed. Especially striking is the fact that the head increased in size over the years. That is the why the snout, still very pointed in the late 1950s and throughout the 1960s, lost its point to some degree. The prevalent taste during the late 1950s asked for a rounder teddy bear. His body became pudgier, the arms shorter and less bent. Arms and legs became much thicker in the 1960s. The bears measured at the belly 28cm (11in) in the 1930s and 1950s, but in the 1960s the belly line was increased to 32cm (13in). The hump hardly changed. The *Original Teddy* was very common in a caramel color, common in yellow, rarer in white and dark brown.

Collectors are especially looking for dressed bears. The name *Teddyli* alone is a declaration of love to the wonderfully dressed bear doll. Those bears had a swivel head made of wool plush or mohair. The first bear dolls were made as early as 1933. *Teddylis* are very rare in good condition.

The *Zottelbär* (*Shaggy Bear*) *Zotty* was a truly revolutionary novelty introduced by Steiff in the year 1951. He was available in 17/18, 22, 28, 35, 43 and 50cm (7, 9, 11, 14, 17 and 20in). He was made of brown-tipped, long and curly mohair, was jointed and had an open mouth made of felt. His chest was made of a light beige (yellowish) in-set and the felt paws pointed backwards. The stuffing was called "super soft." He remained a sales hit for decades and was often copied by competitors (in most cases without the lighter chest). The *Zotty* model featuring brown-tipped mohair remains in the program until 1978. A very rare model is the white *Zotty* measuring 28 and 35cm (11 and 14in), also with a light beige chest. We were only able to find him in the main catalog of 1961/62. *Zotty* was also available as a sleep animal, measuring 17 and 28cm (7 and 11in), also made of brown-tipped mohair. His name was *Floppy Zotty* and he is very soft. He is not very popular with collectors.

From left to right:
Raccoon *Raccy*, 17cm (7in), no voice, also available in 10cm (4in). After 1957.
Indian Panda Bears *Pandy*, 17 and 25cm (7 and 10in). Beautiful models with different mohair. Only made in 1963/64.

Three teddy bears made of Dralon plush, soft stuffing, no voice.
from left to right:
Dark brown *Cosy Teddy*, 30cm (12in), lighter chest, light brown short pile Dralon plush around snout, seams sewn with nylon or perlon threads. After 1966, available in dark brown or white, as early as 1957 in caramel with white chest.
Petsy, almost a baby still, caramel with white chest, not jointed, 22cm (9in), after 1961. After 1964, *Petsy* was delivered with babies' diapers.
Toy duck, 11cm (4in), standing, multicolored, after 1952.
This *Cosy Teddy* is especially nice only if he has not been played with and was never washed, smiling happily to himself. 40cm (16in), caramel-colored chest, short snout of white Dralon plush, open mouth, after 1966. Not very common in this white and brand new condition. Dark brown *Cosy Teddy Bears* are common, caramel-colored bears very common.

Breuni Bär, an advertising figure for the Breuninger Department Store in Stuttgart, 14cm (6in), in-set felt snout. Bendable arms and legs, black glass eyes, felt clothing, no voice. Produced in small numbers, therefore very rare, 1950s.

left:
Panda Bear, standing on four legs, *Pandy*, 12cm (5in), only in that size, no voice, 1955-1958, rare.
Next to *Pandy*, *Young Bear*, caramel-colored, 12cm (5in), no voice. This young bear was also available in 17 and 25cm (7 and 10in), without swivel head, 1950-1972, common.

right:
from left to right:
Cosy Orsi, 20cm (8in), Dralon, open mouth made of felt, not jointed, after 1955.
Betthupferl Teddy (*Bedtime Teddy*), 15cm (6in), Dralon/felt. After 1969.
Hockey player, 30cm (12in), Dralon, red felt trousers, after 1972.

Jackie Bear, made especially for the 50th anniversary (1903-1953) of the teddy bear, was a new model in 17, 25 and 35cm (7, 10 and 14in) and was introduced in 1953. *Jackie* is even rounder, pudgier and more short-legged than the *Original Teddy* of the 1950s. The pink thread running horizontally across the vertically embroidered dark brown nose is as characteristic as the dark brown, sprayed belly button. She remains part of the program until 1955 and is rare.

After 1952, the Orsi, the *Weichbär* (soft bear), 22cm (9in) became available. He is a little on the fat side and sits with his legs at an angle. His arms are attached with disks and he has a swivel head. After 1959, a version measuring 35cm (14in) was added.

Young bears standing on four feet are a welcome distraction for collectors who see mostly jointed bears. These were available in caramel-colored mohair in 12, 17 and 25cm (5, 7 and 10in) without wheels, in 28cm (11in) with wooden wheels, and above 28cm (11in) with red disk wheels. Only the bear measuring 12cm (5in) features a swivel head. All the other sizes have fixed heads. The soles were made of beige felt with four claws on each foot. Young bears without wheels were a part of the program from 1950 to 1972 and are, therefore, still rather common. Young bears on wheels have even been available since 1939.

The koala bear is another one of the Steiff bears. The bear in size 12cm (5in) had bendable arms and legs, sizes 22 and 35cm (9 and 14in) were jointed. Koalas were in the program between 1955 and 1962. They have been finished with great care and have wonderful expressions but are unfortunately very hard to find, except for the smallest one.

Interesting items for a collector are advertising items that were produced by Steiff on demand by clients. Among the bears, *Breuni Bär* was a rare and interesting caricature. He was designed especially for a competition by a large department store in Stuttgart.

The Indian panda bear, *Pandy*, is a further creation of great interest. Steiff has managed to make him very expressive due to the special and labor intensive cut and the use of mohair of different colors. He is much sought-after but hard to find since he was only in the program during 1963/64.

While searching for new models that were related to teddy bears, but digressed from his usual looks, new drafts were constantly presented. *Zotty Zolac* (dangling animal), zoo bear *Zooby* and *Lully Bear* are good examples. All three went into production eventually.

Three prototypes that were made in small numbers as trials but never made it into the program are illustrated at the bottom of page 75. Such prototypes are very rare and are very often extremely hard to recognize as Steiff products since they are usually not marked. They can only be identified by the characteristics of production that were typical for Steiff and the materials and cuts used.

Koala bears like to climb. A family of koalas in sizes 12, 22 and 35cm (5, 9 and 14in). 12cm (5in) without voice, bendable arms and legs. The largest bear has a very friendly look on his face, due to the suggestion of a small lower lip made of felt, 1955-1962.
Teddy bear collectors were debating for a long time whether koala bears were worth collecting. But by now they have become a part of the bear family, even though they are members of the family of marsupials.

left:
Soft bear *Orsi*, 22cm (9in), caramel, is helping the Easter Bunny. *Orsi* has soft stuffing, arms attached with disks and fixed legs attached at an angle. Beige in-set snout, open mouth made of beige felt. The original *Cosy* is wearing a blue bib made of felt around his neck. After 1952, 22cm (9in), after 1959, even 35cm (14in). The rabbits inside the basket are from the 1960s, the yellow wool chicks were made in 1954.

right:
from left to right:
Zotty Zolac, 40cm (16in), jointed dangling bear, soft stuffing, yellowish-beige chest, 1964-1967, rare.
Zoo bear, *Zooby*, 28cm (11in), arms attached with disks, open mouth made of felt, soles made of dark imitation leather, white claws made of felt, 1964-1967, rare.
Baby Bear Lully, 30cm (12in), open mouth made of felt, stubby paws and feet sewn in yellow, white chest, very soft stuffing, common. From 1961 to the 1970s.

After 1966, there was a new model of the *Original Teddy* in the colors honey (beige) and caramel (light brown) in sizes 19, 26, 36, 41, 51 and 66cm (7, 10, 14, 16, 20 and 26in). One outstanding characteristic is the shorter mohair around the snout and eyes. Among collectors, this phenomenon is known as "shaved bear," but also as pictured: *Owl Bear* or *Masked Bear* because of the shape of the added short-pile plush. After 1966, this type was available stuffed at first with excelsior, its paws and soles made of felt. But between 1968 and 1972, a switch was made to soft stuffing and paws and soles made of synthetic velours. The hand-sewn seam is on the back of the bear. Arms and legs are short, body and head are more flat and wider. This type of bear is still available today. It is very common and not very popular among collectors. Bears made of Dralon had been made by Steiff since the mid 1950s. But they were probably not as successful as their colleagues made of mohair. *Cosy Teddy* may have been the most popular one among them.

Three Steiff prototypes
from left to right:
Teddy bear made of caramel mohair with very pointed and narrow paws made of synthetic velours, soft and uneven stuffing, no voice, 27cm (11in). Hand-sewn seam on back. The typical seams on upper arms are missing. They are directly underneath the disk, close to the body. The tiny ears are too small in relation to the rest of the body. The shape of the snout decoration is unusual, as well. Late 1960s/early 1970s.
Original Teddy, type of the 1960s, honey-colored mohair, 43cm (17in). We did not find this bear in this color in any catalog. It is interesting, however, that the bear does have a button and a flag (no. illegible) which would indicate serial production. Mohair of this color was only used in the production of the following model with the shaved type, after 1966. It is possible that the honey color was tested in the earlier models and individual pieces were offered for sale.
Teddy bear with mink character. Cut and shape same as 1960s type, soft stuffing, synthetic plush, gray base with brown tips (similar material but of higher quality was used for *Minky Zotty*), 30cm (12in). He appears to be much pudgier than his colleague *Original Teddy* of the same cut and made of mohair (1960s) due to his soft, long pile plush. We did not find this bear in any catalog. He most probably was made in the early to mid 1960s.

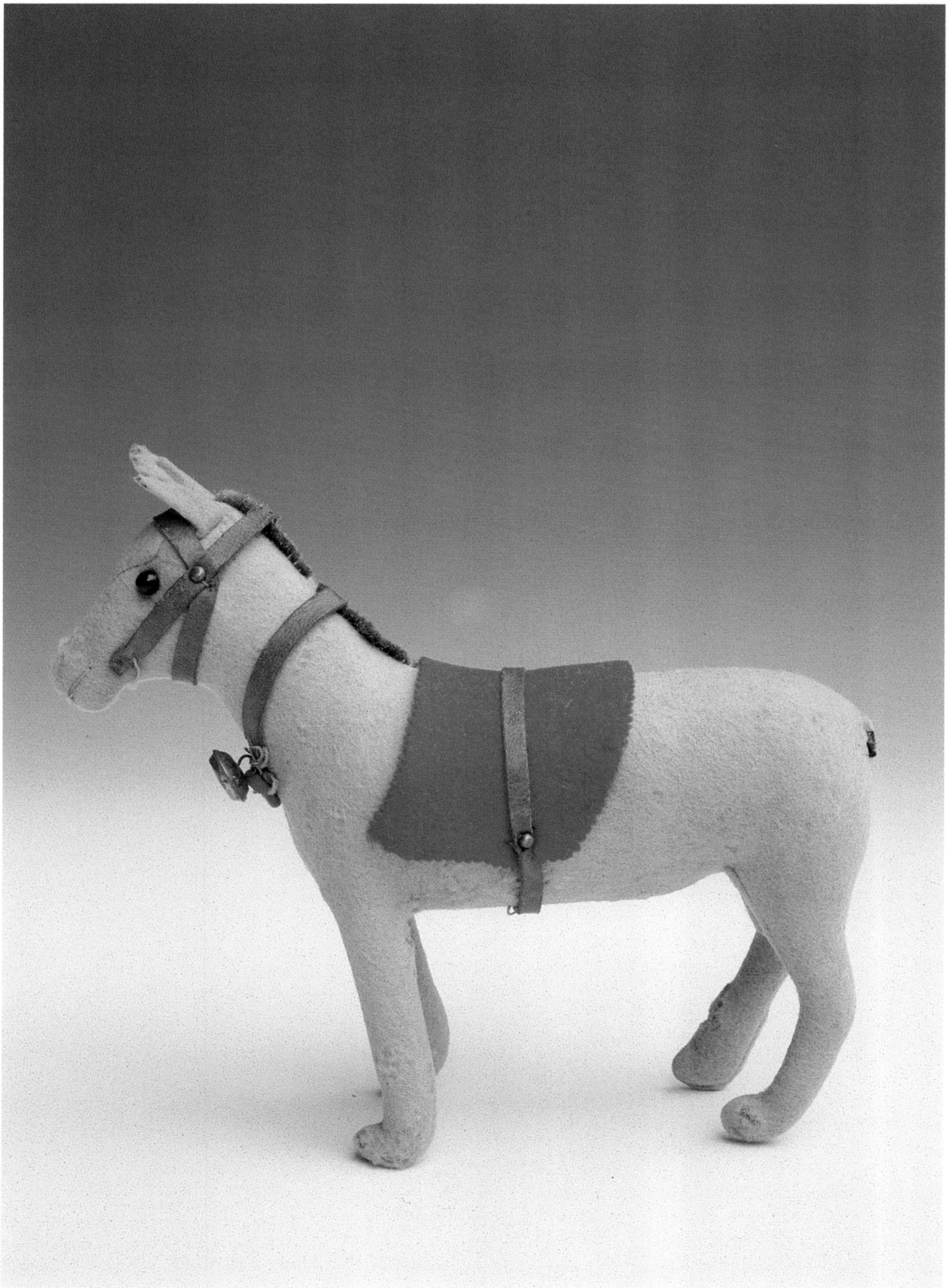

Domestic and Farm Animals

Note: Unless indicated otherwise, all domestic and farm animals feature the same main characteristics:
— no swivel head,
— mohair,
— excelsior stuffing,
— no voice,
— measurements in cm indicate the height, measured standing up.

House pets and farm animals always were among the largest animal groups within the Steiff program. We have, therefore, intentionally excluded some of the domestic and farm animals and given them their own chapters in order to give the reader a better overview. In this manner it will be easier to find certain animals. Special chapters have been devoted to the variety of dogs and cats, and roosters, hens, chicks and geese have been included in the chapter on birds.

Real lambs wool used to be the material early Steiff sheep were made of, but later they were made of wool plush and felt. Sheep have always been very popular since they make for a cute and cuddly companion. Lambs used as pincushions were used as early as the last century. And very popular were sheep on wheels that could be pulled. The first Steiff sheep were stuffed with leftover pieces of felt, later with wool. The wheels made of poured iron were rather primitive in the early days and were only improved with the years. The axles for animals on wheels ran through the hooves or feet of the animals until around 1905. The shape of the sheep which seemed rather inelegant in the beginning, was improved gradually. Silk ribbons were attached to their necks, some with an imprint of the Steiff name and bells. During the 1920s, the iron wheels were replaced by wooden ones. And towards the end of the 1920s, all wheels were changed to disk wheels. Only the smaller sheep kept their wooden wheels up to World War II. Wooden and iron wheels were usually varnished with a blue color. After 1951, a new lamb (standing) was introduced to the repertoire: *Lamby*, made of white wool plush. For years it remained the favorite gift for children (not only for Easter), and it remained in the program for 26 years. It is, therefore, very common. Only for a short time, after 1954, a version in a lying position and in two sizes was manufactured.

Illustration on page 76:
Donkey, shoe-button eyes, brown leather reins, red felt blanket. This type of donkey was produced from the turn of the century until 1910.

from left to right:
back:
Shepherd, 35cm (14in), rubber head, burlap body, after 1958. Also available in 19cm (7in), after 1969.
Young lamb, 14cm (6in), white lamb plush, green and black glass eyes, squeeze voice, mid 1930s.
Lamby, 14cm (6in), standing, white wool plush, green and black glass eyes, typical post-war model, 1951-1976, very common.
Lamb on wooden wheels, length: 25cm (10in), white wool plush, lying position, green and black plastic eyes, after 1966.
Lamb, height: 10cm (4in), length: 15cm (6in), white wool plush, green and black glass eyes, after 1954, only in the program for a short time.
Floppy Lamb, length: 25cm (10in), white wool plush, embroidered eyes (closed), soft stuffing, after 1954, very common.

Lamby, black and white with green and black glass eyes, white head and black or white tail was available in sizes 10, 14 and 22cm (4, 6 and 9in) in 1954 and 1955, exclusively. It is very rare compared to the all-white version. The black and white *Lamby* is often mistaken for the Persian lamb *Swapl* which is black and white, as well. In the Easter catalog of 1957, *Swapl* was introduced made of wool plush in sizes 10 and 14cm (4 and 6in), and made of curly mohair plush in sizes 22, 28 and 35cm (9, 11 and 14in). The eyes are blue and black and it remained part of the program in sizes 10 to 22cm (4 to 9in) until 1962. Further types of sheep were introduced in 1959, *Snucki*, the moorland sheep, and in 1966, *Wotan*, the ram.

Around the turn of the century, a very impressive billy goat with beard, with or without wheels, was made available. In the 1930s and 1950s, more goats were manufactured, but none of them that impressive anymore.

Pigs made of velvet and felt with or without iron wheels were also available around the turn of the century. In 1909, Steiff introduced a pig featuring a ball-joint neck. Almost at the same time they came out with a pink pig made of mohair, 50cm (20in) on iron wheels with a pull voice. "The pig produces its 'oink' when the left ear is pulled repeatedly." This is the description we found in the catalog of 1911. Another interesting animal is a squeaking pig that can be squeezed under one's arm to make it produce a sound remarkably similar to the real-life grunting of a pig. The shapes of the pigs around 1910 and in the mid and late 1920s are much closer to reality than the pigs made in the 1950s and 1960s. But those are still cute to look at and are often given away for good luck. They are, therefore, not that rare.

left:
from left to right: Lamb on iron wheels, 16cm (6in), wool plush/felt, squeeze voice, shoe-button eyes, pink silk ribbon with Steiff name in golden letters, 1908-1922.
Very early Steiff sheep on iron wheels, 10cm (4in), wool plush/felt, pearl eyes, virgin wool stuffing, around 1895.

right:
from left to right:
Persian Lamb, *Swapl*, 22cm (9in), curly mohair plush, open mouth made of felt, blue and black glass eyes, squeeze voice, 1957-1962.
Persian Lamb, *Swapl*, 10cm (4in), wool plush, blue and black glass eyes, 1957-1962.
Lamb *Lamby*, 10cm (4in), wool plush, blue and black glass eyes, only made in 1954/55.

from left to right:
Snucki, the moorland sheep, 22cm (9in), green and black glass eyes, squeeze voice, after 1959.
Wotan, the ram, 22cm (9in), wool plush, green and black plastic eyes, squeeze voice, after 1966.
Zicky, the goat, 10cm (4in), green and black glass eyes, squeeze voice, horns made of felt (or of wood, in goat of 14cm), after 1952.
Goat, 22cm (9in), blue/green and black glass eyes, squeeze voice, after 1934.

Oxen and cows have very beautiful natural shapes and felt versions of those animals were available around the turn of the century. Mohair oxen, with patches of brown and white were made from 1910 until the 1950s and offered for sale with the wheels appropriate for the times. Horns and hooves were sometimes made of leather. *Oxy*, the ox, was for sale during the 1950s for a short time.

Donkeys were more popular during the first two decades of this century than any time later. The catalog of 1916/17, for example, lists 33 different donkeys, mainly made of felt. Between 1938 and 1940, *Muli*, the mule, was introduced into the program for a short while. A new donkey was added after 1950. After 1960, *Grissy*, a donkey made of Dralon was offered for sale. Except for *Grissy*, donkeys in sizes larger than 22cm (9in) are rare.

Horses were a part of the repertoire even before the turn of the century. Children liked them especially as riding animals and animals on wheels. At first, they were mounted onto iron wheels, but after 1914, wooden wheels were introduced gradually and towards the end of the 1920s, most of them were replaced by disk wheels. Horses were mainly made of felt, short-haired plush, mohair or velvet.

Until the mid 1920s, there was a large variety of horses. In 1911, there were circus horses, dappled-gray and white horses. And there was a variety of accessories. There were different saddles and rockers that made a transfer from a riding animal into a rocking horse possible. These were built very solidly. In the 1930s and 1940s, however, the selection of horses was not that glamorous. After 1936, there were colts made of mohair. After 1937, they were made of wool mohair. In the years during and after the war, beautiful toy horses were made of rayon plush. After World War II, the colt, 28cm (11in), model 1936, was made of rayon plush, later of mohair. A new model was introduced with the black and white pony

left:
Pig, 10cm (4in), pink velvet with red snout of felt, black glass eyes, soft stuffing, 1910-1935.
Squeaking pig, height: 22cm (9in), length: 38cm (15in), shoe-button eyes. Hidden within the snout is the sound pipe for the grunting voice. Red gauze has been inserted into the snout so that the grunting is easily heard. 1916-1940.

middle:
Pig, 17cm (7in), shoe-button eyes, squeeze voice, around 1910.
Pig, 22cm (9in), on wooden wheels, shoe-button eyes, velvet snout, squeeze voice, mid/end 1920s.

right:
Squeaking pig from main catalog of 1924.

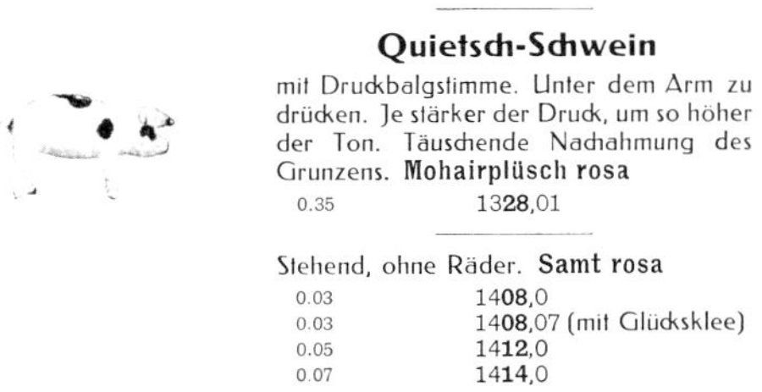

Quietsch-Schwein

mit Druckbalgstimme. Unter dem Arm zu drücken. Je stärker der Druck, um so höher der Ton. Täuschende Nachahmung des Grunzens. **Mohairplüsch rosa**

0.35 1328,01

Stehend, ohne Räder. **Samt rosa**

0.03	1408,0
0.03	1408,07 (mit Glücksklee)
0.05	1412,0
0.07	1414,0

top: Pig, 22cm (9in), blue and black glass eyes, open mouth made of felt, curly tail made of felt, squeeze voice, 1951-1962.
bottom:
from left to right:
Pig, 7cm (3in), blue and black plastic eyes, synthetic velours, 1970s.
Pig, 10cm (4in), blue and black glass eyes, 1960s.
Jolanthe, the pig, 10cm (4in), blue and black plastic eyes, synthetic velours, green clover leaf made of felt, soft stuffing, 1970s.
Pig, 10cm (4in), blue and black glass eyes, early 1960s.
Pig, 7cm (3in), blue and black glass eyes, early 1970s.

Oxen made of mohair with brown and white patches were available between 1910 and the early 1950s in several variations.
left: Ox, 22cm (9in), black glass eyes, horns made of velvet, squeeze voice, mid 1930s.
right: Ox on wooden wheels, 28cm (11in), gray felt underlying shoe-button eyes, horns and hooves made of leather, squeeze voice, mid 1920s.
Teddy bear, 22cm (9in), with lasso (not original), mid 1920s.

Left: *Oxy*, the ox, 22cm (9in), white and black glass eyes, velvet snout, velvet fold on chest, squeeze voice even in 10 and 14cm (4 and 6in) versions, 1954-1958, rare.
right: *Bessy*, the cow, 25cm (10in), white and black plastic eyes, open mouth made of felt, udder and horns made of felt, squeeze voice, 1958-1962, rare in this size.
front: *Bessy*, the calf, 12cm (5in), white and black plastic eyes, after 1958, common.

which was produced between 1951 and 1976 in 12 and 17cm (5 and 7in). The same model, this time with an opened mouth, was offered for sale as a horse, measuring 22, 28 and 35cm (9, 11 and 14in). But contrary to the pony, the horse did not stay in the program very long. Riding horses and horses on wheels that are white and brown, mounted onto blue disk wheels and measuring 43-100cm (17-39in) were sold with green felt blankets and red saddles and reins during the 1950s and 1960s. *Sheddy*, the Shetland pony, was introduced in 1960. Despite the fact that it is made of Dralon material, its features are very expressive.

left:
from left to right:
Donkey, 22cm (9in), black glass eyes, reins of red leather, squeeze voice, after 1950, rare. This model was also available in 12cm (5in), made of velvet, after 1950. Common.
Teddy bear, 10cm (4in), early 1960s.
Donkey, 14cm (6in), black glass eyes, reins of red leather (missing). After 1956.
Grissy, the donkey, 22cm (9in), Dralon, black plastic eyes, open mouth made of felt, orange, after 1960.

right:
from left to right:
Horse on wooden wheels, 28cm (11in), brown and black glass eyes, burlap, blue felt blanket, saddle and reins made of red leather, early 1930s.
Horse on iron wheels, 35cm (14in), felt, shoe-button eyes, red felt blanket, saddle and reins made of brown leather, after 1911.

from left to right:
Colt, 27cm (11in), brown and black glass eyes, squeeze voice, after 1936 in mohair.
Colt, 15cm (6in), brown and black glass eyes, velvet, from 1952.
Toy horse, 23cm (9in), brown and black glass eyes, rayon plush, very expressive form of wild horse, squeeze voice, 1938-1941.
Toy horse as above, 18cm (7in), no voice.

from left to right:
Horse, 22cm (9in), 1952-1958, brown and black glass eyes, also in 28cm (11in), and from 1954 to 1958 in 35cm (14in), all with open mouth made of felt and squeeze voice. Rare. Sizes 12 and 17cm (5 and 7in), on the other hand, with mouth closed, are very common. They are advertised as ponies in the catalogs between 1951 and 1976.
Ferdy, the toy horse, 18cm (7in), brown and black plastic eyes, after 1965.
Sheddy, the Shetland pony, 22cm (9in), Dralon, brown and black plastic eyes, after 1960.

Dogs

Note: Unless otherwise indicated in the captions, the following main characteristics are valid for all dogs:
— mohair,
— brown eyes with black pupil,
— snout decoration embroidered in black,
— squeeze voice,
— excelsior stuffing,
— no swivel head,
— measurements in cm always refer to total height (standing).

The large variety of dogs produced by Steiff in over 100 years is not even surpassed by the teddy bear phenomenon and its countless versions. Dogs, together with cats, are the favored household pets not only of children, but adults like them to decorate the apartment or to replace a live animal. But dogs have not always been the most favorite animals. One glance at early company statistics shows that dogs were not even produced until 1890. In the 1892 catalog, hunting dogs, bull dogs, poodles, dogs as "small fun-animals with soft stuffing with rubber string," and poodles as a part of the game of skittles were listed among others. Around the turn of the century, greyhounds, Great Danes, bull dogs (*Mops*), fox terriers, dachshunds (*Dackel*) and poodles were also available on iron wheels. Due to the teddy bear boom, the creation of new models of dogs moved into the background until 1924. Except for several variations of the fox terrier, St. Bernards were added in 1905, a sitting spitz and a spitz on wheels in 1908, and in the same year, a jointed bull dog made of rough plush. The only changes made were in the use of materials. Early in the century, felt and velvet were used. Often, the same model was sold in a short-haired plush and/or mohair version. During the early 1930s, however, most models were made of mohair, and the velvet or felt versions were gradually faded out. After World War I, paper materials and nettle fiber were used more and more.

Illustration page 82:
Variations on *Bully*, 7 to 43cm (3 to 17in). *Bully*, the bull dog was in high fashion between 1927 and 1936. He was available in the most varied models, materials and colors:
— standing, riding animal with wooden or disk wheels, on eccentric wheels,
— sitting, *Schlenker Bully* (*Bulliette*) (dangling *Bully*),
— as hand puppet, children's purse, pincushion and musical animal (*Music Bully*).
Early *Bullys* came with a hair collar. The lighter face mask was usually made of velvet; in small animals felt was used. The most common color combination was white/black, followed by white/golden (orange) and white/brown. The rarest colors are white/blue. All *Bullys* have a swivel head, except 7cm (3in) *Bully* and hand puppet.

left:
Spitz on iron wheels, 40cm (16in), pull voice, after 1908.

right:
Dachshund on eccentric wheels, 18cm (7in), around 1919. The nettle fiber as well as the brown glass eyes (not painted) with black pupils indicate that the animal stems from a time in which high quality materials such as mohair were scarce. This model was also available in felt or velvet and on iron wheels after 1910.

from left to right:
Sputnik dog *Laika*, 18cm (7in), corner eyes, very rare, only in the program during 1958.
Polar spitz, sitting, 12cm (5in), wool plush, snout and ears made of velvet, no voice, after 1951, rare.
Miniature spitz, white, 17cm (7in), after 1936, also available in sitting position.
Wolfspitz, beige and brown, 18cm (7in), after 1935, also available in standing position.
Spitz, 16cm (6in), after 1908, snout, ears and legs made of felt, shoe-button eyes, red wool string and pompons, original.

Molly, introduced in 1925, was a popular new development and was produced without interruption until 1970, except for war-related production stops, in the most varied versions. This model probably introduced a unique dog era in the history of plush animals. Almost every species of dog and any fad was offered in plush and often they were given the most imaginative names.
The following list including dates of issue gives an overview over the most popular dog models between 1925 and 1938.
1925 *Molly*,
1927 *Bully* (bull dog), *Pip*, *Zotty*,
1928 *Charly*, *Treff* (basset),
1929 *Strupp*, *Chow-Chow Brownie*, *Prince*, *Snip*, *Terry*, *Baldo*, *Cheerio*,
1931 *Scotty* (Scotch terrier), Sealyham, *Rattler* (schnauzer),
1932 *Lord* (Great Dane),
1933 *Peter*, Skye terrier, *Ajax* (wire-haired fox terrier), *Arco* (shepherd), *Chin-Chin*, setter, *Dackel*, *Waldi*, *Putzi*, burlap *Treff* and burlap *Arco*,
1935 wolfspitz, *Tommy* (Sealyham),
1936 *Puli* (Hungarian shepherd), Bedlington, *Troll* (hunting dog), *Tino*, *Zwergspitz* (miniature spitz),
1937 *Griffon*, *Waldili*, Irish blue terrier,
1938 wire-haired dachshund *Flock*, *Peky* (Pekinese).

Charly, children's purse with zipper, length: 20cm (8in), brown and white, squeeze voice inside tail, after 1929. *Music Charly* with pressure-activated mechanism, 26cm (10in), after 1928, rare.
Both dogs have swivel heads.

from left to right:
The smallest fox terrier, *Foxy*, 7cm (3in), white and black, no voice, around 1933.
Scotch terrier, *Scotty*, 9cm (4in), gray/black, no voice, swivel head, pink nose decoration. Collar tag imprint: "Scotty D.R. Patent US patented Jan.9.32," after 1931.
Sealyham, 10cm (4in), no voice, swivel head, after 1931.
Basset, *Treff*, 10cm (4in), no voice, swivel head, after 1928.

left:
from left to right:
Fox terrier, *Foxy*, 26cm (10in), white and black, after 1936.
Fox terrier, *Foxy*, 12cm (5in), swivel head, spotted silk plush, no voice, end 1930s.
Fox terrier, 32cm, beige with brown ear, black colored mohair around right shoe-button eye, after 1908.

right: Poodle, 22cm (9in), white wool plush and velvet, after 1933.

Bull dog, 28cm (11in), jointed, swivel head, shoe-button eyes, brown rough plush with painted pattern, inside of ears brownish-red felt, white mohair chest and front paws, after 1908. Sometimes delivered with muzzle and leash.

below:
left: *Bully*, 7cm (3in), white and brown velvet, white face mask made of felt, no voice, leather collar with five Steiff buttons.
right: Same as above, white and blue, hair collar, very rare, both around 1930.

from left to right:
Molly, 16cm (6in), white and brown tipped, 1925-1970. The model in the picture is from around 1960, with swivel head.
The smallest *Molly*, 7cm (3in), no voice, around 1929.
Molly, 20cm (8in), mechanism in neck, 1931-1934.
Peter, 17cm (7in), white and gray spotted wool plush, with swivel head, after 1933.
Pinscher, 27cm (11in), brown tipped mohair, after 1916.

left:
Colorful Charleston animals as puppets for play and display in cars.
from left to right:
Molliette in pink and yellow; *Cheeriette* in blue; *Original Teddy*, blonde, 1929; *Molliette* in green; *Fluffiette* in orange; *Rabbiette* in lilac and *Bulliette* in blue.
From Steiff main catalog, 1929.

middle:
from left to right:
Setter, 19cm (7in), brown, after 1933.
Griffon, 15cm (6in), wool plush, mixture of grays, after 1937.
Hungarian shepherd, *Puli*, 22cm, white, blue and gray, after 1936.
Wire-haired dachshund, 13cm (5in), yellow and brown shades, after 1938.

right:
from left to right:
Chin-Chin, 16cm (6in), beige, after 1933.
Pekinese, *Peky*, 10cm (4in), light brown, after 1953, very common.
Peky, 26cm (4in), beige and brown, black and white glass eyes, after 1965.
Peky, 10cm (4in), beige and brown spotted, only 1938-1940.
All of the above with swivel head.

The variety of these dogs can only be understood by reading the Steiff catalogs of the 1920s and 1930s. Let us take as an example the catalog of 1929. There are 27 versions of *Molly* in sitting position, standing up or on wooden wheels alone. In addition, there are *Mollys* to be hung from cribs or as "Charleston Animals" (dangling animals) in 18 versions, *Kasperl Molly*, six versions of animal purses, as pincushions in two sizes, and as *Musical Molly*. For this model alone, there are 56 variations!

With this example, the variety of ideas and the size of the dog program becomes clearest. There are, however, species that were only in the program for a very short time and which were only available in one or two sizes.

After World War II, around 1947/48, Airedales and fox terriers were made of silk plush, but in the 1949/50 catalog, they were already listed as made of mohair plush, as were Scotty, Sealyham, *Molly* and *Waldi*. This indicates that the old and successful models from the 1930s were produced again. The young dachshund, *Bazi*, sitting, 14 and 17cm (6 and 7in), was the only novelty. It is interesting to notice that the fox terrier, Airedale terrier, Scotty and Sealyham were offered in silk plush versions in the Easter Catalog of 1950 once again. Obviously, the transition between silk plush and mohair plush was gradual and was stretched out between the years 1947 and 1950/51.

Most pre-war dog models were not taken up again after World War II. The only remaining dogs were *Waldili*, *Waldi*, *Molly*, Airedale and fox terrier. Arco, Sealyham, Scotty as well as setter and St. Bernard on disk wheels were phased out during the 1950s and were partially replaced by other models. The repertoire of dogs during the 1950s and 1960s was at least as impressive as the program during the 1920s and 1930s. In order to give the collector an overview over the numerous post-war models, we have listed the novelties by year:

from left to right:
back:
Fox terrier, *Fox*, on eccentric wheels, 24cm (9in), silk plush, white with black and brown spots, 1948.
Airedale, *Fellow*, 22cm (9in), brown and black silk plush, 1948.
Fox terrier, *Foxy*, 17cm (7in), white with black and brown spots, early 1960s, very common. Model available after 1937.
Fox terrier, 17cm (7in), white with black and brown spots, in program only in 1954/55, rare.
front:
Airedale terrier, *Terry*, 8cm (3in), brown and black, no voice, after 1951.
Fox terrier, *Foxy*, 8cm (3in), white with black and brown spots, no voice, pre-war after 1937, post-war after 1951, very common.

1949 *Bazi*, sitting (young dachshund, later *Jungdackel*),
1950 *Sarras* (boxer), *Tosi* (poodle), *Bazili* (doll), *Music Bazi*,
1951 *Bully*, *Cockie* (white and brown, sitting, cocker spaniel), polar spitz, *Spitz*, sitting,
1952 *Snobby* (French poodle), *Cockie* (standing, light brown), *Beppo* (dachshund),
1953 *Peky* (Pekinese), *Snobby* (poodle, jointed), *Dally* (dalmatian), *Floppy Cockie*,
1954 St. Bernard, standing, *Tessie* (schnauzer), *Hexie* (dachshund),
1957 *Arco* (new model of shepherd, standing, from 17cm (7in), with tongue), *Arco*, lying position,
1958 *Biggie* (standing beagle), *Laika* (Sputnik dog),
1959 *Revue Susi* (cocker spaniel),
1960 Collie, lying position, *Mopsy*,
1962 Basset, *Rolly* (dalmatian), 1963 *Lumpi* (dachshund),
1964 *Bernie Samarit* (St. Bernard with cask),
1965 *Raudi* (wire-haired dachshund), *Biggie* (sitting, beagle),
1966 *Corso* (afghan),
1968 *Electrola Fox*.

During the 1950s and 1960s, dog miniatures, 10cm (4in), were very popular and some of them are very common as collectors items. During the 1960s, dogs were still the largest animal group in the entire Steiff repertoire and they take up the most space in the catalogs. The large variety of dogs and the great imagination of the Steiff designers is truly admirable. But it can also be said that the dogs from before 1940 have more expressive features, they are worked with greater attention to detail and look more natural. One typical characteristic for Steiff

left:
from left to right:
Wire-haired fox terrier, *Ajax*, 25cm (10in), pressed mohair plush (with wave), after 1933.
Wire-haired fox terrier, *Ajax*, height: 10cm (4in), length: 27cm (11in), white wool plush, unpainted brown glass eyes with black pupil, after 1933. Also offered in lying position and on pillow.
Skye terrier, 22cm (9in), beige and black, corner eyes, after 1933, rare.

middle:
Rattler with mechanism in neck, gray, 12, 20, 33 and 8cm (5, 8, 13 and 3in), corner eyes, 8 and 12cm (3 and 5in) without voice. Rattler measuring 12cm (5in) features collar tag with inscription: "Schnauzer." All animals with mechanisms in neck have a cardboard tag attached to their tails with the following inscription: "Turn here and I will turn my head" in three languages, 1931-1940.

right:
from left to right:
Miniature poodle, *Maidy*, 22cm (9in), curly mohair plush with Persian structure, corner eyes, nose black and pink, claw decorations pink, inside of ears made of mohair, only made during 1959.
Poodle, *Tosi*, karakul haircut, wool plush, corner eyes, no voice, US flag, only 1950-1952, rare. Same dog available in four sizes and in white.
French poodle, *Snobby*, 28cm (11in), wool plush, swivel head, US flag, only 1952, rare. Also available in 17cm (7in) and white.

Family of St. Bernards
from left to right:
St. Bernard, 10cm (4in), white and light brown wool plush, no voice, 1929.
St. Bernard, on wooden wheels, 24cm (9in), white and brown, 1929.
Same model, sitting position, 10cm (4in), no voice, swivel head, only in 1936, rare.
St. Bernard, 10cm (4in), white and light brown spotted, no voice, after 1954.
Bernie Samarit, 20cm (8in), with original wooden cask, white and light brown spotted, 1964-1967, rare.
Bernie, 14cm (6in), sitting position, white and light brown spotted, no voice, after 1963.

from left to right:
Dachshund, *Lumpi*, leaping, 18cm (7in), black and brown, after 1963.
Young dachshund, *Beppo*, 15cm (6in), black and brown spotted, jointed, 1952-1962.
Young dachshund, *Bazi*, 14cm (6in), light brown, standing, no voice, flag: "Made in US Zone Germany," 10cm (4in) after 1950, 14cm (6in) after 1951.
Young dachshund, *Bazi*, 10cm (4in), sitting position, after 1950. In 14 and 17cm (6 and 7in) after 1949, otherwise as described above.
Dog doll, *Bazili*, 23cm (9in), body made of burlap, flag: "Made in US Zone Germany," 1950-1955, very rare in this condition.
All dogs with swivel head, except *Lumpi*, the dachshund.

from left to right:
Shepherd, *Arco*, 10cm (4in), ears made of felt and snout made of velvet, no voice, 1951-1956.
Arco, 22cm (9in), open mouth without tongue, inside of ears made of felt, flag: "Made in US Zone Germany," 1933-1956.
Arco, 11cm (4in), ears made of felt, no voice, after 1957.
Arco, 24cm (9in), open mouth, after 1957. Most striking difference to the model of 1933: tongue, inside of ears made of mohair, different color pattern.

dogs is the hand-sewn seam running along the dog's stomach. Riding animals are an exception to that rule. In pre-war models (standing), the squeeze voice is activated by pressing on the dog's side, in post-war models, by pressing on its stomach (exceptions: *Maidy*, the miniature poodle and the prototype of the standing dalmatian). In sitting models, the voice is activated in pre-war dogs by pressing on the side or the front, in post-war models generally by pressing on the front.

left:
from left to right:
Chow-Chow, *Brownie*, 34cm (13in), beige, inscription on back of collar tag: "Zeppelin Mascot," after 1929.
Polar spitz, *Chow*, 24cm (9in), beige wool plush, flag: "Made in US Zone Germany," rare.
Same model in 12cm (5in), but snout is inset and ears are made of velvet, no voice, both after 1951.

right:
from left to right:
Afghan, *Corso*, length: 40cm (16in), no voice, soft stuffing, 1966-1968, not very common.
Collie, sitting position, 22cm (9in), no voice, after 1962.
Collie, lying position, length: 40cm (16in), after 1960.
Shepherd, *Arco*, length: 37cm (15in), after 1957.
Collie and *Arco* both have open mouth made of felt and red felt tongue.

from left to right:
Schnauzer, *Tessie*, 14cm (6in), no voice, after 1954, common.
Bull dog, *Bully*, 20cm (8in), velvet snout, US flag, after 1951.
Dog, *Mopsy*, 22cm (9in), white and black plastic eyes, after 1960, common.
Boxer, *Sarras*, 22cm (9in), snout made of mohair/velvet, inside of ears made of felt, after 1950.
All dogs with swivel head, except *Sarras*, the boxer.

from left to right:
Cocker spaniel, *Cockie*, 16cm (6in), light brown, open mouth made of velvet, 1951-1957.
Cockie, 18cm (7in), brown and white, model following the previous, after 1957.
Cockie, 18cm (7in), *Revue Susi*-type, but in standing position, light brown, white and black plastic eyes, after 1960.
front: *Floppy Cockie*, 18cm (7in), soft stuffing, after 1954, common.
All dogs with swivel head, except *Floppy Cockie*.

from left to right:
Dachshund, *Hexie*, bow-legged, 12cm (5in), white and black glass eyes, no voice, swivel head, after 1954.
Dog doll, *Waldili*, dressed as a hunter, with rifle, 22cm (9in), black plastic eyes, body made of burlap, swivel head, 1937-1974. Post-war versions are common.
Dachshund, *Waldi*, 14cm (6in), black glass eyes, 1933-1978! 45 in the program and, therefore, the most common Steiff dog of all.
Wire-haired dachshund, *Raudi*, 24cm (9in), white and black plastic eyes, swivel head, after 1956.

from left to right:
Cocker spaniel, *Music Cockie*, 18cm (7in), white and black, with Swiss musical work to wind, 1955-1962, rare.
Cockie, 30cm (12in), plastic corner eyes, brown and white, open mouth made of felt, 1957-1959, rare.
Cockie, 14cm (6in), white and brown, open mouth made of velvet, 1951-1959.
Butch, 32cm (13in), corner eyes, closed mouth, flews made of felt. Inscription on collar tag: "Butch the cover dog Copyright by Albert Staehle." late 1950s, rare.
Revue Susi, 17cm (7in), white and black plastic eyes, light brown, after 1959, very common. Also available in 12cm (5in) (very common) and in 28cm (11in).
All dogs with swivel heads.

from left to right:
Dalmatian, *Rolly* (modeled after Walt Disney design), 12 and 22cm (5 amd 9in), white and black plastic eyes, in larger model, white rings of wax cloth underlying the eyes, 22cm (9in) version has in-set velvet snout, 12cm (5in) version has machine-sewn snout decoration, no voice, after 1962, rare.
Dalmatian, 23cm (9in). To date, no reference found in any catalog. Therefore, this is probably an advertising item or a prototype of the late 1950s. Unusual for a post-war model is the fact that the voice is activated by squeezing on the side. This feature usually identifies the pre-war dalmatian.
Dalmatian, *Dally*, 10cm (4in), open mouth made of velvet, swivel head, after 1953.

left: Poodle, *Snobby*, jointed, 22cm (9in), corner eyes, after 1953 in black and white, after 1954 in gray, very common.
right: Poodle as advertisement for the Walther Company, 34cm (13in), wool plush/mohair. Not typical for Steiff animals: Face is made of rubber with painted eyes. 1950s, rare.
Both dogs have swivel heads.

right:
Electrola Fox (*His Master's Voice*), 12, 17 and 25cm (5, 7 and 10in), Dralon with ears made of mohair, 12 and 17cm (5 and 7in) without voice, after 1968. 12cm (5in) version until 1972, 17cm (7in) version until 1969, 25cm (10in) version until 1970, rare.

from left to right:
Basset, 12cm and 22cm (5 and 9in), brown and black plastic eyes with white edge, no voice, swivel head. Rare since only produced during 1962 and 1963. A further basset was an advertisement for the shoe company Hush Puppies, similar cut, but no swivel head, around 1965.
Beagle, *Biggie*, 11cm (4in), corner eyes, no voice, after 1958, not very common.
Biggie, 10cm (4in), machine-sewn snout decoration, no voice, swivel head, after 1965.

left: Caricature of dog, *Putzi*, 22cm (9in), wool plush, eyes and nose made of shoe buttons, red felt tongue, soles made of burlap with cardboard insert, bushy brown eyebrows, after 1933, only in the program for a short time, very rare.
right: *Mopsy*, the ballet dog, 18cm (&in), Dralon with mohair chest, inside of ears made of black velvet, white and black glass eyes, red felt tongue, only in 1961/62, rare, both with swivel head.

Cats

Note: Unless indicated otherwise in the captions, the following main characteristics are valid for all cats:
— no swivel head,
— mohair,
— green eyes with black slit pupil,
— excelsior stuffing,
— nose and claw embroideries in pink or red,
— no voice,
— measurements in cm refer to total height (standing).

Plush cats and their predecessors made of felt and velvet have been very popular with children ever since they were invented. Next to dogs, these common house pets were favored because they were funny and cuddly and because they would only hiss when pressed. In the first catalog of 1892, cats were already offered with and without voices. They were available in sitting and standing positions, on iron wheels, as parts in a game of skittles or as pincushions. Around the turn of the century, cats in lying positions were sold as rattles for children. The expression of the cats from the last century is, in general, rather simple. But this improved with the years and the cats became very true to nature. This is true for cats made before 1955. After that year, as a rule, the shapes of the bodies and especially the typical facial expressions were once again simplified.

At first, shoe buttons and pearls were used for eyes. But as early as 1892, cats with more naturally-looking glass eyes could be purchased for an additional fee. The eyes were yellow and green with black slit pupils. They were not perfectly round, but had a straight edge at the top. After World War I, round glass eyes in blue and green with black slit pupils were used. They can be found for example in *Fluffys*. After World War II, the color of the eyes change to a watery light green with black slit pupils. An exception is the Siamese cat, *Siamy*. This cat was given blue and black glass eyes.

The early cats from before the turn of the century were usually of one single color, white, gray or black. Some of them were tabbies. They were made of felt or plush. The markings were painted onto the coat with brush and color. After 1905, the cats' legs, head and even tails could be moved, thanks to disk joints. In 1911, Angora cats, cats made of lamb plush and cats dressed as ladies, babies and *Puss-in-Boots* were introduced as novelties. Tumbler cats and cats to be hung from cribs were added. In the 1913 catalog, the first cat on wooden eccentric wheels was introduced. It was made of felt and had the painted markings of a tabby. The repertoire of cats remained practically unchanged until the mid 1920s, due to the war.

Typical cats as described in the 1914 Steiff catalog. Advertisement from the *Illustrierte Zeitung*, 1914.

Illustration page 92:
back: left: *Lizzy*, gray and white, 23cm (9in), after 1968.
right: *Snurry*, beige and brown, 12cm (5in), soft stuffing, embroidered eyes (closed), swivel head, after 1964, not common.
front:
from left to right:
Tabby mounted on red wooden eccentric wheels, squeeze voice, 15cm, late 1930s, not common.
Fiffy, white and gray, 14cm (6in), soft stuffing, swivel head, after 1955, not common.
Floppy Kitty, very common, 17cm (7in), embroidered eyes (closed), soft stuffing, after 1954, not very popular among collectors.

Gray *Tabby* made of velvet, on iron wheels, painted with brush, 19cm (7in), light green glass eyes (upper edges cut off at an angle), beige snout decoration, soft stuffing, inner steel frame to increase stability, tail with excelsior stuffing. Axles through paws, indicating that this must be a very early model from around 1900. Similar models were available until the mid 1920s. Very rare.
Gray cat made of felt with painted stripes on wooden wheels with natural varnish, 22cm (9in), shoe-button eyes, squeeze voice, after 1913, rare.

In 1926, *Fluffy*, in sitting position, was introduced. It was produced in nine sizes between 7 and 43cm (3 and 17in). The long mohair on the chest and the snout was white and the tips of the hairs on the back were colored blue and gray. This "tipped" mohair gave *Fluffy* a very natural look. For a short time, during the early 1930s, there was a model of *Fluffy* made of gray and white mohair plush. But the tipped *Fluffy* remained in the program until shortly after World War II and was a very popular cat. The blue and gray tipped model made of mohair has often been bleached by sunlight so that *Fluffys* often turned beige or a light gray with the years.

From 1928-on, a cat in lying position with painted light brown stripes became part of the program. It was made of mohair and velvet and was later given the name *Tabby* (see *Tabby* 1928, appeared as a replica in 1986). Versions in standing positions and *Tabbys* on eccentric wheels were added and from in the late 1930s, they were only available with gray stripes.

In 1930, the Siamese temple cat, *Siamy*, was introduced to the great delight of cat fans. Made of beige mohair with in-set dark brown plush, the character of this noble cat was reflected very well.

Susi, with gray stripes and in sitting position, was another well-known and very popular cat of the 1930s. It was also sold after World War II in a slightly modified version. Between 1931 and World War II, *Kitty*, a jointed cat with a mechanism in the neck, was produced. When the tail was turned, the head turned, as well. There were *Kittys* with mechanisms in the neck in sitting and standing positions, but they were not as well- known, since they were only part of the program for a short while in the 1930s. In the early 1950s, *Kitty* was sold as a jointed cat without mechanisms in the neck once again. Body and head were slender and paws and snout were white. The character of a cat was much better reflected in this model than in the following one (1955-1970), which appears to be over-simplified. In this late model, paws and snout were not inserted, the body was pudgier and the dark stripes on the back were interrupted.

Tapsy and *Tabby* are often confused.
left: *Tapsy*, 8cm (3in), no squeeze voice, 15cm (6in) with squeeze voice, mohair with brown stripes (sprayed), for the first time in the supplementary catalog in 1959, common.
right: *Tabby*, 7cm (3in), gray stripes, markings on back not interrupted, late 1930s.
Tabby, 14cm (6in), description as above, but with squeeze voice, markings on back interrupted.
Tabby was sold until 1977, was one of the most popular cats, very common and not very popular among collectors.

Also worth mentioning are the fully-dressed cat dolls in 22 and 28cm (5 and 11in) that were offered in the 1930s. They were similar to *Waldili* and were dressed in various boy's and girl's outfits.

After World War II, after 1948, *Susis* and *Tabbys* were made of silk plush according to pre-war cuts. In 1949, *Fluffy* and *Kitty* (no mechanism in neck, but jointed) were added.

In the early 1950s, silk plush was replaced by mohair. The black caricature *Tom Cat* was offered in 8 and 10cm (3 and 4in) made of velvet and in 14, 17 and 22cm (6, 7 and 9in) made of mohair plush. The *Tom Cat* was available as early as the turn of the century, however, with a much stronger arch. Also among the novelties was, in 1950, a musical cat in standing position and fully dressed with a pressure-activated Swiss musical work. Music plays when the cat is squeezed. The *Musikkatze* is considered rare since it was only in the program until 1952. *Tabby, Susi* and *Kitty* were offered in 14 different variations, once again in mohair after 1951.

Cats from the post-war years until around 1955 resemble in proportion and expression the pre-war models to a T. And often, if the button is missing, they are mistaken as such. It can be helpful to look for the US flag on the right front leg (from the cat's point of view) in order to determine the age more accurately.

Two new developments were the black and white *Gussy* in two sizes (1952) and *Siamy* in sitting position with an open mouth. *Siamy* was only offered in the 1954/55 catalog after World War II. It has a swivel head and blue glass eyes.

from left to right:
Fluffy, 8cm (3in), gray and white.
Fluffy, 21cm (8in), swivel head, squeeze voice, 1926-1950.
"Soft, young kitten made of wool plush, gray and white, 17cm." This was the description in the 1935/36 catalog, squeeze voice, swivel head, back of ears made of gray felt, predecessor of *Susi*.
Susi, gray and white tabby, made of mohair, 18cm (7in), swivel head, squeeze voice. Interesting combination of markings: Post-war button, sign with angular bear's head, US flag, 1951-1953, after 1936 part of the program.
Susi, later version, after 1956, 20cm (8in), swivel head, squeeze voice. Difference to earlier model: wider head, markings on back interrupted, snout decoration embroidered horizontally, front paws not made of mohair and inserted, but turning into the leg without seam.
Susi is one of the most common cats and was part of the program until 1978.

Siamese temple cat, *Siamy*, light beige/dark brown, 27cm (11in), blue and black glass eyes, closed mouth, squeeze voice, swivel head, 1930-around 1940, rare in such good condition.
Gray cat, six joints: legs, head and tail with disk joints, 15cm (6in), amber-colored glass eyes with angular upper edges, squeeze voice, swivel head, after 1905 until about the mid 1920s. Very interesting feature: seam running through center of face, rare.

Kitty, the musical cat in sitting position and *Fiffy*, in lying position in 12, 17 and 25cm (5, 7 and 10in), were further novelties after 1955. As early as 1952, there was a predecessor to *Fiffy*: a gray and white cat made of mohair in lying position, available in 22cm (9in). This must have been a test run since the cat was only in the program for one year. Further interesting models are the brown and beige *Tapsy*, standing (1959), *Kalac*, the tom cat (1964) and *Snurry*, the cat in lying position with embroidered eyes that were closed (1964). The following cats made of Dralon are also worth mentioning: *Cosy Kitty* (white and gray, standing, 1955), *Cosy Minka* (white, standing, 1962), *Cosy Sulla* (gray and white, standing, 1965), Persian cat, *Diva* (sitting, white or gray, 1967), Angora cat, *Diva* (lying position, white or gray, 1968).

Cats form the largest group and collectors will find them relatively often. This is especially true for models such as *Tabby, Susi, Floppy Kitty* or the black tom cat. *Siamy, Fiffy* and musical cats are harder to find.

left: *Kitty*, 18cm (7in), jointed, with mechanism in neck, gray and white tabby markings, uninterrupted, on back, nose embroidered vertically, squeeze voice, 1930s.
back, right: *Kitty*, 17cm (7in), jointed, no mechanism in neck, markings on back interrupted, nose embroidered horizontally, pudgier shape of head and body, 1955-1970, 10cm (4in) version has mohair ears and snout.
front, right: *Kitty*, 10cm (4in), jointed, no mechanism in neck, gray and white tabby markings on back uninterrupted, nose embroidered vertically, slender body and head, 1950-1954, 10cm (4in) version has little felt ears and in-set velvet snout.
All with swivel head.
Mouse, *Pieps*, 8cm (3in), gray, after 1958, also available in white with red eyes.

The first velvet version of the caricature of the tom cat with high arch and high tail appeared among the novelties in 1903/04.
from left to right:
17cm (7in) version with blue and green glass eyes, ears made of velvet, produced between 1926 and 1934.
Tom cat, 14cm (6in), difference to above model: shorter mohair for body and tail, green glass eyes, no claw decoration, 1950-1976, common.
Siamy, brown and beige, sitting, 11cm (4in), blue glass eyes with black, round pupil, open mouth made of felt, brown ears made of felt, swivel head, in-set face mask made of velvet, only made in 1954/55, rare.
White and black *Gussy*, 17cm (7in), swivel head, open mouth made of velvet, velvet ears, squeeze voice. Also available in 12cm (5in) with closed mouth. After 1952, not very common.

from left to right:
Betthupferl Katze (bedtime cat), 15cm (6in), gray and white, little red coat made of felt, after 1969.
Puss in Boots, Lix and *Lixie*, 13cm (5in), body made of rubber (in most cases defective since rubber is very old), head and tail made of mohair, clothing made of felt and linen, after 1954, very cute, very rare in good condition.
Musical cat, *Kitty*, 20cm (8in), white and gray stripes, inside of ears made of felt. Swiss musical works inside the body, wound by turning the tail, melody: "Guten Abend, gute Nacht." 1955-1958, rare.
All with swivel head.

from left to right:
Kalac, the tom cat, black and white, 40cm (16in), jointed as dangling animal, yellow and black plastic eyes, swivel head, only in 1964, rare.
Dangling cat, 32cm (13in), blue and gray, made of Orlon and Dralon, very soft stuffing, red scarf made of felt, after 1972.
Hoppelkatze, 24cm (9in), mounted on frame with red disk wheels, rubber tires, velcro underneath paws allows removal from frame, claw decoration sprayed, after 1967.

Angora cat, *Diva*, made of white Crylor, 30cm (12in), yellow eyes with black, round pupil, after 1968.
Persian cat, *Diva*, gray long-haired Dralon plush, 35cm (14in), swivel head, yellow glass eyes with black pupil, after 1967.

Maxi

Forest and Field Animals

Note: Unless otherwise indicated in the captions, the following main characteristics are valid for animals of the field and forest:
— mohair,
— excelsior stuffing,
— no squeeze voice,
— black eyes,
— no swivel head,
— measurements in cm refer to total height (standing).

In order to keep the volume of this chapter down to a manageable size and to give a better overview to the reader, we have dedicated a separate chapter to the large group of rabbits. It is interesting to see that animals who live in the forest and the field (with the exception of rabbits) were not very numerous among the animals produced by Steiff up to 1950. True, there are deer, foxes, squirrels and a few others, but in comparison with the breadth of other species, these numbers are rather insignificant.

Animals of the woods and fields were not discovered by Steiff designers until the 1950s and 1960s. Once they were discovered, they were copied in plush versions. The main goal in this case was not necessarily to show the funniness and to stress how cuddly those animals are, as may be the case with deer and squirrels. Animals such as snails, lizards, spiders or ferocious wolves were made, as well. Firstly, we will take a closer look at the largest group, the deer. Around the turn of the century, they were available made of burlap and short-pile plush, mainly as riding animals or on wheels (see page 13). One interesting item is a brown buck in lying position made of velvet. It features an elephant button from 1904/05. Deer made of felt or short-pile plush and mounted on iron or wooden wheels were produced until World War I. During the mid 1920s, there were no deer in the program. Only towards the end of the 1920s was another model made. This time mohair plush was used and the animal was mounted on wooden or disk wheels, 28-50cm (11-20in). And it was not until the mid 1930s that the repertoire started to grow. Complete deer families were now part of the program: a buck with antlers, different fawns and in 1938, a doe was added. These models hardly changed their forms until the 1950s, in some cases even into the 1970s. Materials used were the only change. At first, mohair was used, the legs, however, were sometimes made of velvet. Starting during the late 1930s, wool plush and rayon plush were the favored materials. Walt Disney's *Bambi* was a huge success. It was "born" in 1951 and was available in sizes 14 and 22cm (6 and 9in). It remained a hit for years. All deer made after the mid 1930s have one common characteristic: a light pink thread running across the vertical black nose decoration. All deer made between 1935 and 1975 are very common with the exception of the deer in lying position, made in the 1930s.

Illustration page 98:
Skunk, *Skunk*, 10cm (4in), mohair/velvet, brown and black glass eyes, after 1962.
Mole, *Maxi*, 10cm (4in), soft stuffing, with red or blue shovel, after 1964.
Dormouse, *Dormy*, 10cm (4in) in diameter, soft stuffing, after 1966.

top:
Roebuck, 10cm (4in), velvet, shoe-button eyes, antlers made of felt, soft, virgin wool stuffing, very little excelsior, elephant button, 1904/05, very rare.

bottom:
left: Fawn, 12cm (5in), velvet, after 1951.
right: Walt Disney's *Bambi*, 22cm (9in), after 1951.

The first chamois were offered in 1939. They were available in three sizes and were made of mohair with horns of black leather. There was also a chamois kid made of wool plush without horns. After 1962, there were chamois in 17cm (7in) with horns made of felt and a kid, 12cm (5in), without horns. The first capricorns were added in 1963 in the sizes 14, 22 and 28cm (6, 9 and 11in). Reindeer (after 1956) and moose (after 1963) were manufactured by Steiff, as well. Their markings are beautiful and their antlers look very natural and impressive. Reindeer stayed in the program for 15 years; moose, however, were only sold for two years and are, therefore, rare.

The jointed Steiff foxes were added in 1910. They had a very natural look. The same model, this time on eccentric wheels, was introduced in 1916. Both versions (each in three sizes) remained in the repertoire until the late 1920s. From the start of the 1930s-on, a new model of fox made of wool plush was sold. It was offered in sitting position and on eccentric wheels for a very short time, and in standing position until the end of the 1950s, but now it was made of mohair. The following model was the leaping fox, *Xorry*, who was available from 1969-on. Collectors should also be very interested in the very rare couple of fox dolls, *Fixili*.

Squirrels were made as early as the turn of the century and were sold in a velvet version. The variety of squirrels can be seen in the illustration on page 102. Squirrels are considered common.

Again and again, new models of animals in forests and field were developed. Young wild boars (velvet) in 1952, young wild boars (mohair) and wild boars, 20cm (8in), in 1962, wild boars, 15cm (6in), in 1969, various hedgehogs, the dormouse in 1966, the mole in 1964, a skunk in 1962 and a gold hamster in 1955. Especially interesting to the collector are those models that were in the program for only a short time, such as the wolf (only in 1964), the badger (only in 1963/64), and the lynx (only in 1963). Collectors also like snails, lizards, spiders and bats. They, too, were in the program for a very short time, were probably sold in very small numbers and their chances for survival were not very good, given the sensitive materials they were made of. Some interesting Dralon models were made in the 1960s, e.g. ermine, weasel and chinchilla.

from left to right:
Roebuck with antlers, 35cm (14in), squeeze voice. After 1936, form made of wool plush, completely made of mohair after 1954-1973. Our example is from the mid 1960s.
Fawn, 22cm (9in), spotted, glass eyes, after 1954.
Roebuck with antlers, 35cm (14in), legs made of velvet, shoe-button eyes, squeeze voice after 1938.
Doe, 28cm (11in), squeeze voice, mohair, 1954-1970.

from left to right:
Fawn, standing, 14cm (6in), spotted, after 1954.
Fawn, lying, 12cm (5in), squeeze voice, after 1936.
Fawn, standing, 22cm (9in), spotted wool plush, US flag. This form was made before the war in mohair with velvet legs. After the war, there were different rayon plush versions. 1949-1953 in wool plush, as depicted. Following model just like fawn, far left.
Kid, lying, length: 35cm (14in), mohair with Dralon chest, after 1966.

Chamois, 17cm (7in), black leather horns, squeeze voice, 1939-1941, very rare.

left: Lady bug on wooden wheels, height: 9cm (4in), length: 15cm (6in). Wire legs move when pulled to create the impression of a crawling bug. Mid 1920s.
right: June bug on iron wheels, height: 8cm (3in), length: 16cm (6in), shoe-button eyes, felt/mohair, antennae missing, after 1915.

top: Chamois, 17cm (7in), green and black glass eyes, ears and horns made of felt, after 1962.
left: Capricorn, *Rocky*, 28cm (11in), green and black plastic eyes, horns made of felt, squeeze voice, after 1963.
middle: Capricorn, *Rocky*, as above, but 14cm (6in), no voice.
right: *Original Teddy*, 22cm (9in), mid 1920s.

from left to right:
Female fox doll, *Fixili*, 25cm (10in), brown and black glass eyes, swivel head, burlap body, squeeze voice, traditional costume, US flag, after 1950, rare.
Fox on eccentric wheels, 20cm (8in), brown and black glass eyes, fixed head, squeeze voice, after 1916.
Fox, 14cm (6in), jointed, brown and black glass eyes, swivel head, squeeze voice, after 1910.
Fox, as above, but 20cm (8in).

from left to right:
Fox, standing, 17cm (7in), brown and black glass eyes, swivel head, squeeze voice, after early 1930s in wool plush, 1951-1959 in mohair.
Under hunter *Waldili's* arm, fox model as on left, but 10cm (4in), no swivel head.
Following model, *Xorry*, 18cm (7in), leaping, fixed head, size 28cm (11in) with squeeze voice, after 1960.
Dog doll, *Waldili*, 28cm (11in), pre-war version after 1937, rare.

from left to right:
back:
Walt Disney's squirrel, *Perri*, 17cm (7in), felt paws, nut made of velvet, 1959-1980, available in 12cm (5in) until 1983.
Squirrel, 20cm (8in), squeeze voice, velvet nut, 1936-1956.
Squirrel, *Possy*, light brown, 22cm (9in), squeeze voice, velvet nut, 1957-1976, in gray 1957-1970.
front:
Squirrel, 11cm (4in), velvet/mohair, 1936-1941.
Squirrel, brown, 10cm (4in), velvet/mohair, 1950-1957, also available in gray.
Squirrel, 10cm (4in), velvet/mohair, shoebutton eyes, turn of the century.

left: Young wild boar, 10cm (4in), blue and black eyes, after 1962.
right: Wild boar, 20cm (8in), blue and black plastic eyes. squeeze voice, after 1962.
front: Two young wild boars, 7cm (3in), velvet with varying intensity of color, after 1952.

back: Wild boar, height: 70cm (28in), length: 125cm (49in), brown and black glass eyes, tusks poured in PVC. Made as display animal in the 1960s.
front:
from left to right:
Two wild boars, 20cm (8in), blue and black plastic eyes, brown and black glass eyes, respectively, squeeze voice, after 1962.
Wild boar, 15cm (6in), brown and black plastic eyes, soft stuffing, after 1969.

from left to right:
Moose, *Moosy*, 25cm (10in), squeeze voice, only in 1963 and 1964.
Moosy as above, but 14cm (6in), no voice.
Reindeer, *Renny*, 22cm (9in), squeeze voice, 1956-1970.
Reindeer, *Renny*, as above, but 14cm (6in), no voice.

Family of hedgehogs
from left to right:
Three small hedgehogs, length: 6cm (2in), mohair/felt, after 1966.
Hedgehog, *Joggi*, length: 10cm (4in), lying position, mohair/Dralon, after 1966.
Joggi, 12cm (5in), at attention, swivel head, after 1951.
Joggi, 15cm (6in), lying position, after 1962.

from left to right:
Marmot, *Murmy*, height: 6cm (2in), length: 18cm (7in), (tail included), after 1960, rare.
Hamster, *Goldy*, 10cm (4in), swivel head, after 1955, common.
Goldy, 14cm (6in), fixed head, open mouth made of velvet, soft stuffing, after 1955.
Marmot, *Piff*, 17cm (7in), swivel head, squeeze voice, open mouth made of felt, after 1962.

top:
left: Badger, *Diggy*, at first listed as "*Diggi*" in the catalog, at attention, 15cm (6in), brown and black plastic eyes, after 1959.
right: *Diggy*, lying position, height: 13cm (5in), length: 32cm (13in), brown and black plastic eyes, squeeze voice, very complex cutting pattern requiring four different types of mohair plush, claws made of felt, only in 1963, rare. Smaller version (height: 6cm [2in], length: 16cm [6in]) in 1963 and 1964 in program.
bottom:
left: Wolf, *Loopy*, 25cm (10in), brown and black plastic eyes, squeeze voice, only in 1964, rare. Also available in 35cm (14in), open mouth, tongue and teeth.
right: Lynx, *Luxy*, 25cm (10in), yellow and black plastic eyes, squeeze voice, Dralon chest, only in 1963, rare.

from left to right:
Spider, *Spidy*, length: 12cm (5in), wire/chenille legs (similar to pipe cleaners). Only three glass bead eyes (cross spiders have eight eyes), 1960-1962.
Spidy as above, but 22cm (9in) in length, wire legs covered with mohair. Only seven glass bead eyes. Both are rare.
Bat, *Eric*, 10cm (4in), body of mohair with wire/chenille arms and legs, ears made of felt, wings made of plastic foil, 1960-1962.
Eric as above, but 17cm (7in), wire arms and legs, covered with mohair. Both are rare.

Lizards, 20 and 30cm (8 and 12in) in length, velvet, 1959-1962, rare.
Snails, 10cm (4in), top in green or brown spotted velvet, underside in beige wax cloth material, house made of PVC, 1962-1963, rare.

from left to right:
Ermine, *Wiggy*, 12cm (5in), Dralon, after 1962.
Chinchilla, *Gogo*, 15cm (6in), Dralon, tail made of mohair, swivel head, after 1965.
Weasel, *Waggy*, 12cm (5in), Dralon, after 1962.

Steiff
Original
geschützt
Germany
Jmporté
d'Allemagne

Rabbits

Note: Unless otherwise indicated in the captions, the following characteristics are valid for all rabbits:
— Squeeze voice,
— mohair,
— excelsior stuffing,
— brown eyes with black pupils,
— swivel head,
— nose and mouth embroidered in pink/brown (decoration),
— measurements in cm always refer to total height (standing).

The Steiff sales statistics published in the anniversary publication of 1930 indicates that rabbits had been produced since 1890. In one year alone, 1088 rabbits were sold. These figures put the rabbits on second place in popularity after only one year, closely behind elephants (1215 pieces). In the first catalog of 1892, rabbits appear in many versions:
— made of felt as parts in a game of skittles,
— made of felt or plush with steel frame, with and without iron wheels, jumping and with or without voice,
— in sitting position with and without voice, with soft stuffing for small children,
— rabbits on an elastic string ("weichgestopptes Scherztier," i.e. "softly stuffed fun animal"),
— as pincushion on a knitted bed of moss,
— on a three-wheeled bike with and without a basket on their backs.

A large percentage of the rabbits featured from the very start a silk ribbon, matching in color, with a bell around its neck. The variety of rabbits was increased every year. Rabbits in lying and sitting positions as well as rabbits at attention were added to the program. New materials were introduced as well: short-haired plush, mohair plush, lamb plush and velvet. Around the turn of the century, very soft rabbits made of velvet were sold as children's rattles. These are rabbits in sitting position with a soft stuffing. Inside their bodies there is a hollow space with a ball inside which creates a rattling noise when the animal is shaken.

Illustration on page 106:
Rabbit, never played with, 25cm (10in), at attention, in original condition. White lamb plush, black glass eyes with underlying red felt, no voice, no swivel head, inside of ears made of pink velvet. The rabbit is wearing a red felt jacket with yellow stitching. The original blue handkerchief is still in the pocket. The red felt slippers with leather soles are also original (see illustration on page 109). In its left ear, button and white flag with item No. 4522,6. After 1905, the model depicted from around 1914. Very rare in untouched and complete condition.

Rabbit No. 80 (with basket on back), on three-wheeled bike with patent wheels. Taken from the catalog of the "Filz und Spielwaarenfabrik Giengen" ("Felt and Toy Factory in Giengen") in 1892 (reprint).

Rabbit on eccentric wheels, height: 13cm (5in), length: 25cm (10in), felt, no swivel head, shoe-button eyes with underlying red felt. Original silk ribbon around neck, inscription: "Steiff" in golden letters. Hanging ears are very interesting. Lead weights have been inserted to keep them hanging in position. This model also available in mohair versions and in felt, rare, 1913.
Rabbit, 9cm (4in) high, 13cm (5in) long, black glass eyes with underlying red felt, no swivel head, without voice, rare, 1916.

The markings were painted by hand. Shoe buttons were used for eyes except for smaller animals. There, black and red beads were used. Nose decorations were embroidered with red, pink or beige cotton yarn or bead yarn. Natural bristles were used for whiskers. At the beginning of the 20th century, cute animals meant for petting and dressed rabbits were added to the original version of the rabbits. The company's catalog of 1911 displays dressed rabbits wearing tails made of colorful felt and felt slippers with leather soles. There are also rabbits at attention with backpacks. One highly valued toy is the "Holländer Hase" (Dutch rabbit) whose arms, legs, heads and ears can be moved. He was newly produced as a replica in 1988. But rabbits were still available in the form of pincushions, tumblers and wobbling animals (*Rolly Polly*). Rabbits to be hung from cribs were also made of felt and velvet. Shape and variety of rabbits hardly changed until the mid 1920s. But between 1916 and 1920, due to World War I, an austerity program had to be implemented as far as the number of models was concerned. In the years between 1918 and 1921, good material was scarce and replacement materials such as paper and nettle fiber had to be used. Only very few models made of those materials were manufactured according to pre-war patterns. After the time span between 1921 and 1926, the program hardly changed and the pre-war patterns were once again used.

from left to right:
Brown rabbit in lying position, felt, 6cm (2in), red bead eyes, around 1900.
Velvet rabbit as rattle, 9cm (4in), shoe-button eyes, white with painted brown spots. Soft stuffing, interior rattle, around 1900.
Velvet rabbit with white and black spots, sitting position, 7cm (3in), black bead eyes, around 1900.
All without swivel head and without voice, very rare.

from left to right:
Rabbit, 15cm (6in), brown tipped mohair, inside of ears are beige, soft stuffing, long adjustable ears with inserted wire, late 1920s.
Rabbit at attention, 26cm (10in), mohair with increased percentage of wool, eyes made of colored glass with black pupils, no swivel head, inside of ears made of felt, early 1920s.
Rabbit at attention, 27cm (11in), orange, chest and inside of ears in white, very long feet and ears, soft stuffing, 1929, rare.
White rabbit, sitting position, 18cm (7in), ears adjustable (inserted wire), soft stuffing, 1929.

After 1927, the rabbits became more colorful: golden, orange, lilac, pink and light blue. The rabbits' clothes added some color, too. Novelties were now Charleston animals as toy and car dolls, among them *Rabiette*, the rabbit, with long dangling arms and legs. The rabbit's head is made of brown tipped mohair plush, the body of velvet in blue, pink or lilac. Fists and feet are made of lightly colored mohair plush. In 1931, the first rabbits with new head movement were introduced. They featured a copyrighted mechanism in the neck. In the early 1930s, wool plush was used more and more in the production of rabbits. As a consequence, they became about 10 percent cheaper than the mohair models. Clothing became more interesting during the 1930s, as well. Under the heading "Animal Dolls," the 1933 catalog offered rabbit dolls in 14, 22 and 28cm (6, 9 and 11in) in white or maize for sale.
The so-called "funny" clothing was available in six versions:
— sports shirt with blue pants,
— pajamas,
— playsuit with red pattern,
— bathing suit, red/yellow,
— loose dress,
— blue playsuit.

Rabbits made of rayon plush were available after 1938. They were made in white with black spots or blue and gray/orange/white, the colors running together, in sitting position or at attention. In the main catalog of 1939/40, 63 different rabbits were described and some of them were depicted. This large repertoire was reduced during the war until the production of plush animals was halted completely in 1943.

But in the post-war catalog of 1949/50, nine rabbits were listed already. They were made exclusively from mohair plush. At first, there was no time for the design of new models and, therefore, the pre-war patterns were used exclusively. Since the sales of rabbits are seasonal, Steiff began to issue a special Easter catalog after 1950. More and more new models were added to the program after that. Among the most successful creations was *Niki*, the rabbit, made of gray/white mohair who had full moving ability. We found him in the Easter catalog of 1951. In 1985, a limited edition of a *Niki* replica of the 1952 model was produced, this time in brown/white. Interestingly enough, there is no catalog reference for the brown/white *Niki*!

Leather sole of a felt slipper belonging to rabbit No. 4522,6 (page 106). Inscription: "Knopf im Ohr. Regstd. No. 423888, Made in Germany."

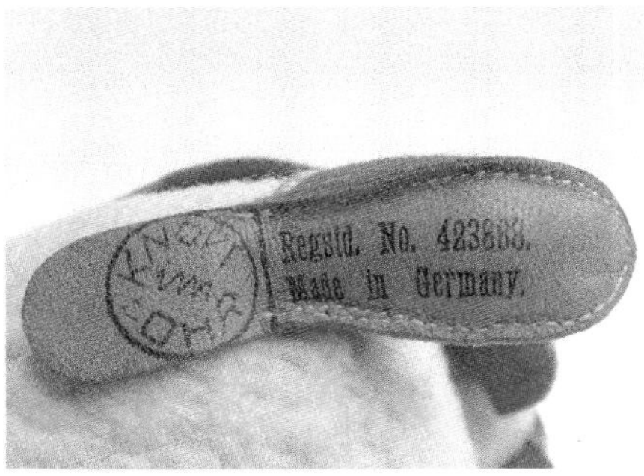

from left to right:
Rabbit in sitting position, 15cm (6in), rayon plush, inside of ears made of felt, no voice, after 1938.
Rabbit doll, 27cm (11in), head made of light brown wool plush/mohair, backs of hands and feet made of wool plush, inside of ears made of white felt, skirt made of red/green wool muslin, green felt vest, short white blouse sleeves, white voile apron, white linen underwear, red scarf made of muslin, only in 1939/40. Very rare in complete condition.
Rabbit, 19cm (7in), Alpaca plush, maize/ white, very soft stuffing, pink painted claws, early 1930s, very rare.
Rabbit, *Ossi*, 15cm (6in), brown and white spotted mohair, inside of ears made of white felt, only in 1939/40.

Rabbits were quite successfully modeled after the living animal in various positions. The four most common positions are:
left to right:
jumping rabbit, 8cm (3in), no swivel head, inside of ears made of felt, in this size produced from 1951-1974. After 1974, sold as *Hoppy*.
Rabbit at attention, 10cm (4in), inside of ears made of felt, 1951-1974. After 1966 sold as *Manni*.
Rabbit, *Sonny*, in sitting position, 10cm (2in), inside of ears made of mohair, 1966-1976.
Rabbit in lying position, 6cm (2in), white and black plastic eyes, swivel head, inside of ears made of white velvet, 1952-1970. All rabbits very common.

Bibbie and *Bib*, the rabbit couple. Female *Bibbie*, 12cm (5in), made of rubber or PVC, head made of beige mohair, ears made of velvet, some of them had ears sewn to have inside of ears pointing to front or back. Originally, *Bibbie* was carrying a wicker basket of natural color on her back. A small white woolen pompon marks her tail on the backside of her dress. Her clothing consists of a red/white linen skirt. As far as we know, there are four different patterns available. *Bibbie* is wearing white felt underwear. Her top consists of a red linen blouse with white collar made of felt and a yellow felt jacket. No voice, 1954-1962, rare.
Rabbit doll, *Bib*, materials and finish same as *Bibbie*. Clothing: yellow jacket, brown felt pants, beige linen shirt, orange silk ribbon around his neck. Woolen miniature, little rabbit made of wool, ears made of felt, 1960s.

from left to right:
Bedtime rabbit, 15cm (6in), no voice. This series consists of four rabbits in the following colors: orange, red, green and blue. Further bedtime animals: cat, teddy bear, dog and fox, after 1968.
Rabbit, *Ossili*, 30cm (12in), inflexible legs, bendable arms, open mouth made of felt. Green apron, red tie made of felt, soles of feet made of rubber material similar to suede, after 1962.
Female rabbit, *Yella*, 20cm (8in), inflexible body, bendable arms. Red and white striped cotton skirt with blue shoulder straps made of felt, after 1966. Matching male is named *Yello* (not illustrated).
Bedtime rabbit, as above, but with green skirt.

Rico Rabbit, 43cm (17in), jointed, blue hat and scarf (missing).
The rabbit on the right, *Lulac*, is shaped similarly. Version measuring 60cm (24in) in length (highly unusual), only during 1965 and 1966 in the program. *Lulac* measuring 43cm (17in) is fairly common since it was produced for the relatively long time between 1952 and 1973. Versions after 1973 were partially or completely made of synthetic fiber. Blue and black squinting eyes.
Rabbit on eccentric wheels (pull-animal), 8cm (3in), after 1957. Rare in this size.
Front: Baby rabbit, *Sassy*, 22cm (9in), soft stuffing, inflexible body, after 1955, very common, also available in 30cm (12in).

from left to right:
back:
Rabbit, *Pummy*, 25cm (10in), mohair/Dralon, after 1963, common.
Niki, sitting position, 25cm (10in), Dralon, soft stuffing, after 1969, very common.
Transformation Rabbit, 25cm (10in), fully-flexible hind legs and can, therefore, be put into lying, sitting, jumping and attentive positions, after 1957. Also available in 17cm (7in).
Rabbit, *Ossi*, 23cm (9in), mohair/Dralon, after 1962. Also available in 18cm (7in).
front:
Sleeping animal, *Floppy Hansi*, 17cm (7in) long, eyes embroidered, no swivel head, no voice, soft stuffing, after 1954, very common.
Timmy, 10cm (4in), Dralon, black felt ears, no swivel head, soft stuffing, after 1965.
All without voice.

from left to right:
Rabbit boy, *Nikili*, 26cm (10in), head made of mohair, open mouth made of felt, arms attached with disks, black pants, red felt vest. 1958-1962, rare.
Rabbit, *Niki*, jointed, 35cm (14in), measured in sitting position, gray/white, open mouth made of felt, US flag, available in five sizes, 1951-1962.
Rabbit girl, *Nikili*, 26cm (10in), same as boy but with skirt, no vest, 1958-1962.
Rabbit, *Niki*, jointed, 17cm (7in), measured in sitting position. Same as 35cm (14in) version, but no voice.

Another big hit was the dangling rabbit, *Lulac*, who was introduced into the program in 1952. According to the catalog, its stuffing is "super soft," it is made of mohair and after 1974, two versions were available, one made of mohair/Dralon, one made of synthetic fibers exclusively. Those last two versions do not really belong to the field of collecting. The 43cm (17in) version of *Lulac* made of mohair is found frequently due to his long time within the program. The 60cm (24in) version, however, is very rare since it was only in the program in 1965 and 1966. Within the Floppy series which was especially designed for small children, *Floppy Hansi*, a rabbit in lying position, was introduced in 1954. Collectors are not interested in this item.

Dralon, introduced in the 1950s, brought on a new age in the history of plush animal production. The first rabbit made of Dralon was called *Cosy Mummy*. During the following years, new Dralon rabbits were added almost annually. During the early 1960s, there were models made of mohair with Dralon inserts, e.g. *Ossi*, the rabbit, in 1962. Dressed rabbits are very much sought-after by collectors (rabbit dolls). Cute names such as *Hansili, Nikili, Ossili, Bib* and *Bibbie* are a collectors' delights. The larger rabbits could be dressed and undressed. The disadvantage is that today the rabbits are most often found without their clothes. Rabbit dolls are very hard to find in untouched and complete condition. The skiing rabbits, *Hupfi* and *Knupfi* and *Rico Rabbit* in winter outfits, prove that rabbits are no longer only Easter items. Rabbits are, compared to other species, relatively common. But even here, as is the case with other animal groups, some models were only manufactured for a very short time and are, therefore, very rare. Among them are the dressed rabbits, *Nikili, Hansili, Bib* and *Bibbie* as well as velvet, rattle and felt rabbits.

Knupfi, the crippled skiing rabbit, 18cm (7in), white and black plastic eyes, green/red Perlon velours, with plastic ski pole, arm in a sling, leg in a cast.
Hupfi, the skiing rabbit, description as above, colors: blue/red, but with two plastic skis, two ski poles.
Both skiing rabbits after 1968; they are rare complete with equipment.

Animals Living In and By the Water

Note: Unless otherwise indicated in captions, the following main characteristics are valid for all animals living in and by the water:
— no voice,
— mohair,
— excelsior stuffing,
— no swivel head,
— nose and mouth embroideries in pink/brown (decoration),
— measurements in cm refer to total height (standing).

Animals living in and by the water are not very numerous in the Steiff repertoire. Aquatic birds have been included in the chapter on birds.

Frogs in stretched out, lying position were available as early as the turn of the century. In 1913, seals measuring 17 and 22cm (7 and 9in) were introduced and during the 1930s, frogs in sitting positions in green, red and yellow were added. But besides those, no other water animals were produced until the 1940s. It was not until the 1950s and 1960s that this group of animals received more attention by Steiff. In 1953, a green velvet frog in sitting position measuring 8cm and 10cm (3 and 4in) was produced. Today, he is available in different shades of green and brown, depending on the fading effect sunlight has had on the velvet.

After 1959, a mohair frog in sitting position was added to the program, 28cm (11in). The same model was available in 20cm (8in) after 1961. His green and yellow markings are very striking. Another frog, this time in lying position (*Krabbel Frosch*, i.e. crawling frog) with soft stuffing was available after 1962. However, his looks are less natural since he has no markings. His back is made of green, his belly of yellow mohair. After 1970, a dangling frog, 35cm (14in), made of velvet with a head made of PVC was offered for sale. The dangling *Frog Prince* made in the mid 1950s is a very interesting item. He is only available as a prototype (see chapter on Curios and Other Items).

Slo, the turtle was available after 1955. It featured a rubber shell and was sold in lengths of 10 and 14cm (4 and 6in). Towards the end of the 1950s, the shell material was changed to PVC. After 1958, a turtle made of mohair with soft stuffing measuring 22cm (9in) with beautiful markings was introduced. The markings of *Gaty*, the crocodile, available after 1957 in lengths of 34 and 73cm (13 and 29in), are also very beautiful.

Illustration on page 114:
Cosy Sigi, the seahorse, 20cm (8in), Dralon, green and black glass eyes, soft stuffing, also available in 28cm (11in), only in 1959. Even though it is made of Dralon, it is considered a collectible. Very rare.
Crabby, the lobster, 10 and 17cm (4 and 7in), felt, black eyes, 1963-1966.

from left to right:
Crocodile, *Gaty*, height: 6cm (2in), length: 34cm (13in), mohair/felt, green and black eyes, after 1957.
Frog, *Froggy*, 10cm (4in), velvet, brown and black eyes, after 1953.
Turtle, *Slo*, length: 10cm (4in), shell made of PVC, black eyes, after 1955.
Frog, *Froggy*, length: 20cm (8in), brown and black eyes, after 1961.

from left to right:
Multi-colored fish, *Flossy*, length: 22cm (9in), measurement excluding tail fin, brown and black eyes, mouth made of felt, 1961-1964.
Bluefish, *Flossy*, and goldfish, *Flossy*, as above, but 1960-1978, very common.

Robby, the seal, available in 10 and 14cm (4 and 6in) after 1954, and in 22cm (9in) after 1958, was a very popular aquatic animal and was offered into the 1970s. This also means that it is very common. Not quite as common is *Paddy*, the walrus, available in the same sizes after 1959. And in the Floppy series, *Floppy Robby*, the seal, was in the program from 1964-on in 28cm (11in) and with soft stuffing.

Bluefish and goldfish were made after 1960 in lengths of 10, 22 and 50cm (4, 9 and 20in), measurement excluding tail fin. Fish in 22cm (9in) were made until 1978 and in 10cm (4in) even until 1981. They are considered very common. Much rarer is the multi-colored fish (yellow/brown/white) available in the same sizes, but only between 1961 and 1964. A blue riding fish with steering mechanism was introduced to the program in 1965.

Family of beavers, *Nagy*, 10, 17 and 25cm (4, 7 and 10in), black eyes, tail made of felt, 17 and 25cm (7 and 10in) versions with squeeze voice and swivel head. 10 and 17cm (7 and 10in) after 1958, 25cm (10in) after 1960.

Seal, *Robby*, 14cm (6in), black eyes, after 1954.
Walrus, *Paddy*, 14cm (6in), white and black eyes, plastic tusks, after 1959.

Crabby, the lobster, is very popular with collectors. It was made of felt and in lengths of 10 and 17cm (4 and 7in) between 1963 and 1966. It was also available in a mohair version, but this version was only offered in 1963/64. The lobsters have legs of chenille wire and antennae made of red elastic string.

After 1957, "Snuggy-Sitztiere" (stools) were introduced. They were the turtle, *Snuggy Slo* (43cm [17in]) after 1957, the starfish, *Starly* (35cm [14in]) after 1959 and the giant frog, *Froggy* (40cm [16in]). They feature a strong steel frame and beautiful markings.

Molla

Animals of the Wild

Note: Unless otherwise indicated in the captions, the following main characteristics are valid for all animals of the wild:
— squeeze voice,
— mohair, monkeys made of mohair/felt,
— excelsior stuffing,
— no swivel head, monkeys with swivel head and jointed,
— measurements in cm always refer to total height (standing).

Since the very early days of the Steiff company, animals of the wild have taken a very important place in the repertoire. Since the history of plush animals started with an elephant, we will first take a closer look at those pachyderms made of felt. In 1880, Margarete Steiff made her first animal of felt, a pincushion elephant. He was brought back as a replica in 1984.

Already in the first catalog of 1892, 14 different elephants were advertised. They were made of felt, had tusks made of bone or wood and were available with or without iron wheels. Around the turn of the century, felt elephants were sold on three-wheeled bikes, as elements of a game of skittles and as tumblers. The carriage of the animals on wheels was improved gradually and around 1905, mohair elephants were sold alongside the ones made of felt. Most riding elephants are covered by a red shabrack (cover) made of felt and decorated with various patterns. Jointed elephants were available as well as an elephant with a built-in clockwork that would let it turn head-over-heels. After 1914, riding elephants were sold with iron or wooden wheels. Caricatures in red and blue made of mohair added to the variety of the program around 1910. Plush versions were available until the mid 1920s. Around 1920, elephants were made of nettle fiber. Iron wheels disappeared as well around the mid 1920s and only wooden wheels were made until the introduction of disk wheels during the late 1920s. Felt elephants were made until the early 1930s. Also produced during this time span were elephants made of nettle fiber and the circus elephant. He is at attention, features snap joints and a mechanism in the neck and a mouth that can be opened and closed. For the occasion of the company anniversaries in 1930, 1955 and 1980, anniversary elephants were issued in limited numbers. Toy elephants made of burly wool plush were added to the program during the mid 1930s, elephants made of wax cloth during the late 1930s.

Illustration page 118:
Giraffe, 75cm (30in), natural-looking spots, black eyes, no voice, open mouth made of felt, interior steel frame, after 1961. This model available in wool plush in 28 and 35cm (11 and 14in), mid to late 1950s.
Giraffe, 150cm (59in), brown and black eyes with long lashes, swivel head, open mouth made of felt, interior steel frame, 1960s. Dromedary, 35cm (14in), wool plush, face and legs made of velvet, brown and black eyes, after 1933. Until 1952, only available in 28 and 35cm (11 and 14in). After 1953, also available in 14cm (6in) (common).
Dromedary, height: 70cm (28in), length: 90cm (35in), brown and black eyes, red velour cover with yellow decorations and inscription: "molla" (advertisement), brown leather saddle, US flag, no voice, interior steel frame, early 1950s.

from left to right:
Elephant on iron wheels, 16cm (6in), gray felt, red cover with yellow decoration, tusks and open mouth made of felt. Shoe-button eyes with underlying felt, no voice, after 1908.
White chimpanzee, 10cm (4in), 1950s.
Elephant, washable animal, 12cm (5in), gray wax cloth, cover and tusks are painted, soft stuffing, black eyes, no voice, 1938-1940, very rare.
Toy elephant, 14cm (6in), gray burly wool plush, cover with colorful stripes and wool pompons, black eyes with underlying felt, open mouth made of felt, 1934-1940, rare.
Elephant on blue wooden wheels, 20cm (8in), gray felt, red and yellow shabrack made of felt with bells, tusks and open mouth made of felt, black eyes with underlying felt, no voice, around 1930.

from left to right:
Toy elephant, 22cm (9in), gray, red felt cover with yellow and green decoration, black eyes with underlying felt, open mouth made of felt, US flag, block letter button without underscoring F, letters far apart, 1938-1952, mostly in silk plush.
Elephant, 22cm (9in), gray, red felt cover with bells, tusks and open mouth made of felt, black and white eyes, no voice, from 1952 to early 1970s, very common.
Soft elephant, *Jumbo*, 22cm (9in), gray, at attention, red felt bib, soft stuffing, arms attached with disks, legs inflexible, open mouth made of felt, bell on trunk, swivel head, after 1952. After 1958 also available in 35cm (14in).
front: Elephant, 10cm (4in), gray, red felt cover, plastic tusks, black and white eyes, no voice, 1950-1977, very common.

Between 1950 and 1952, new models were introduced. Their shape was simplified. They were available in 1957 in the sizes 7, 10, 17, 22 and 35cm (3, 4, 7, 9 and 14in) in standing position without wheels, in 28cm (11in) on blue wooden wheels and in six sizes between 35 and 100cm (14 and 39in) on blue disk wheels as riding elephants. From size 28cm (11in), the elephants carried a headdress made of red leather with a bell. In 1955, the 7cm (3in) version was sold as the anniversary issue. He had a red cover made of a material similar to rubber with the inscription: "1880-1955, 75 Jahre Steiff."

After 1956, the same model was sold with the same cover. But the inscription now simply read: "Steiff." The model was made until the early 1960s. Later, the cover changed again to a plain red felt cover. The soft elephant, *Jumbo*, in sitting position measured 22cm (9in) and featured a red bib. He was added to the program in 1952. The same model in 35cm (14in) was available from 1958-on. *Cosy Trampy* was one of the first animals made of Dralon in 1956. The design of the standing elephant remained practically unchanged between 1950 and the early 1970s.

The many species of monkeys have always been the children's favorites. Around the turn of the century they were already available in a game of skittles

from left to right:
Chimpanzee, 24cm (9in), brown tipped, brown and black eyes, end 1920s, very rare.
White chimpanzee, 17cm (7in), with tail, green and black eyes, face, hands and feet made of felt and painted purple, no voice, after 1925.
Orangutan, *Orangu*, 12cm (5in), rusty brown, brown and black eyes, no voice, 1931-1933.
Orangutan, *Mimocculo*, 35cm (14in), rusty brown. Large white, brown and black glass eyes that can be moved. Mechanism is controlled from right ear. Open mouth made of felt, 1931-1933, very rare.

from left to right:
Chimpanzee with driver's cap, 24cm (9in), brown, brown and black eyes. Radiator mascot for cars with brass steering wheel. The monkey is sewn to a wire rack that could be clamped onto the hood, around 1913.
Chimpanzee (*Jocko* model,) 25cm (10in), yellow mohair with brown horizontal lines (dyed), brown and black eyes, 1920s.
Musical chimpanzee (*Jocko* model) with pressure-activated work, 35cm (14in), dark brown, brown and black eyes. Pressure point for the musical clock is on his stomach, marked by a piece of red felt, open mouth made of felt, 1951-1958.
front: monkey head pin, 6cm (2in), brown and beige felt, clown's hat with red woolen pompon, white ruff made of felt, shoe-button eyes, no voice, around 1916.
All of them are very rare.

and dressed monkeys, riding monkeys wearing tails and sitting monkeys with elastic strings were sold, as well. In 1901, monkeys wearing clowns' costumes and flexible monkeys made of plush or felt were offered. After 1908, there were jointed monkeys in white or brown wearing jerseys in various colors. Also around 1908, a new pattern for a chimpanzee was designed (sold from the early 1930s-on as *Jocko*) and was manufactured until the 1970s. Typical for *Jocko* are the legs (at an angle.) Face, ears, hands and feet were made of felt and he does not have a tail. The eyelids were taken in, which was one of the most striking features together with the white beard made of plush. The chimpanzee is one of the most common Steiff animals since it was in production during more than 65 years. This is not the case with the dressed chimpanzees (see top of page 14), clockwork chimpanzees (turning head-over-heels), and pantom chimpanzees (marionettes), as they were offered as early as 1910.

We found a very ingenious description of a novelty in the catalog of 1911/12: "Chimpanzee with car cap as driver. Strings that are pulled through the monkey's feet can be used to attach him to the filler screw plug on the hood." In 1913, he was available with a steering wheel and sewn to a wire rack in sitting position which could be clamped onto the hood of cars. During the same year, *Record Peter*

from left to right:
Chimpanzee, *Jocko*, 25cm (10in), brown, brown and black eyes, after 1908 and until 1970s. This is a model with US flag, 1950/53, very common.
Desert fox, *Xorry*, 12cm (5in), sitting, brown and black eyes, no voice, after 1957.
Jocko, 10cm (4in), white, black eyes, no voice, 1950s.
Jocko, 15cm (6in), brown, brown and black eyes, no voice, 1950s and 1960s, very common.
Jocko, 15cm (6in), white, green and black eyes, no voice, 1950s.

Baboon, *Coco*, 14cm (6in), gray with red bottom made of felt. Standing on inflexible hands and feet, green and black eyes, with tail, no voice, after 1951, common.
Baboon, *Coco*, 35cm (14in), long-haired mane around shoulders, strong facial features, striking eyelids, brown and black eyes, with tail, 1951-1962, rare.

left: Gibbon, 22cm (9in), brown and beige, dangling arms and legs, no disk joints, body made of mohair, face made of Dralon, hands and feet made of Dralon and felt, ears made of felt, no voice, inflexible head, white and black eyes, no tail, after 1962.
right: Multi-colored monkey, *Mungo*, 28cm (11in), body multi-colored (white, green, brown, orange, blue), hands, feet, face and ears made of white Dralon, face sprayed brown and blue, blue and black eyes, bendable arms and legs, with tail, no voice, after 1957.

was the big attraction among the plush animals. He was a chimpanzee sitting on a so-called push-pull car on wooden wheels. When pulled, the animal appears to be rowing. He was available in brown mohair in the sizes 20, 25 and 30cm (8, 10 and 12in) and in red felt with a fez, both versions with voices. The version in mohair plush was in the program for a very long time. At first, the wooden wheels were varnished for a natural finish, from the mid 1920s to the mid 1960s they were varnished red and after 1966, the wheels have black rubber tires with red spokes made of plastic. Until the mid 1920s, there were hardly any changes in the monkey program except for the time during the war. However, dressed chimpanzees, chimpanzees as drivers as well as clockwork monkeys and pantom chimpanzees were not produced after World War I.

After 1925, white chimpanzees with tails, a bicycle monkey with a clamp to be used as a mascot and another *Record Peter* made of white mohair were added to the program. Experiments were under way to dye mohair in various colors. Therefore, at the end of the 1920s, a chimpanzee with yellow and brown horizontal stripes and a chimpanzee made of tipped mohair were produced. Both are very rare.

After 1931, a baboon made of brown tipped mohair and with painted paws and mechanism in the neck was made in seven sizes ranging from 22 to 70cm (9 to 28in). There was also a model of a brown tipped chimpanzee with mechanism in the neck in six sizes between 13 and 29cm (5 and 11in). The jointed Orangutan, *Orangu*, was the novelty of 1931. He was available in the sizes 8, 10, 12 and 14cm (3, 4, 5 and 6in). In the supplementary catalog of 1931, he was introduced in the sizes 17, 22, 25, 28, 35, 43 and 50cm (7, 9, 10, 11, 14, 17 and 20in) with moving "Mimoccul" eyes. By moving the right ear, the eyes move to the right or to the left or roll around. This orangutan was sold with a collar tag with the inscription "Mimocculo." Another chimpanzee, his face made of pressed felt, is also very rare. He was available for a very short time during the 1930s and only in 30cm (12in). Between the mid and the late 1930s, the selection of monkeys had dwindled to the brown and white chimpanzee and the brown *Record Peter*. And even after World War II, the Steiff repertoire included only these successful models. The white chimpanzee was only available in the sizes 10 and 15cm (4 and 6in), the brown one in 10, 15, 35, 50, 60 and 80cm (4, 6, 14, 20, 24 and 31in). After 1951, *Coco*, the gray baboon, was sold in standing position, measuring 10, 14 or 22cm (4, 6 and 9in). A version on eccentric wheels, 25cm (10in), and a jointed gray baboon were also available. The multi-colored monkey, *Mungo*, was introduced in 1957. He featured hands, feet and a face made of

left: Monkey, *Record Peter*, on push-pull car with red wooden wheels, 25cm (10in), dark brown, brown and black eyes, 1913-1970, available with various wheels.
right: Monkey, *Record Peter*, on push-pull car, wooden wheels with natural varnish with Steiff imprint, body made of red felt, fez with black tassel, 20cm (8in), shoe-button eyes. 1913 to early 1930s, very rare in good condition.

from left to right:
Lioness, *Lea*, 11cm (4in), no voice, after 1956.
Lion, *Leo*, 12cm (5in), dark brown tipped mane, no voice, after 1956. Lion cub, 10cm (4in), beige and brown spotted, with swivel head, no voice, after 1933, this model from early or mid 1950s.
Lioness, jointed, height: 17cm (7in), length: 21cm (8in), swivel head, 1910-1958.
in background: Steiff cage wagon, length: 28cm (11in), after 1955, with five lion cubs, 10cm (4in), mohair and wool plush, no voice, 1950s.
All have brown and black eyes.

from left to right:
Young lion, leaping, height: 14cm (6in), length: 30cm (12in), beige and brown spotted, green and black eyes, no voice, also available in 10 and 17cm (4 and 7in), after 1954.
Lion, *Leo*, lying position, 50cm (20in), mane made of brown tipped mohair, brown and black eyes, also available in 22 and 35cm (14in), after 1955/56, common.
Leo, sitting position, brown and black eyes, no voice, after 1958.
Young lion, lying position, 43cm (17in), beige with brown spots, green and black eyes, also available in 17, 28 and 60cm (7, 11 and 24in), after 1953/54.
Leo, standing, 17cm (7in), brown tipped mane, brown and black eyes, no voice, also available in 10 and 28cm (4 and 11in), after 1964.

left: Tiger, jointed, height: 20cm (8in), length: 26cm (10in), swivel head, green and black eyes, 1916-1935.
right: Lion cub, lying position, height: 14cm (6in), length: 24cm (9in), wool plush, green and black eyes, swivel head, 1939-1941, rare.

from left to right:
Young lion, lying position, length: 28cm (11in), beige with brown spots, green and black eyes, after 1953/54.
Ocelot, length: 28cm (11in), beige and dark brown, yellow and black eyes, after 1964, rare.
Leopard, length: 28cm (11in), beige and brown, green and black eyes, after 1954.
Tiger, length: 28cm (11in), beige, gold and brown, green and black eyes, after 1953/54, common.

left: Okapi, 14 and 28cm (6 and 11in), velvet, black eyes, no voice.
Okapi, 43cm (17in), mohair, brown and black eyes, after 1958.
right: four zebras in different versions:
12cm (5in), velvet, no voice, after 1952.
22cm (9in), silk plush, no voice, 1947/48.
22cm (9in), wool plush, 1936 until early 1950s.
28cm (11in), mohair, from early 1950s-on.
All have brown and black eyes.

Dralon. In 1962, a gibbon was added, also with a face made of Dralon. Hands and feet were made of Dralon/felt. The gray gorilla, *Gora*, was completely made of Dralon (after 1962). The light brown multi-colored monkey, *Hango*, (after 1963), was also made of Dralon, but his hands and feet were made of felt.

Wild cats can be found in the most various shapes and models in the Steiff collection. Despite the fact that they are predators in nature, they have been sold with great success as children's toys. As early as 1897, lions were sold on iron wheels. At the beginning of the century, they were already available in 120cm (47in). Lions made of velvet were sold as pincushions (see the chapter Curios and Other Items) around 1910. A jointed lion and lioness were available in mohair after 1910. The lion remained practically unchanged in the program until the beginning of the 1960s, the lioness until 1958. Lion cubs in sitting and lying positions made of spotted wool plush were added in 1933. The cub in sitting position was first available in rayon and later in wool plush after World War II. After the mid 1950s and until the early 1960s, the cub was made of mohair. After 1953/54, spotted young lions were offered for sale a in lying position (semicircular) and in a leaping version. *Leo*, in lying position, was added in 1955/56. During the 1950s and 1960s, he was very popular as a decorative accessory in the back windows of cars. *Leo* was only available in two sizes in sitting position: after 1956 in 12cm (5in) and after 1958 in 22cm (9in). The lioness, *Lea*, in sitting position matches the smaller model almost perfectly. She was made after 1956 and is rare compared to *Leo*. Tiger models were rare before the war. Between 1916 and 1935, there was a jointed tiger. Between 1939 and 1941, tigers in sitting and lying positions (semicircular and stretched out) were made of wool plush. A standing lion made of mohair and mounted on wooden wheels was introduced into the program in 1928. After World War II, the tiger collection grew very large:
— jointed in 10 and 14cm (4 and 6in), 1952-1960,
— sitting, mouth closed, 10cm (4in), after 1952,
— sitting, mouth open, 14, 22 and 43cm (6, 9 and 17in), after 1959,
— lying (semicircular) in 17, 28, 43 and 60cm (7, 11, 17 and 24in), after 1953/54,
— leaping in 10, 14 and 17cm (4, 6 and 7in),
— and as Floppy animal in 17 and 28cm (7in and 11in) after 1956.

left: Kangaroo, 50cm (20in), gray, brown and beige, flexible arms, brown and black eyes, swivel head. The baby in the pouch measures 10cm (4in) and is made of velvet, brown and black eyes, after 1935, rare.
right: Kangaroo, 35cm (14in), beige, flexible arms, brown and black eyes, swivel head. Baby, 10cm (4in), mohair, brown and black eyes, 1931-1935, rare.

Other wild cats of great interest are the leopards in lying position in 17, 28, 43 and 60cm (7, 11, 17 and 24in) that were manufactured after 1954 as well as a leaping version in 10, 14 and 17cm (4, 6 and 7in), made after 1955. They have green eyes with black pupils as opposed to the ocelot with its yellow eyes with black pupils. The ocelot was available only in lying position measuring 17 and 28cm (7 and 11in) during 1964 and is, therefore, rare.

Giraffes, zebras and camels were made even before the turn of the century in felt versions, some of them on iron wheels. Felt versions of the giraffe were still available during the 1930s. In the 1933 catalog, a giraffe was offered to shoe stores: "Riding giraffe made of mohair with leather saddle and foot rest for children while they try on the shoes." From the mid 1930s to the mid 1950s, giraffes were made of wool plush. During the 1950s and 1960s, the following models of giraffes were in the program: velvet, 17cm (7in) (only in 1951/52,) after 1953, the velvet version is changed to 14cm (6in). The sizes 28, 35, 50 and 75cm (11, 14, 20 and 30in) were offered in mohair. Display animals were made in 150 and 240cm (59 and 94in).

The dromedary was listed in the catalogs until 1958 as a camel with one hump. It had been around since the 1930s. It is of maize color and is made of wool plush with velvet legs and face. During the 1950s and 1960s, it was available in

left: Rhinoceros, *Nosy*, 10 and 14cm (4 and 6in), white and black eyes, horn made of felt, no voice.
right: Hippopotamus, *Mockie*, 10 and 14cm (4 and 6in), white and black eyes, open mouth made of felt. 14cm (6in) version has two wooden teeth in lower jaw, no voice. All are from after 1954, after 1957 they were all also available in 22cm (9in).

Buffalo, 30cm (12in), beige and brown, brown tipped, thick mane, brown and black eyes, only in 1962 and 1963.
Llama, 40cm (16in), white and gray long-haired mohair, inside of ears made of felt, brown and black eyes, after 1957.
Gazelle, *Yuku*, 35cm (14in), beige, inside of ears made of velvet, black eyes, horns made of poured PVC, tail made of white chenille reinforced with wire, also in 22cm (9in), only in 1962 and 1963, rare.

the sizes 14, 28 and 35cm (6, 11 and 14in). Camels (two humps) were only sold as riding animals with red disk wheels and multi-colored covers.

Okapis made their first appearance in the Steiff collection in 1958. The two velvet versions in 14 and 28cm (6 and 11in) were offered in the catalogs until 1970 and were rather common. The 43cm (17in) model made of mohair was listed in the catalog until 1964 and is rare. The very natural markings are especially striking.

The hippopotamus, *Mockie*, and the rhinoceros, *Nosy*, were manufactured from 1954-on in the sizes 10 and 14cm (4 and 6in), and after 1957 in 17cm (7in).

Kangoo, the kangaroo, was introduced in 1953. The 14cm (6in) version featured felt ears. After 1967, it was listed under *Linda* in the catalog and the 14cm (6in) version now had mohair ears. The collar tag has the imprint "*Linda* (im Steiff Kinderbuch) *Linda* in the Steiff-Children's Book)." Sizes 14 and 28cm (6 and 11in) (*Kangoo* and *Linda*) carried a plastic baby kangaroo in their pouches, sizes 50 and 65cm (20 and 26in) a baby made of velvet. The arms of the 28cm (11in) version were attached with disks.

Three more animals of the wild were available only after World War II. These were the buffalo, the llama and the gazelle, *Yuku*. The buffalo was made only during 1962 and 1963 in 12, 17 and 30cm (5, 7 and 12in). The last size is hard to find. The same is true for the llama which was produced in 17, 28 and 43cm (7, 11 and 17in) after 1957. The gazelle, *Yuku*, was only made during 1962 and 1963 in the sizes 22 and 35cm (9 and 14in) and is considered rare.

Birds

Unless otherwise indicated in the captions, the following main characteristics are valid for birds:
— mohair,
— excelsior stuffing,
— black eyes,
— no voice,
— measurements in cm refer to total height (standing).

Birds and fowl were not among the first animals with soft stuffing that Margarete Steiff created. As a matter of fact, fowl played a very small role in the collection before the early 1950s. Miniature birds made of wool are exceptions (see chapter on Woolen Miniatures). There are several reasons for this fact. Birds are not particularly cute and funny and their value as toys is not very high. They are much more suited for collection and display on a shelf than for cuddling. Birds often have poor standing capabilities due to their anatomy so that they fall easily. This may be why many of the beautiful creations have been ignored by the customers with the exception of ducks and chickens. Consequently, many of the birds were taken out of the program after a very short time, especially during the 1950s and 1960s. This means that for today's collector those items are of higher value, making birds a much desired field of specialization. The most striking aspect of the bird collection is its variety. In the catalog of 1892, games of skittles with chickens and a rooster made of felt were sold, and roosters and hens for small children and ducks attached to elastic string with or without wire feet were listed. Storks and roosters made of felt were sold as paperweights and pen wipers. Colorful ducks to pull, made of felt and mounted on iron wheels, were introduced in the following years. Also very popular were chickens and roosters made of colorful pieces of felt. The feet were made of wire that was wrapped with thread. In later models, they were covered with yellow felt. This type of felt rooster was in the program until the mid 1920s and remained practically unchanged. It is important for the collector to know that the colors and shades of early felt animals have been put together in many variations without any clues in the catalogs. Leftover pieces of felt and cloth that were available at any given moment were used for the production. Swans on iron wheels and felt storks, both listed in sizes ranging from 14-100cm (6-39in) in the 1901 catalog, were very striking. Flying doves made of felt or velvet with interior rattle were hung by elastic string above children's cribs and standing doves were also popular around 1901. The Steiff designers were full of innovative ideas around 1911. Egg warmers in the shape of rooster or hen heads as well as pot holders and a coffeepot cosy (see chapter on Curios and Other Items) were produced and sold. Doves and chicks were also available as pincushions and carnival hats were sold in the shape of roosters, hens and parrots. Another novelty in 1911 was a jointed goose made of mohair. Due to the fact that its legs could be moved, it looked very lifelike.

Illustration on page 128:
Stork, *Adebar*, 35 and 60cm (14 and 24in), white, black and orange felt, black and brown eyes, 1954-1966, in the program for a relatively long time but still rare, also available in 17cm (7in) with wire legs and plastic beak, 1954-1969.

from left to right:
Chick, 8cm (3in), white and yellow, painted, felt beak, wire feet wrapped with yellow string, 1911-1931.
Rooster, 21cm (8in), felt, black bead eyes, legs wrapped with string, later models covered with yellow felt, after 1897, until mid 1920s.
Chicken, as above.
Rooster, 17cm (7in), small wings attached on sides, green tail made of felt, wire legs covered with gray felt, squeeze voice, 1931-1940.

from left to right:
front:
Typical post-war rooster, 10cm (4in), red wire legs, green felt tail, 1953-1974.
Chicken, beige and brown with black stripes and spots, 10cm (4in), beige felt tail, red wire legs, 1953-1974.
Rooster, 10cm (4in), yellow and beige with rusty brown felt tail, light brown wire legs with small spurs made of wire, 1930s.
back:
Chicken, 16cm (6in), white and brown, inserted black felt tail, wire legs covered with beige felt, 1966-1976, common.
Typical colorful post-war rooster, 30cm (12in), green felt tail, wire legs covered with beige felt, 1953-1977, very common.
Chicken, 17cm (7in), beige and brown with black stripes and spots, stuffed beige felt tail with black stripes, wire legs covered with beige felt, 1953-1965.

Dove, flying, as children's rattle to be hung above crib (original on elastic string), length: 27cm (11in), felt, shoe-button eyes, feet decorations embroidered, after 1898, in this size until 1912.
Dove, 22cm (9in), white Dralon with fanned tail made of synthetic velours, rubber beak, pink plastic feet, after 1969.
Dove, gray mohair, description as above, but wide tail feathers instead of fan, also after 1969.

Since the introduction of eccentric wheels in 1913, ducks gained in natural appearance. Starting in that year, ducks waddled through almost all the catalogs in the most interesting and various appearances until the 1970s. The voice department was very creative and after 1916 produced young mohair ducks with a quacking voice. These ducks were now equipped with quacking voices and eccentric wheels. Until the mid 1920s, there were no basically new developments among birds and fowl. In the 1924 catalog, we found a picture of a swinging duck with wooden handle whose chirping voice sounds when it is swung back and forth (see page 48, top). Gray ducks made of felt on eccentric wheels were also offered. Several of these ducks could be attached to each other to form a chain. The following wooden toys on eccentric wheels were new after 1924: Ducks, roosters, hens, chicks, a finch, a titmouse and a sparrow. Practically no songbirds had been made up to this point. In 1928, a penguin with beak, wings and feet made of leather was introduced, and in 1929, tiny ducks in standing position dressed in felt jackets and bonnets were added. In 1931, another novelty was introduced. *Kingpeng*, the penguin, with mechanism in the neck was manufactured. But this was practically the only novelty among birds in the 1930s.

left: Raven, *Hucky*, 12cm (5in), black. Red beak made of felt, black eyes with underlying red felt, black felt tail, red wire legs (stable), 1952-1970, common, also available in 17cm (7in). In 8cm (3in) as woolen miniature. Sizes 12 and 17cm (5 and 7in) with swivel head.
middle, top: Titmouse, 10cm (4in), yellow and blue with plastic feet, beak made of PVC. Same model available as sparrow, bullfinch or goldfinch after 1969.
middle, bottom: Plush bird, finch, 12cm (5in), wings and tail made of felt, wire legs, plastic beak, swivel head, after 1955, rare.
right: Songbird, bullfinch, 10cm (4in), multi-colored, beak made of PVC, wings and tail made of stiffened braid of hair, wings and legs bendable, 1959-1962, rare.

from left to right:
Toy duck, 11cm (4in), multi-colored, bill and feet made of orange felt, squeeze voice, after 1953, also in 14cm (6in). Swimming toy duck in yellow was offered in 10 and 13cm (4 and 5in). All are very common.
Young duck, yellow wool plush, gray stripes, black eyes with underlying felt, bill and feet made of golden felt in pre-war models, orange in post-war models, squeeze voice, 1933-1962.
Toy duck, 17cm (7in), yellow, bill and feet made of orange felt, tail made of brown felt, after 1952, also available in 10cm (4in). Standing duck available in blue and white, 11 and 18cm (4 and 7in). All are common.
Multi-colored pull duck or quacking duck on eccentric wooden wheels, 17cm (7in), bill and feet made of orange felt, automatic quacking voice, after 1933.

After 1952, a black and white penguin with a red felt beak and red felt feet was added to the program. He stayed until 1956 and is rare. The wings of this model were still made of velvet and completely black. The following model of 1956, however, was white, gray and black and had a red beak, beige feet and wings made of mohair. In 1952, *Hucky*, the raven, made of mohair until 1970, the striking turkey, *Tucky*, and the goose in standing position in 12 and 17cm (5 and 7in), as well as the yellow duck in standing position were introduced. They were followed in 1953 by rooster and chicken (very common). After 1954, *Wittie*, the owl, became very popular as did *Adebar*, the stork. Finch and titmouse made of plush are rare. They were made after 1955 in 12 and 17cm (5 and 7in) with wire feet. Also rare are the following songbirds with bendable wings and feet: finch, blue tit and bullfinch, made between 1959 and 1962. It is a largely unknown fact that chickens and ducks were also available as Floppy animals. They were only made in 1958 in the sizes 17 and 28cm (7 and 11in) and are rare. Another impressive addition was *Piccy*, the pelican, in 1959. Further important birds of the 1960s were the colorful parrot, *Lora*, in 12 and 22cm (5 and 9in) after 1962, the canaries *Hansi* and *Franzi* made of green or blue velvet, respectively, after 1962 and doves made of gray mohair or white Dralon after 1969.

Chick, *Kiki*, 12cm (5in), dress with red and white stripes, yellow head and arms made of mohair, yellow plastic beak, rubber body, after 1957, rare.
Duck, *Quaggy*, 12cm (5in), blue and white sailor suit, head, arms and body as above, beak and shoes made of orange felt, after 1955, rare.

from left to right:
Goose on eccentric wheels (according to 1916/17 catalog — "Piep-Gänschen"), 21cm (8in), white and gray, red felt underlying the eyes, bill and feet made of orange felt, chirping voice, 1916-1962. Despite the fact that this goose was in the program for such a long time, it is fairly hard to find.
Goose, *Kuschli*, 12cm (5in), gray and white, bill and feet orange. Same model as *Tulla*, but made as advertisement for goose down covers. Instead of the tail made of felt, this goose has a tail made of down feathers and also has down feathers on her head, around 1960.
Goose, 17cm (7in), as above, but tail made of felt. In the regular sales program after 1952. From the 1967 catalog on, this model was called *Tulla*.
Goose, 35cm (14in), white, legs attached with disks, shoe-button eyes with underlying red felt, squeeze voice, bill and feet made of yellow felt, after 1911. This model also available in brown and gray, mixed.

from left to right:
Goose, white and gray, 60cm (24in), blue and black eyes with underlying yellow felt, bill and feet made of orange felt, open bill, flag "Made in US Zone," very nice posture with spread wings. This model was not part of the regular sales program. It was only listed as a display item in the Display Catalog around 1952.
Both gray and white geese in the middle: 28cm (11in), description as above, but no US flag. Rare, since this goose was only in the program between 1958 and 1962.
Goose, description as far left, but 50cm (20in) and without US flag, around 1960.

Family of Owls, *Wittie*, 10, 14 and 22cm (4, 6 and 9in), mohair/felt. In older models, the backsides of the eyes were painted with a fluorescent color. When light fell onto them, they would glow in the dark for a while after the light was turned off, giving them a ghostly look. After 1963, they had green and black plastic eyes with a black edge, swivel head, feet made of sturdy wire, covered with felt. The smallest owl has a beak made of felt, the larger ones have beaks made of PVC and squeeze voice, after 1954, very popular and, therefore, common.

Even today, collectors do not pay too much attention to birds, but collect them as marginal items, even though many models are very true to nature in color and expression.

Turkey, *Tucky*, 14cm (6in), combination of materials is interesting: Body made of mohair, brown tipped. Wings and fanned tail made of beige felt. Markings sprayed on with the help of stencils. Neck and head made of red and blue velvet, brown wire legs, 1952-1962, rare, also available in 10cm (4in).
Pelican, *Piccy*, 17cm (7in), white and pink, bill and feet made of yellow felt, white and black eyes, 1959-1962, rare, also available in 25cm (10in).

from left to right:
Parrot, *Lola*, 12cm (5in), red, blue and yellow, green and black eyes, beak made of PVC, facial mask made of white felt, feet and claws made of beige felt, after 1962.
Lora, as above, but 22cm (9in), neither very common.
Canary, *Franzi*, 13cm (5in), blue velvet with beautiful natural markings, beak and feet made of PVC, after 1967. Later editions (after 1975) made of synthetic velours.
Canary, *Hansi*, green, as above, both very common.

from left to right:
Penguin, *Peggy*, 22cm (9in), white and black, feet and beak made of red felt, black velvet wings, squeeze voice, flag "Made in US Zone," 1952-1956, rare.
Same model, but 14cm (6in), no squeeze voice and no US flag.
Penguin, 15cm (6in), black and white, brown and black eyes with underlying beige felt, Beak, wings and feet made of black leather, markings painted in red, squeeze voice, after 1928, very rare, also available in gray and white.
Family of penguins (*Peggy*), 10, 14, 22cm (4, 6 and 9in), white, gray and black and partially dyed yellow, red felt beak, brown and black eyes, feet made of beige felt, rubber material similar to suede or synthetic velours, wings made of mohair, in 22 and 35cm (9 and 14in) with squeeze voice and swivel head, after 1956, common.

Dolls

Early Steiff dolls, *Betzinger Bauernpaar* (farming couple), from around 1894. Excerpt of anniversary publication to celebrate 50 years Margarete Steiff GmbH.

Under the guidance of Margarete Steiff, the company began to develop the first dolls in 1890. They were offered in the 1892 catalog to accompany donkeys on iron wheels without giving a closer description or as "Harlequins" with unbreakable heads and bodies made of felt with multi-colored pieces of cloth. Around 1894, the first doll collection was issued. Seventeen different types were advertised, some for individual sale, others available in couples. They were described as follows: "Dolls whose bodies and clothing are made of felt, unbreakable heads, Height: 26cm (10in)." The heads were most likely not manufactured in-house, but ordered from the German doll industry.

Some dolls with felt heads were produced as early as 1894. The 1901 catalog offered besides animals on bicycles (elephant, rabbit, monkey), also a man and a woman on a bike, without giving more detailed information about their characteristics. Doll monkeys were produced in various outfits. New pull toys were a polar explorer in Eskimo outfit with a polar bear and a bear leader with a dancing bear. Both dolls were also available individually, without the bears. In America, new materials for the doll production were introduced. They were now made of various materials and are called "KÜnstlerpuppen" (Art Dolls).

Around 1903, Richard Steiff created dolls of felt and velvet. One seam ran vertically down the middle of the face and the eyes were made of black shoe buttons. They were simple figures and some of them have a grotesque and amusing look. These caricatures made people laugh and were bought not only for children, but quite often as display objects for adults.

Around 1907, Richard Steiff designed a new generation of dolls. They were called toy dolls and had childlike faces. Richard did not appreciate the hard porcelain too much so he forced his soft felt into new shapes. His doll of the future seemed to live and was very pretty, making it a huge success. How can the success of this "Charakterpuppe" (doll full of character) be explained? The production of the first "Charakterpuppen" introduced a revolutionary doll reform. Steiff was supposedly the first company to manufacture dolls with soft stuffing. All of a sudden the dear old dolls had lost their doll faces and were given human faces. But as long as people were able to remember, dolls had always looked the same. They had the same fresh and healthy facial color and the same expression, i.e. they were doll-like with no facial expression. At first, people claimed that these

Illustration on page 136:
left: "Charakterpuppe," farm boy, 28cm (11in), blue glass eyes with black pupils, black felt shoes, knitted socks, black velvet trousers, white linen shirt, brown felt vest, black felt hat, face made of felt with vertical and horizontal seam, arms and legs made of felt, body made of linen, with voice, dark brown mohair wig. On his back he is carrying a basket attached with silk ribbons with a velvet pincushion inside, around 1910. In this untouched condition, very rare.
right: "Charakterpuppe," *Erich*, 35cm (14in), hands and face made of felt with vertical and horizontal seam, arms and legs made of linen, blue suit made of fine cotton cloth, apron made of coarse linen, white cotton underwear, white cotton socks, shoes are not original, blue glass eyes with black pupil, blonde mohair wig. The original edition was wearing a hat. Available after 1913 in 28, 35 and 43cm (11, 14 and 17in), after 1916 in 50cm (20in).

left:
Gnome, *Puck*, 30cm (12in), oversized, dark brown shoes made of felt, short beige linen pants, brown shirt made of felt, gray and blue felt jacket, high pointy cap made of golden mohair. Body and legs made of linen, face with vertical seam, hands made of felt. Widely laughing mouth with painted stubble underneath. Long and silky hair and beard made of mohair. Small black glass eyes with cunning look, also available in 20 and 40cm (8 and 16in), after 1915.
Caricature doll, *Struwwelpeter (Stru) 30*, 30cm (12in), black shoes made of wax cloth, green pants, rusty brown body made of felt with added short skirt decorated with black braids made of felt, black leather belt with metal buckle, white felt collar with blue bow. Face made of felt with horizontal and vertical seam, small black glass eyes. Characteristic for this figure is the disheveled white and gray mohair wig and the very long fingernails made of leather, after 1910. Very rare in this untouched condition.

right:
from left to right:
Caricature doll, *Leutnant Inf Leutn 60*, 1911, 60cm (24in). Uniform made of blue felt, overly long, skinny black legs with red decoration running horizontally, monocle on red string in the right eye, face made of felt with horizontal seam, black shoe-button eyes, intricately crafted sword. Very rarely found complete with accessories.
Caricature doll, *Soldier of the Infantry, Inf 50*, Inf 50, 1911/12, 50cm (20in), in fatigues, also available in 43cm (17in). Infantry soldiers were also available in cloth suit or cloth coat and denim pants. Blue and red felt hat, face with vertical seam in middle, hands made of felt, horizontal seam at mouth. Body, arms and legs were made of linen. Head, arms and legs attached with disks, knee joints, high boots made of wax cloth with leather soles and Steiff buttons, blue glass eyes with black pupils.
Caricature doll, *Sailor*, 50cm (20in), 1913. Dark blue felt pants, white linen shirt, blue collar and cuffs, dark blue sailor's cap made of felt with black ribbons. Face with vertical seam and hands made of felt. Body, arms and legs attached with disks, knee joints, high boots made of wax cloth and leather soles with Steiff buttons, blue glass eyes with black pupils, painted moustache. All three dolls have painted brown hair.

new dolls were not made for children, but for adults. Exhibits in department stores and toy stores helped exposure of the dolls to the public. They became a tremendous success and the demand was constantly rising each year. In 1907, Franz Steiff obtained an American patent on dolls' heads made of felt. In 1908, the "Charakterpuppe," now with hair made of mohair, plush and felt body with soft stuffing, was brought to the spring fair in Leipzig where it caused quite a stir.

The special report of a trade magazine put it into words: "...and this is how the toy industry was led from the boring monotony of its doll house magic into the joyous world of Steiff's models. These dolls make every child's heart beat faster. They are indestructible and cute. They are parading by in the most varied costumes. There were girls from the villages and girls from the city. And these fat boys with red cheeks whose round, glass-bead eyes were challenging the world were a welcome change from the sweet and boring dolls with fragile heads and yellow dust inside their bodies." Around 1910, there was a call for more artistic expression in crafts in Germany which also had repercussions in the toy industry. Richard Steiff, together with his brothers, Paul, Hugo and Otto, were discussing whether it would be appropriate to transfer real people's humor to the toys. This is how village musicians, a schoolmaster and his boys and all kinds of characters from city and country were developed. They were bringing humor into the children's imagination. One fine day Albert Schlopsnies, an artist from Munich, came to the Steiff factory and showed some of his marionettes. He wanted to convince Steiff to manufacture those items as toys for kids and adults. However, they were never produced since the company found other tasks and responsibilities for the artist. Richard Steiff recognized the artist's talent needed by Steiff for the production of new models of dolls. The scholar of the Young School of Munich (JungmÜnchner Schule) did not let him down. Coming from Eastern Prussia, the young man had once ridden his bike all the way from Tilsit to Munich in order to show his sketches and drawings to Franz Stuck. Albert Schlopsnies' uncle had not had any patience for the dreams of his nephew and his artistic future. But Franz Stuck immediately recognized and supported this talented artist. In 1910, Richard Steiff was able to win him as a consultant for his company. During this year, pantom animals were introduced. These are animals that are moved using the same techniques that are used to move marionettes. Many moving display groups for store windows were composed, predecessors of the mechanical showpieces whose production was also started in that same year. A new chapter in Steiff's art of design was written, thanks to Schlopsnies' talented hands. New ideas, new areas were explored, and the repertoire of "Charakterpuppen" and caricatures was expanded enormously.

During the fall of 1910, the Wertheim department store in Berlin displayed the big Steiff Circus (see page 18, middle). For a long time, this event remained in everybody's memory. The circus features several arenas and Schlopsnies had modeled it exactly after the *Airkus Sarrasani*. Many groups were powered by mechanisms and performed the movements of the acrobats.

The 1911 catalog described dolls as follows: "Caricature dolls are the most popular of their kind. Our 'Charakterpuppen' made of felt led to a true reform on the doll market. We have invented not only the dolls but also their name since they grasp the child's attention with their individual characteristic facial expression. This is a great change from the previous lifeless faces. The dolls dress is true to the original and very tasteful. The dolls can be undressed. The shiny, curly hair can be combed and brushed while wet." Jointed caricature dolls depicting many different professions were very popular and were sold in various traditional costumes. There are, for example, mountain farmers, farmers from Brittany and farmers from Dachau. In 1910, *Struwwelpeter* was available in 30cm (12in) under the description "caricature doll" and in 1911 as novelty in sizes 35 and 43cm (14 and 17in) as "artists caricature doll." Steiff soldiers in national and international uniforms were invading the children's rooms in 1911. German, Italian, French and Austrian officers, staff sergeants and regular soldiers were made. American, Dutch, Belgian and English soldiers were added later. The equipment and uniforms of the different soldiers are very complex and copied perfectly. Rifles, swords, field packs and even the lieutenant's monocle are right where they belong. The major is a very striking figure, carrying a sword and many decorations on his chest. His shoes are made of the finest leather. Very often, the soles were nailed not only with shoemaker's nails, but also with as many as 25 Steiff buttons per sole. There were policemen of various nationalities. Soccer players, sailors and *Graf Zeppelin* (*Uncle Zeppelin*) were also offered in 1911. "Charakterpuppen" were dressed in various traditional costumes and were, therefore, called "Trachten Originale." Among them were fishermen, Dutchmen and hunters. Besides those, there were bathing dolls and beach dolls, pupil dolls, winter sport dolls and, among "various dolls," there were babies and Eskimo dolls. Accessories such as skis, sleds, school furniture, doll furniture, farmers' chairs, beds and circus chairs were available and could be shipped as decorations. The child's room could be transformed into a complete barracks square with the help of accessories such as equipment, bars, fountains, assault stands, crossbeams, sentry boxes and targets. Even among the "artists caricature dolls" listed separately from the caricature dolls in the 1911 catalog, soldiers and policemen were offered for sale.

At the trade show in Munich in 1912, the showpiece "The Dingharting Fire Fighters" was displayed (see page 18, bottom). A special publication described very enthusiastically the striking scenes: "The spectators were standing in a large crowd in room no. 6 of hall 1 with smiles and grins on their faces. There was a fire in the village and the fire fighters were in full action! The scene is action packed; everybody is busy. The impressive inn is engulfed in surprisingly realistic flames and the water hoses are handled by eight men. The water is shot into the flames, the fire chief with his important-looking nose and incredibly arrogant and superior expression moves his head from the left to the right."

from left to right:
Type of doll from 1910 to the mid 1920s with mohair wig, vertical and horizontal seams running through the face, "Mommy" voice, arms, legs and head attached with disks.
Type of doll from 1910 to 1916/17 with painted hair, vertical seam running through the face, arms, legs and head attached with disk, body made of linen, knee joints, boots made of material resembling wax cloth with leather soles and Steiff buttons.
Type of doll from 1937-1952, face made of pressed felt, mohair wig, head and legs attached with disks, dangling arms, squeeze voice, body made of burlap, blue and white glass eyes with black pupils.

Infantryman, 50cm (20in), blue glass eyes with black pupils, only vertical seam running through face, hair, mouth and eyebrows painted, 1911/12.
Eskimo, 43cm (17in), shoe-button eyes, vertical and horizontal seam, separately sewn mouth, mohair wig, after 1911.
Doll with face made of pressed felt, no seam, blue and white glass eyes with black pupils, mohair wig, after 1937.

Eskimo, 43cm (17in), vertical and horizontal seam in face, arms, legs and head attached with disks, body made of blond mohair, squeeze voice, shoe-button eyes, felt gloves and shoes, black mohair wig. Steiff skis and poles as accessories, after 1911.

Until today, Steiff has held onto the tradition of displaying very complex showpieces. Every year the visitors of large toy fairs are delighted with the most beautiful displays of imaginative scenes and decorations.

Further doll models were added to the collection in 1913. Professions such as tailor, cobbler and butcher and new types of boys and dolls in uniforms were made. A clown and an American Indian, both 100cm (39in), were certainly pretty to look at, but they were not sold in large numbers. *Twee Deedl*, an American fairy-tale figure only stayed in the program for a very short time.

In 1915, *Puck*, the gnome was added to the dwarves *Snak* and *Snik*. *Puck* was available in 20, 30 and 40cm (8, 12 and 16in). Even more dolls in uniform (soldiers, young heroes, see page 19) and a Mexican measuring 100cm (39in) were added later. Fully-equipped ski dolls were given to winter sport fans. Two of the funniest caricatures were *Schidünn* and *Schidik* (*Skiskinny* and *Skifat*). Figures created by Wilhelm Busch in his stories were numerous within the program and really resemble the originals.

During the war, 1916/18, further models of soldier dolls became more popular again. Belgian, Austrian, Turkish, Italian and Russian soldiers and a cossack in dress uniform were manufactured.

The collection of "Charakterpuppen" with childlike faces grew continuously. Between 1916 and 1926, dolls with typical German first names such as *Berta, Erika, Grete* and *Lisa* were added to the program.

In 1922, Steiff asked Albert Schlopsnies to design another huge showpiece, the "Städtle" (small town). This was not a toy, but was mainly displayed to show artistic and technical ability at the German trade show. It was meant to prove that the cloth dolls with their typical movements, characteristic facial expressions and perfect and original color coordination stand for the outstanding quality that was traditional at the Steiff company. The *Neue Süddeutsche Illustrierte* published a special report in August of 1922. This is an excerpt: "If the supervisory personnel at the German trade show were to keep a list of the questions their people had to answer most often, the most asked question would most likely be: 'Where is the Städtle?' Not only thousands of people holding their curious and impatient children by the hand are looking immediately for the closest path to the Städtle, but also guests who came without children do not want to miss the room at the entrance to hall 1. This is the large toy market in the middle of which the loveable, lively, funny, colorful and mystic yet down to earth and real Städtle has been set up and opened to traffic."

In 1921/22, Albert Schlopsnies developed a new type of doll. It was called Schlopsnies doll and it was manufactured using the Aprico method. The head was made of celluloid and was purchased from the Schildkröt company in Mannheim (Rheinische Gummi und Celluloid Fabrik Co.). It was one of Schildkröt's regular items. But the special thing about this head was the fact that Steiff painted its inside and stuffed it with excelsior. This technique requires the head to have an opening. Schlopsnies dolls have a round plate on the back of their heads measuring 6.5cm (2in) in diameter. The doll's hair was painted blonde or dark. Those dolls measured 40cm (16in) and had a felt body. The Schlopsnies doll did not have a voice. Head and arms were jointed with disks and the arms were sewn to the body, hanging down alongside the doll (dangling

Two scenes from the showpiece "Das Städtle," 1922, Bavarian Trade Show, Munich.
top: Carpenters on the roof.
bottom: at the inn "Zum Ochsen": Daily arm wrestling contest, organized by the Committee for the Promotion of Tourism.

arms). This doll was considered the novelty of the epoch and was described to the minutest detail in a special Steiff Schlopsnies Doll Catalog in 1922: "With the Steiff Schlopsnies Dolls we have achieved an unprecedented level of artistic and technical perfection. The Steiff Schlopsnies doll is completely unbreakable. The body is covered with the finest wool felt and has a soft stuffing. The shape of the body corresponds to the characteristic proportions of a three-year-old toddler. The clothing was designed by the best artists and finished very carefully to the smallest detail. Only the highest quality was used in the selection of materials and it fulfills the child's wish to dress or undress the doll whenever it feels like it. The child also recognizes his own clothing in the doll's. The main characteristic of the doll, however, is its unbreakable head crafted in the entirely novel 'Aprico Method' (German patent pending). This indestructible paint makes it possible to re-create the mild and lovely scent of a child's face in the most natural way. The peachy skin, however, is completely resistant to scratching (even sandpaper or knives cannot harm it) and is washable. Every doll carries the trademark 'Armring' (bracelet) and a bear head pendant around the neck. These advantages of the Steiff Schlopsnies Doll make it a valuable educational toy and lets it take first place among all artists dolls." The dolls were available in each model as a boy and a girl in various outfits. However, the doll was not a great success. It was only in the program for barely five years. After the mid 1920s, it was no longer offered for sale.

top:
Caricature doll, *Schidik*, 28cm (11in), according to catalog 35cm (14in), felt, jointed, brown glass eyes with black pupils, woolen scarf and spats, leather shoes, backpack, Steiff skis and poles, 1916-1927. His counterpart was the skinny and slanky *Schidünn* in 40cm (16in).

bottom:
Dwarf on push-pull car, *Record Puck*, 20cm (8in), brown glass eyes with black pupil, mohair hat, body made of felt, mohair beard, hands and head made of linen, probably replacement material used in the place of felt, chirping voice, 1921/22-1927. Good Luck Manikin, 28cm (11in), felt, black and white squinting eyes, head can be turned and is made of pressed felt, mohair beard and wig, no voice, dangling arms, spotted felt hat, 1937-1940.

left:
Schlopsnies doll, *Agnes*, in winter clothes (replaced), 40cm (16in), felt body with excelsior stuffing, no voice, celluloid head made by Schildkröt (branded), with Steiff's Aprico paint method (on inside), head and legs jointed with disks, dangling arms, 1922-1925.

In 1929, only three caricature dolls with faces made of felt remained: A clown with soft body and swivel head in a blue velvet suit available in sizes 26, 35 and 43cm (10, 14 and 17in) and the dwarves *Puck*, 20 and 30cm (8 and 12in) and *Snik*, 25, 35 and 43cm (10, 14 and 17in). Those three still appeared in the 1933 catalog under the heading "Caricature Dolls." In addition, three felt soldiers with swivel heads were advertised: A lieutenant, a soldier and a SA soldier. They all measured 22cm (9in).

As a novelty, the catalog H 33 (1933) listed the fairy-tale figure *Schwefelmännchen* (*Sulphur Manikin*) in 25cm (10in), made of yellow felt with green felt hat. Among the "Charakterpuppen, the production of a Hitler boy (HJ28) and a Hitler girl (HMäd28) was considered, but they were not taken into the sales program. Another new "Charakterpuppe" with celluloid head was introduced in

Gewicht Kilo		Nummer	Stückpreis

95

Steiff-Schlopsnies-Puppen

Prächtige Künstlerpuppen

Körper in der bewährten, jedoch wesentlich verfeinerten Ausführung der Charakterpuppen, natürlich proportioniert und fast unverwüstlich. Das Hauptmerkmal ist jedoch der wunderschöne, unzerbrechliche Kopf in der neuen „Apriko"-Bemalung D.R.P., die es ermöglicht, den lieblichen, zartglänzenden Hauch (Pfirsichhauch), der Kindergesichtchen eigen ist, aufs natürlichste wiederzugeben. Ferner gibt ein klares, glänzendes Auge dem Gesicht den unbefangenen kindlichen Ausdruck. Die Kleidung ist besonders geschmackvoll aus nur Qualitätsstoffen hergestellt. Von ersten künstlerischen Kräften entworfen und bis in alle Einzelheiten durchgearbeitet, ist der kindliche Wunsch erfüllt, die Puppe in derselben Weise an- und auskleiden zu können wie sich selbst.

40 cm groß, Schutzmarke: „Armring".

ohne Kart.	mit Kart.	
		Dirndlkleider
orangekarierter Spielanzug bzw. Dirndlkleid		
0.38	0.57	Peter
0.37	0.56	Anna
grüne Leinenhose bzw. Kleid und bunt karierte Jacke bzw. Mieder		
0.38	0.58	Sepp
0.37	0.57	Resi
		Sommerkleider
weiß Leinenanzug bzw. Kleid		
0.37	0.57	Ernst
0.37	0.57	Elsa
buntkarierter Spielanzug bzw. Kleid		
0.37	0.57	Viktor
0.39	0.59	Vera
blaue Filzhose, rosa/weiß karierte Bluse bzw. Kleid		
0.40	0.60	Marius
0.38	0.58	Madeleine
weiß Samtanzug bzw. Kleid		
0.38	0.58	Carlos
0.37	0.57	Klara
weiße Batistbluse, rosa Samthose bzw. Kleid		
0.36	0.56	Rolf
0.38	0.58	Ruth
		Herbstkleider
rot/schwarz karierter Anzug bzw. Kleid		
0.38	0.58	Richard
0.37	0.57	Rita
rote Hose bzw. schwarz/roter Trägerrock, weiße Bluse		
0.38	0.58	Theo
0.37	0.57	Adele
weiße Hose und Seidenbluse bzw. Kleid, je gesticktes Bolerojäckchen		
0.38	0.58	Kolja
0.40	0.60	Marga
		Winterkleider
rosa Filzanzug bzw. Mantel		
0.41	0.61	Herbert
0.40	0.60	Henriette
farbiger Strickanzug bzw. Kleid		
0.41	0.61	Otto
0.42	0.62	Lene
Skier sind extra zu bestellen		
Lammplüschjacke und weiße Filzbreeches bzw. Filzrock		
0.44	0.64	Axel
0.42	0.62	Agnes
		Schlafanzüge
weißer Schlafanzug bzw. Nachthemd		
0.36	0.56	Bubi
0.37	0.57	Meedi
Hemdchen bzw. Hemdchen, Leibchen, Windelhös'chen		
0.35	0.55	Hemdmatz
0.35	0.55	Hosenmatz
		Clown
Clownanzug aus Samt blau/gelb		
0.41	0.61	Der Weiße

Schlopsnies dolls in different outfits. Excerpt from the Steiff main catalog, 1924.

1935. The head was again made by Schildkröt. This time it was a newborn baby measuring 28cm (11in). However, it did not remain in the program for very long. Just like the Schlopsnies doll, the baby's head was stuffed with excelsior. The arms were made of fine wool felt and the arms are simply sewn to the body (dangling arms). This doll's special features were the snap joints (see *Circus Bear* on page 39) and the "Mommy" voice. This type was available in four versions, wearing a knitted jacket and bonnet: *Greta* in light green, *Rose* in pink, *Angela* in orange (all of the above with white skirts) and *Blonda* in light blue with a blue skirt. But these dolls were only part of the program for three years. The first caricature doll with a face made of felt was a clown. According to the 1936 catalog, it could be wiped clean since it was waterproof, the body had a soft stuffing and featured dangling arms and legs and it wore a suit made of blue cloth with patterns, a ruff around the collar and a clown's hat. It had a voice and brown glass eyes with black pupils. To follow the *Schwefelmännchen*, the *Glückspilz* (*Lucky Fellow*) was introduced in 1937 among the caricatures. During the same year, *Mat*, the sailor, was produced, measuring 35cm (14in), with a head made of pressed felt and dressed in a blue felt suit and blue hat. He was only available for one year. New Steiff dolls were advertised in the Novelty Catalog published in April 1937: "To continue the tradition of our highly popular Steiff doll we are now offering a new doll, perfectly manufactured and with beautiful expression. No head seam and made of pressed felt with glass eyes, the hair is made of mohair, woven into the head and styled to perfection. Underwear and outer wear are modeled after children's outfits and manufactured very carefully, using only the best of materials. Again, the dolls can be dressed and undressed. The body is made of high quality felt with dangling arms and jointed legs that enable the doll to stand or sit down. Height: 35cm (14in). With voice. Sold in individual box." At first, four versions were available:

— *Mella*, loose dress, pink coat and hat,
— *Rosemarie*, loose dress with blue pattern,
— *Heidi*, striped dress with belt,
— *Gudrun*, polka dot blouse, light blue skirt.

Every year new models were added. In 1938, couples in traditional costume were introduced: *Seppl* and *Lisl*, *Bärbl* and *Hansl* and the boys, *Frieder* and *Rudi*.

Larger versions in 43cm (17in) were also introduced. They were produced until the early 1940s and again after the war until 1952. During that year, however, the repertoire only included eight versions in 35cm (14in).

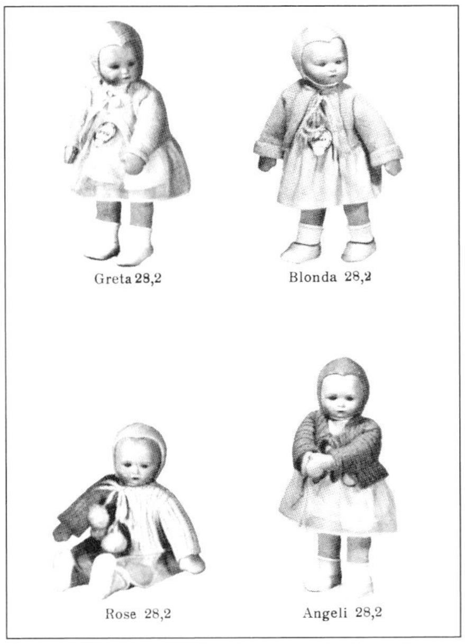

"Charakterpuppen" with celluloid heads made by Schildkröt, 28cm (11in), felt body with snap joints (legs), "Mommy" voice and in various outfits, after 1935 in the program only for a short time. Excerpt of the 1936/37 Steiff main catalog.

Typical felt dolls with faces made of pressed felt, 35cm (14in), burlap bodies, dangling arms and legs with disk joints made of felt, mohair wigs, glass eyes, squeeze voice, 1937-1952. These dolls were available in different dresses, suits and costumes so that war and post-war dolls can be found today in various outfits made of different materials and patterns. There were also a few models in 43cm (17in).
from left to right:
Hansl, *Mella*, *Frieder*, sitting doll with linen body (name unknown) and original wreath on head made of woolen flowers.
In back: Doll of unknown name.
right: *Cenzi*.

Clowns with faces made of pressed felt.
from left to right:
Caricature doll, clown (dangling doll), 35cm (14in), brown glass eyes with black pupil, felt body, linen suit, mohair wig, ears made of pressed felt (folding ears,) after 1936.
Clown, *Kasperl*, hand puppet as above, but clothing of different floral pattern, after 1936.
Caricature doll, clown, as above, but blue and white glass eyes with black pupils, ears painted, 1939-1941.

More than 20 years passed before Steiff finally produced more dolls in the early 1970s. A molding technique using foam was the production method that Steiff used for synthetic dolls (washable) and now offered for sale. Further toy dolls followed but they are not considered collectibles yet.

The Steiff event of the year was the new Margarete Steiff doll in 1987. Steiff was once again trying to take up the tradition of producing high-quality dolls to play with or to collect, a tradition that reaches back to 1892.

Certain models from the years before World War I were produced in a series of replicas. Since they were issued as limited editions, they are of great interest to the collector. This revival of an old tradition was a brilliant idea. Many new collectors of Steiff products or dolls with porcelain heads do not know that Steiff used to manufacture dolls. It is also a little known fact that the Steiff catalog of 1911/12 listed over 270 versions of dolls. Unfortunately, they are very rare in mint condition. Despite the fact that Steiff gained international reputation due to its production of teddy bears, the company has to be considered among the largest manufacturers of dolls in the world because of the production of a great variety of artistically highly valuable dolls.

Figures

Note: Unless indicated otherwise in the captions, the following main characteristics are valid for all figures:
— swivel head made of rubber/PVC,
— no voice,
— painted eyes.

In this chapter we would like to list the main characters that were produced with a rubber/PVC head. Animals with heads made of mohair or velvet are described in the respective chapters.

Figures with rubber/PVC heads were not available before the end of World War II. The legendary hedgehog, *Mecki*, "trademark" of the magazine *HöR ZU* stood at the very beginning. *Mecki* and his wife, *Micki* (named after Diehl film), were first listed in the catalog of 1951, both in 17, 28 and 50cm (7, 8 and 20in) with burlap bodies. The children, *Macki* (boy) and *Mucki* (girl), 12cm (5in), were introduced in 1953. Their bodies were made of rubber/PVC. The hairline of early models runs straight across the forehead. As early as 1952, however, the hairline comes to a point in the middle of the forehead. *Meckis* and *Mickis* between 1951 and 1953 have much darker faces than the later models. The shirt patterns in 1951/52 were slightly different: they changed from red and white stripes to checkered. Blouses changed from large patterned to finely checkered and skirts from red and white patterned to red and black checkered.

The rubber heads of figures made before the 1950s often show fissures and are porous. This is simply a sign of old age; deterioration of the old rubber that cannot be prevented or stopped. During the late 1950s and early 1960s, rubber was gradually phased out and heads and bodies were made of PVC. Figures made of PVC preserve a lot better. After 1962, *Mecki* and *Micki* were also sold as bendable figures in 9cm (4in). From the mid 1960s-on, they were available dressed in soccer outfits. They were called *Fuba*. The version dressed in a dirndl was called *Alpa*. The funny-looking *Mackys* were only for sale in 1978. They were dressed and bendable *Meckis* in 10cm (4in), depicting different professions or sports. *Mecki* is one of the most successful sales items produced by Steiff after the war and is considered very common.

Family of *Meckis*
from left to right:
back: Parents.
Mecki, 28cm (11in), early version made of old rubber quality, straight hairline, striped shirt in red and white, wooden pipe varnished with white color, arms and legs jointed with disks, flag: Made in US Zone, after 1951.
Micki, version as above, but blouse with large checkerd pattern.
Mecki and *Micki*, 28cm (11in), typical model as sold after 1952. Clearly visible is the pointed hairline. Both have a small pocket with a printed identification card, e.g. "Name: Micki. Profession: Wife of Mecki, editorial hedgehog of 'HöR ZU,' the largest German magazine! Residence: Everywhere, but especially in the hearts of the readers."
front: Children.
Macki (boy,) 12cm (5in), head and body made of rubber or PVC, bendable arms, after 1953.
Mucki (girl,) description as above, but girl's outfit.
Mecki and *Micki*, 17cm (7in), same version as parents in the back, right side, but inflexible legs, after 1952.
Micki and *Mecki* as bendable figures, 9cm (4in), after 1962.
Bendable *Meckis*, *Fuba* and *Alpa*, 9cm (4in), dressed in soccer gear or dirndl, respectively, after 1964.

top:
Dwarves: *Gucki* (burgundy cap), *Lucki* (bright red cap) and *Pucki* (dark green cap). All of them with swivel head and rubber bodies, felt and linen clothing, mohair beards, 13cm (5in), after 1953/54-1973, common in this size.

bottom:
from left to right:
Clown, *Clownie*, 14 and 19cm (6 and 7in), red felt hat, green felt vest, only in those two sizes and during 1954/55, rare.
Moritz and *Max*, 11 and 10cm (4in), bendable figures, after 1962.
Clown, *Clownie*, 19 and 14cm (7 and 6in) black felt hat, blue linen trousers, 1954-1975, also in 43cm (17in), 1953-1975.
Sailor, *Mat*, 19cm (7in), with accordion, also in 14cm (6in), both only in 1954. Rare in mint condition, since only available in old rubber quality.

left:
Fire fighter, 43cm (17in), rubber head with glass eyes, hands and clothing made of felt, rubber helmet deformed, mid 1950s, rare. Fire fighter, 37cm (15in), head made of PVC, painted eyes, felt clothing, hands made of synthetic velours, 1980s. Advertisement for Ziegler, manufacturer of fire equipment.

right:
Santa Claus, 13cm (5in), red felt clothing. Made in 13 and 18cm (5 and 7in) from 1954 until 1962 and in 31cm (12in) between 1953 and 1962.
Neander, the caveman, 13cm (5in), clothing made of brown mohair resembling fur. Single plastic tooth on a string, worn around the neck, also in 19cm (7in), after 1968.
Maggi Cook, Fridolin, 17cm (7in), advertisement, mid to end of the 1950s, rare.
Stonsdorf Dwarf, 13cm (5in), advertisement, green apron with imprint: "Echt Stonsdorf," early 1960s.

During 1953/54, the funny dwarves *Gucki, Lucki* and *Pucki* were introduced. They were available in 13, 18 and 30cm (5, 7 and 12in), as well as in 55cm (22in) for decorative purposes. In the catalog of display animals, they were offered in 120cm (47in).

The smaller sizes have swivel heads made of rubber/PVC and the bodies of the dwarves measuring 13cm (5in) were also made of the same materials. The 18 and 30cm (7 and 12in) versions had bodies made of burlap. The arms of the 18cm (7in) version were jointed with disks and the legs were inflexible. The 30cm (12in) version had both arms and legs that were jointed with disks.

Another important figure was the clown, *Clownie*, issued in the mid 1950s in two versions. The rare version is wearing a green felt vest and was only offered for sale in 1954/55 in the sizes 14 and 19cm (6 and 7in). The version that was introduced in 1953/54, however, is common. This clown is wearing linen trousers. He was available in the sizes 14, 19 and 43cm (6, 7 and 17in) until 1975. The 43cm (17in) version had glass eyes and his head could not be turned.

Santa Claus was available in 13, 18 and 31cm (5, 7 and 12in) during 1953/54. His head was manufactured using the same mold that was used for the dwarves. For a very short time during the 1950s there was a cowboy in 12 and 17cm (5 and 7in) as well as *Larifari* (named after Diehl film) in 32cm (13in). The following figures stayed in the program a little longer: A shepherd in 35cm (14in), introduced in 1958. Another version, 19cm (7in), was added in 1969. *Cappy*, the dangling doll, measured 28cm (11in) and was available after 1963, and finally the sandman, *Sandy*, in 29cm (11in), available after 1965. *Max* and *Moritz*, bendable figures, as well, are considered less common. They were produced after 1962 in 10 and 11cm (4in), respectively. *Neander*, the caveman, was available in 13 and 19cm (5 and 7in) after 1968.

Advertisements are especially interesting to collectors since they were not part of the official sales program. There was, for example, *Fridolin, the Maggi Cook*, the *Stonsdorf Dwarf, Tele Maxl* and *Niki Tiki*. A fire fighter made of the old rubber quality in 43cm (17in) is also considered rare. He is very well equipped with tools and helmet. Steiff figures are very appealing due to their intricate and detailed clothing and their friendly facial expressions and characters.

Hand Puppets

Note: Unless otherwise indicated in the captions, the following main characteristics are valid for all hand puppets:
— Animal puppets are made of mohair,
— regular puppets faces are made of rubber/PVC,
— clothing made of felt or cotton fabric,
— years indicated refer to first year of publication in a Steiff catalog,
— lengths between 25 and 34cm (10 and 13in), mimic animals measure 40cm (16in).

Hand puppets were also called Kasperle puppets and many more names. At the beginning of this century, puppet players were still working in their profession, moving from one town to the next and performing their art. They were considered masters of a precious craft of great tradition. Only through the play do these puppets come to life since the player gives them heart and soul. The unmoving mask awaken with life and the silent puppet begins to speak. Reality is created, invisible and untouchable as it may be, it is still felt by every spectator as he watches.

In 1913, the first chimpanzees, bears, dog (*Charly*) and cats, all made of mohair, were introduced. In 1916, a fox with a closed mouth and a fox terrier were added.

During the early 1920s, chimpanzees with heads made of brown mohair and red felt dress were introduced. Towards the end of the 1920s, the collection was extended by adding dogs such as *Molly, Bully* and *Treff* and *Petsy Bear*. The chimpanzees, *Bully* and *Molly*, were available with voices for an additional fee. The voice could be activated with the playing hand during a performance. *Siamy* (Siamese cat) and *Teddy Baby* were added in the early 1930s. The Steiff catalog of 1936/37 listed a lion and a clown, both with a head made of pressed felt that could be wiped clean and a colorful dress. This was also the first time the term "Bi-Ba-Bo" was used to describe these Kasperl animals. Until the early 1940s, the repertoire remained unchanged. Only three Bi-Ba-Bo animals were added in 1949: a chimpanzee, a teddy bear and a lion. In the early 1950s, however, a rabbit, *Molly* (dog), a cat, *Sarras* (boxer) and a new model of a fox terrier were added. The first hand puppets with heads made of rubber/PVC were introduced in the mid 1950s. Those were *Mecki*, the hedgehog and *Gucki*, the dwarf as well as new animals, a tiger, *Bully* (post-war version) and a black tom cat. During the *1960s* and *1970s*, a large spectrum of new models of animals and figures was

from left to right:
1st row: *Teddy* 1951, bear *Seebär* 1972, *Teddy Baby* 1931-1935. After 1936 listed as *Teddy*.
2nd row: Clown *Clownie* 1967, Dwarf *Gucki* 1953, chimney sweep *Blacky* 1964, *Santa Claus* 1955.
3rd row: *Mecki* 1954, multi-colored monkey *Mungo* 1958, chimpanzee, mohair head, red felt dress, 1936, chimpanzee (*Jocko*-type) 1913.

left:
from left to right:
1st row: Pekinese *Peky* 1963, dog *Mopsy* 1960, boxer *Sarras,* 1951, dog *Bully* 1952, poodle *Snobby* 1956.
2nd row: *Scotty* 1933, dachshund *Lumpi* 1965, fox terrier *Foxy* 1951, dog *Cockie* 1957.
3rd row: Mimic animals *Dally, Tessie, Biggie*, only in 1958/59, rare.
4th row: dog *Molly* 1927, cat 1913, black tom cat 1952, cat (inside of ears made of felt) 1959. A similar cat was made during the 1930s, inside of ears made of mohair plush.

middle:
from left to right:
1st row: squirrel *Hopsi* (from primer "Hopsi") 1962, rabbit 1950, wolf *Loopy* 1956, fox with open mouth 1952, fox *Smardy* 1964.
2nd row: lion made of wool plush 1936, young lion 1951, lion *Leo* 1958, tiger 1952.
3rd row: penguin 1967, raven *Hucky* 1962, rooster 1968, hen 1968, owl *Wittie* 1955.
4th row: snake *Snaky*, only 1965-1967, parrot *Lora* 1967, crocodile *Gaty* 1956.

right:
from left to right:
1st row: *Hand Happy* 1961, devil 1973, *Maxifant* and *Minifant* 1975.
2nd row: *Kasper* 1971, robber 1973, policeman 1973.
3rd row: witch 1968, *Hänsel* 1968, *Gretel* 1968, *Lulia* 1973.
4th row: frog *Froggy* 1963, princess 1968, king 1968, sorcerer 1968.

introduced. The mimic animals *Tessie, Dally* and *Biggie* are rare since they were only produced in 1958/59.

Zipper animals, *Zotty, Nauty* (polar bear), a panda bear and a rabbit were manufactured between the mid 1960s and early 1970s. The body consists of a pocket with a zipper, making it possible to use those animals as hand puppets.

In most cases, hand puppets are bought as marginal items in a collection of Steiff animals or to complete and decorate a doll collection. They are not highly valued since most models are common. Exceptions are: *Blacky*, the chimney sweep, *Snaky*, the hand snake and *Sneba*, the snowman. Those are very hard to find. Not very common are *Peky*, the Pekinese, *Lumpi*, the dachshund and *Santa Claus*. Hand puppets made of mohair are very striking and thanks to the great spectrum of species, there are no boundaries to the players' imagination. A combination of hand puppet animals and dolls, whose heads are mainly made of rubber or PVC, can make for a very sizeable collection. The hand puppet dolls of the 1970s are hardly considered collectibles but they certainly add to a collection of hand puppet animals.

Woolen Miniatures

Woolen miniatures were an inexpensive alternative that were sold by Steiff from the early 1930s-on. They were made of very fine wool, Nomotta, that could be formed and was wrapped around wire frames.

The first woolen miniatures appeared in the supplementary catalog of 1931 as a novelty. Woolen birds, 8cm (3in), with wire feet and glass eyes were available in six different color combinations such as a mixture of orange and white. Beak and tail were made of felt. These birds were replaced in the mid 1930s by other species such as finch, sparrow, titmouse, woodpecker, robin and yellow hammer. Birds form the largest group among the woolen miniatures. A red and a black woodpecker, a swallow, a raven, ducks, a rooster, a hen, a parrot on a perch and a couple of warblers with a double-tone chirping voice whose chirping voice and picking motion were activated by pressing the bellows were introduced in the 1930s. Bird trees and branches and a bird house made of wood with natural varnish were sold, as well.

Lady bugs and June bugs, squirrels, dogs, cats, mice, elephants pigs and lambs were also available. There also was a large selection of different rabbits.

After World War II, various pre-war models were taken back into the program, among them robin, sparrow, titmouse, raven, duck. rooster, hen, little mouse and various rabbits. The bird house was also offered once again and two new models were added, one in the shape of a piggy bank with a slot in the roof.

Exotic birds and above were added in 1953. Around 1956/57, the feet were changed from wire to plastic in all birds except the raven, the duck, the rooster and the hen. They kept their wire feet until the early 1970s. Glass eyes were used until the late 1960s; then they were changed to plastic eyes. Woolen poodles (after 1955) were very popular from the late 1950s to the early 1960s. But besides the addition of this item, the collection remained basically unchanged. Woolen fish of the coral reef and humming birds were introduced in the late 1960s. Both animals were available as mobile. Various woolen miniatures were produced until the late 1970s.

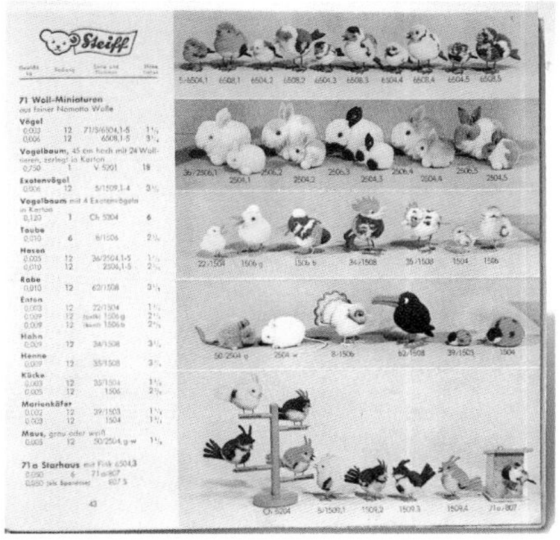

Collection of woolen miniatures around the mid 1950s. Excerpt of the Steiff main catalog, 1954/55.

left:
Rare woolen miniatures of the 1930s. Only the sparrow (middle, front) was produced even after World War II.

right:
from left to right: Yellow and red rabbit at attention, 8cm (3in), brown glass eyes with black pupils, whiskers, arms made of yellow felt, wire feet with felt slippers, after 1937.
White rabbit, 8cm (3in), white and black squinting eyes made of glass. Especially witty caricature of an albino rabbit, after 1938.
White and pink rabbit, 9cm (4in), at attention, pink glass eyes with red pupils, whiskers, after 1936. All of the above are woolen miniatures with ears made of felt and white wool pompon for a tail, very rare.

Wooden Toys and Vehicles

Very early on, the Steiff company recognized that certain accessories for the animals and teddy bears could be made very easily of wood. With the constant improvement and expansion of the wood shop within the company, the basis was created for the production of showpieces, animals on wooden wheels and wooden vehicles or furniture for dolls. Among the first wooden toys in the Steiff repertoire in 1911 were school furniture, furniture for dolls and equipment for the physical training within the barracks square. Ladders as accessories for the circus and balustrades for the arena, chairs and a platform for the orchestra were also made. Carts, handcarts and stagecoaches were added in 1915/16. Good plush was rare after World War I so Steiff expanded the selection of wooden toys. Many wooden toys are varnished in various colors such as pull-toys on eccentric wheels, wobbling figures, wooden trains and boxes of building blocks in natural finish. After 1921, scooters for children were a big success. Wooden planes, cars and streetcars with steering mechanisms were introduced during the mid 1920s.

Between 1928 and 1940, pedal cars made of sheet metals were offered for sale. Steiff produced those in-house. Many accessories were available such as horns, lamps, rear-view mirrors, windshields and much more. Some new models were produced by Steiff in the 1950s but were later removed from the program.

In the early 1930s, wooden toys such as Kubus, Entkett, horse-drawn handcarts and model planes were added. A rowing vehicle, Ruderrenner, was sold very successfully between 1937 and 1971. Wooden wheelbarrows were added in the mid 1930s. A wooden tank, Sand Tank, 34cm (13in), in camouflage paint, "makes clacking-noise when pulled," was only offered in the 1938 catalog. The first truck with steering mechanism was added in 1939. It was produced again in the 1950s and 1960s in various versions.

After World War II, good plush was again hard to come by, which again leads to a greater concentration on wooden toys. Handcarts were sold for government-issued wood stamps. These carts were the most important means of transporta-

Wooden toys were usually shipped in colorful cardboard boxes.
from left to right:
back: Cardboard box showing building blocks to build a town, 1957/58.
Cubes were available in many colors, described as "Hohlkubus" (hollow cube), "Wrfelkubus" (cube), "Satzkubus" (cube set) or "Kubusbox" (box of cubes) from the early 1930s until the early 1960s.
Sack with about 100 building blocks of colorful wax finish as displayed in foreground, after 1951.
"Hohlkubus" cardboard box, 1930s.

Steiff hoop, 60cm (24in) in diameter, stick missing, around 1937.
Hobbyhorse, length: 100cm (39in), leather reins, 1950s. Comparable models available as early as late 1920s.
Children's sports car "Corso," height: 70cm (30in), can be folded, disk wheels, 1946-1950, very rare.
Truck with steering, length: 75cm, steering wheel and wooden seat, rubber tires. Early version with painted radiator grille and headlights, after 1953, rare.
Chimpanzees (*Jocko*-type,) 25, 35 and 50cm (10, 14 and 20in), 1950s and 1960s.

tion in the years after the war. Corso 2870, the folding sports car for children was advertised for DM 24. — in a leaflet in 1947. Corso was very popular between 1946 and 1950. The 1950s and 1960s brought many sturdy toy vehicles that were very impressive. Various tractors and trailers, cage wagons and camping trailers for the circus, trucks, "Unimog," trailers to haul long trees, construction vehicles such as road rollers, concrete mixer and a dredging shovel, construction trailers and a traveling crane were introduced. Some models of this large series (width around 11-14cm [4-6in]) were still available in the early 1970s. A smaller series was introduced in 1968. These vehicles measured around 6-7cm (2-3in) in width. As in the large series, diggers, "Unimog," tractors, trailers and other vehicles were manufactured. Pull animals were added in 1968. They feature a natural varnish and have red wheels. They appear pale and expressionless since they were not painted. But only one year later, the version had been improved. In 1969, pull animals were made of natural wood and the markings were branded into the wood. Domestic and farm animals as well as animals of the wild were part of the program. A European bison 18cm (7in), a zebra 20cm (8in) and a cow showing especially beautiful markings.

Wooden toys are not yet very popular among most collectors. The fact that Steiff used to produce them is not very well known. But because of the careful finish and the detailed work, these toys make for a great section within a collection. Unfortunately, they are hard to find in mint condition because they were so popular. They also were usually played with outside the house, exposing them to the elements.

left:
Living wagon, 28cm (11in), roof can be removed. A matching cage wagon was available in the same size, both after 1955.
Wooden tractor, 20cm (8in) in length, steering mechanism, rubber tires, after 1953.
Trailer to haul long trees, loaded, 36cm (14in) in length, rubber tires, after 1961.
"Unimog," 23cm (9in) in length, steering mechanism, rubber tires, roof can be removed (available in various versions), windshield can be folded down, after 1956.

middle:
Horse-drawn handcart, 35cm (14in) in length, after 1934.
Finch, wobbling animal on eccentric wheels, 12cm (5in), colorful varnish, early 1920s.
"Stratosplan," catapult airplane, span: 14 and 20cm (6 and 8in), waterproof wings with steel frame, soft rubber nose in the shape of a bear head, after 1932.
Colorful cardboard box of a "Stratosplan," 1930s.

right:
Entkett, 32cm (13in) in length, colorful varnish, on eccentric wheels, from the early 1930s until early 1960s.
VW pickup truck with plastic top, 21cm (8in) in length, push steering, after 1960.
"Bimbahn," 35cm (14in) in length, colorful varnish, on eccentric wheels, 1950s. Already available during mid 1930s as "Bimmelbahn."

Handcart, 60cm (24in) in length, disk wheels, after 1950 available in various sizes. Chimpanzees (*Jocko*-type) in 35 and 60cm (14 and 24in), 1960s.
Bear head scooter, Flitzro 73, height: 73cm (29in), 1950s and 1960s. Steiff produced children's scooters as early as 1921.
"Ruderrenner" (rowing vehicle,) length: 80cm (31in), 1937-1971.
Chimpanzee "Jocko," 80cm (31in), US flag, 1953.

Curios and Other Items

In the first catalog of 1892 there were already items listed that differ from the regular toy animals and that are strange and unusual. One item that is worth mentioning is the princess play rug which is described as follows: "The figures are taken from the very popular storybook 'Struwelpeter.' They are made of colored pieces of felt with shades of wool and silk and sewn onto the rug. The effect is glamorous. If the rug is placed on the floor it makes for a soft padding and will also keep the little ones busy, much to every mother's delight."

Many more items that were both beautiful toys and had a practical use in the household were made around the turn of the century. Dachshunds as pincushions or table brushes, animals sewn onto small pillows as well as pot holders and egg warmers were among them. Coffeepot warmers in the shape of an animal head or a market woman, turkey or cook were very popular. A female cook was in the program for 36 years, from 1905 until 1940. A carnival cap was modeled after a parrot's head, available in many colors and sizes.

Another one of Richard Steiff's creations was the Steiff Roloplan in 1908. This was a folding kite made of cloth and without a tail. It created a stir at every aviation show and received many prizes, e.g in 1909 in Frankfurt, in 1910 in Scheveningen and in 1911 it even won the first prize and a diploma from the Aeroclub Belgique. Steiff used these prizes as advertisement and describes the kite as follows: "Roloplan, the kite, registered trademark, is the most perfect kite made of cloth. The ideal toy for kids and adults. It was designed aeronautically correct and ranks way above the paper kites. Its climbing ability with very little wind is without competition. It will not be harmed by the elements, folds into a small package and is easy to transport (each kite comes with a detailed and illustrated description)." The demand was so great during the first few years that a separate kite department had to be opened. Roloplan was available with a wing span of 120-360cm (47-142in) on two levels or 180-360cm (71-142in) on three levels. It was available with text to be used for advertising purposes. Each kite was tested in a flight above Giengen before it was shipped. This was a spectacle that delighted not only children. After 1911, a tripod was developed for Roloplan so that beautiful aerial pictures could be taken when the tripod was used in connection with a camera. During World War I, the Roloplan was even used for military reconnaissance flights. It was offered as "Military Roloplan" in 1916: "...especially resistant to the elements. Many units use it very successfully for target practice." A picture in the catalog was proof of the high load-carrying capacity of the Steiff Roloplan. Three kites, for example, were able to lift up one adult. The catalog points out that these experiments are potentially deadly and that they should not be copied!

left:
from left to right:
Caricature of a dachshund used as table brush, length: 25cm (10in), body made of dark brown velvet, virgin wool and excelsior stuffing, black shoe-button eyes, brush on dog's stomach made from horsehair, around 1900, very rare.
Dachshund pincushion, height: 5cm (2in), length: 9cm (4in), dark brown velvet, virgin wool stuffing, black bead eyes, snout decoration made of red thread, oversized tail, around 1900, very rare.
Dark red velvet pincushion within pink wooden frame with perch, height: 11cm (4in). Two sparrows on perch, 4cm (1.57in), made of Nomotta wool with wire feet, straw in beak, after 1936, rare.

middle:
from left to right:
Three car dolls.
Lucky chimney sweep, 18cm (7in), face and hands made of light beige felt, body and top hat made of black felt, arms and legs bendable due to inserted wire, painted hair, wooden ladder with black varnish, broom missing, 1937-1940, rare.
Chimney sweep, 20cm (8in), body made of black velvet. Face, hands, feet and top hat made of felt, eyes and mouth embroidered, black button nose, red mohair wig, red scarf, metal ladder with black varnish, only 1950, rare.
Policeman, 20cm (8in), face, hands and feet made of felt, body with uniform and cap made of velvet, eyes and mouth embroidered, only in 1950, rare.

right:
from left to right:
Roloplan kite, wing span: 90cm (35in), two levels of linen fabric, wooden sticks, also available in spans of 100 and 120cm (39 and 47in), after 1951.
Roloplan kite, wing span: 210cm (83in), two levels of linen fabric, bamboo sticks, early 1920s.
Eagle kite, wing span: 122cm (48in), linen, wooden sticks, after 1954.

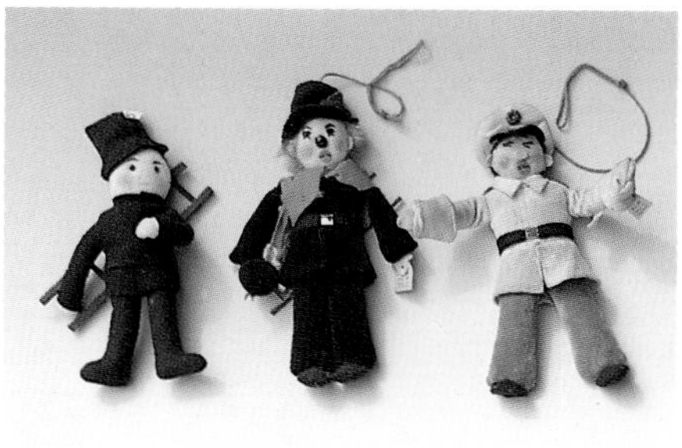

left:
Pincushion made of green velvet framed in silk cord, a lion is lying on the cushion, height: 16cm (6in). Body and face made of velvet, mane made of mohair, black shoe-button eyes. Nose, snout and claws painted with brush, soft stuffing, after 1913, very rare in untouched condition.

right:
Plant louse (also called bacillus or bacteria).
Peck, 10cm (4in), body made of green mohair, tightly stuffed, wire arms and legs wrapped in green felt. Gloves and slippers made of red felt. Black rubber pants. Mouth made of hard rubber with straw made of glued cardboard, 5cm (2in), individual black felt hairs on his head, black glass eyes with underlying white imitation leather, elastic string with loop to hang the figure, advertisement in the mid 1950s, very rare.

When World War I started, war toys were produced for the first time so that the young heroes would be able to copy their fathers' deeds. They could be equipped with field packs and many other accessories to play war, such as rifles made of wood with a barrel made of sheet metal, bayonets, uniform vests made of felt and tobacco pouches in the shape of pants or caps.

In 1929, Steiff published a storybook with the title: *Teddy und Verwandte reisen durch die Lande* (*Teddy and His Relatives Are Traveling Across the Country*). *Teddy*, *Bully* and *Molly* are the protagonists, but many other Steiff animals get their share of the action.

On the last pages of the 1933 catalog, an offer of "Nationale AusrÜstung" (national outfits) was described without illustrations. Brown shirts and pants, berets, triangular scarves, leather belts, belt buckles and shoulder straps were the "Hitler Jungvolk." For the Hitler Jugend, the SA and the SS, the same items were offered in adult sizes, with leather items of higher quality and silver plated metal.

Talisman and mascots was one of Steiff's favorite topics. There are funny and unique car dolls. Lucky witches and chimney sweeps were available after the mid 1930s and cowboys, chimney sweeps, sailors, negroes and policemen during the early 1950s.

Animals and figures from film and television were made of plush during the late 1960s. These are often strange figures that require a lively imagination concerning both the materials and the production.

Animals of the imagination and figures from outer space are in great demand among children who are not necessarily looking for a cuddly animal but rather for something that will guarantee satisfaction in imaginative play. They were usually useful for advertisement purposes for a short time and as a rule did not remain in the program for a long time. Even more recent items of the 1980s are already sought-after rarities.

left:
Lion, standing as figure, we call him "Leoli," 28cm (11in), same body shape as *Mecki*, dressed in beige and brown loden suit, silk tie with pink pattern, blue shirt. Head, mane and oversized tail made of mohair. Tail is tied to the right arm with a pink silk ribbon, brown and black glass eyes, red and black embroidered nose/snout decoration.
Frog Prince, length: 50cm (20in), green and brown velvet, hand-painted, small crown made of felt, soft stuffing, voice, red velvet cape with white mohair collar, large brown and black glass eyes, arms with disk joints, oversized dangling legs.
Both in early 1950s, never produced in series.

right:
White *Original Teddys* visit the *Little Green Man on Mars*.
Teddys from left to right:
front row: 10cm (4in) 1910, 10cm (4in) 1955, 13cm (5in) 1922.
back row: 18cm (7in) 1922, 32cm (13in) 1935, 18cm (7in) 1922.
Little Green Man, IFS Brussels, 35cm (14in), 1982, rare. Teddy bear on his lap: 10cm (4in) 1936.

left:
Rooster head as pot holder, 20cm (8in), hen's head, 16cm (6in), egg warmers, rooster heads, 14cm (6in), hen's head, 12cm (5in). White felt, crest made of red felt, black glass eyes with underlying felt, after 1911, rare.
Female cook as coffeepot warmer, 43cm (17in), hands and face with horizontal and vertical seam, made of felt, black eyes with underlying felt, head covered with thin black cotton fabric, top made of red felt with black polka dots, head and arms attached with disks. Thick green felt skirt with soft stuffing, white cotton apron, from 1905 until 1940, rare in mint condition.

right;
"For the little heroes of World War I." field pack, height: 28cm (11in), wooden frame covered with brown linen fabric, cover made of brown mohair, flaps and straps made of light brown leather with stenciled Steiff signature, 1916/17, very rare.
The little "stowaway" is not part of the original equipment; he is simply hiding.

Brontosaurus, *Brosus*, height: 15cm (6in), length: 34cm (13in), mohair, orange felt crest on his back, open mouth made of pink felt, green and black squinting eyes made of glass, also available in 30cm (12in) height and 70cm (28in) length. Not as common as dinosaur *Dino* to his right.
Dino, height: 30cm (12in), length: 70cm (28in), green and black squinting eyes, voice, ears made of yellow felt, crest on his back pointed and made of mohair, body made of mohair, also available in 35cm (14in) length and 4m (13ft) (showpiece).
A dinosaur at attention was also produced: Tyrannosaurus *Tysus*, 20 and 43cm (8 and 17in). All dinosaurs were made around 1958 in very small numbers, only for sale in the U.S., very rare.

Animals from the Walt Disney movie *Jungle Book*.
left: *Shir Khan*, the tiger, 35cm (14in), Dralon, swivel head, after 1968.
back, middle: *King Louie*, the monkey, 25cm (10in), Dralon/Crylor, swivel head, dangling arms, after 1968.
right, middle: *Baloo*, the bear, 40cm (16in), Dralon, soles made of brown imitation leather with felt claws, swivel head, felt nose, arms attached with disks, inflexible legs, after 1968.
front, middle: *Hathi*, the elephant baby, 20cm (8in), Dralon, open mouth made of felt, inflexible head, after 1968.
right, front: *Bagheera*, the panther, 25cm (10in), woven coat, inflexible head and legs, 1980.

Replicas

Many collectors want to achieve an older and complete collection by looking for toys from before the two world wars. They have to realize that those toys are becoming increasingly more difficult to find. And if they are found, they are often sold for unrealistically high prices. The collection fever that started in America and reached Germany, by way of England, is the reason for the incredible increase in prices.

The Steiff company took advantage of this wave of nostalgia and decided to create a series of replicas. Animals that used to be popular and successful many years ago were now celebrating a comeback. These replicas are a stimulation to the collectors' market since they usually are issued in limited numbers, sometimes accompanied by a certificate, numbered and in a cardboard box. Replicas are made, if possible, according to the same pattern and with similar materials and stuffing as the original animals or teddy bears. All old originals are displayed in the Steiff museum in Giengen or at least listed in the archives. Beginners among the collectors often buy these replicas to bring the touch of old toys into their homes. This facilitates the entrance into the field — a hobby that has led to a worldwide search for old plush animals today. Many collectors were hooked on collecting after they saw the replicas.

To celebrate the 100th anniversary of the Steiff company in 1980, the first replica, the *Original Teddy* of 1903, was produced. The old pattern was copied. He was stuffed with excelsior, had glass eyes and was made of high-quality mohair. It is very questionable, however, whether the first teddy bears really looked this way. A special feature was that for the first time, a bear was produced in a limited edition, 6000 pieces for Germany and 5000 for the U.S.A. This teddy bear is called Papa Bear among collectors. At first, it was ignored in Germany since the wave of teddy bear collecting was only just coming across the ocean at that time. Today, however, this teddy bear is considered to be the most wanted and most highly priced replica. This teddy bear introduced the phrase: "The investment of the man in the street." Even if no plush shares are traded anywhere and even though there are no official exchange rate reports, collectors still know that this replica appreciates considerably and that the trend has not stopped yet.

Some replicas were made exclusively for sale in the United States. They were listed in special catalogs and often those items are hardly known in Germany and almost impossible to obtain. During the last few years, these items have increased. It is obvious that such items are of the greatest interest to the collector. Those are the most wanted and sought-after items. These items were either produced in small numbers or they could only be ordered during a limited time. Replicas are often introduced in America one year before they are publicized in Germany. The small difference between those items lies in the certificates issued in either German or English and the writing on the cardboard boxes.

The three oldest Steiff replicas: from left to right:
Replicas 1903 (*Mother and Child*), issued in 1981, only for sale in the USA. Mommy, 38cm (15in), child 15cm (6in), jointed, both with soft stuffing, black plastic eyes, no voice. The mother is carrying her small child in an orange scarf. Rare in Germany.
Replica 1903 (*Papa Bear*), issued in 1980, first Steiff replica. 43cm (17in), jointed, yellow mohair, excelsior stuffing, black glass eyes, no voice. Rare in original condition (cardboard box and certificate).
Replica 1902/03, *Richard Steiff Teddy*, issued in 1983, third Steiff replica. 32cm (13in), jointed, gray mohair, soft stuffing, black plastic eyes, tilt voice, not common.

German collectors are wondering why certain replicas are made exclusively for the American market and are never sold in German toy stores. Firstly, when such a decision is made, the manufacturer has to keep in mind economic reasons and marketing considerations. The American importer can, therefore, order certain products to be made exclusively for him or he can have them protected for one year. This leads to a more active and lively collectors' market since the new collection is expected with great excitement every year. And last, but not least, friendships between collectors from both countries that started with the exchange of special replicas are continued and expanded. The first replica made exclusively for sale in the United States in 1981 is, therefore, a much desired object. It is a "Mommy and Baby Set," mother and baby with an orange scarf. It was designed on the occasion of the 101st birthday of the Steiff company and appeared in a limited edition of 8000 pieces. It is often confused with the "Giengen Teddy Set."

Another important replica is the *Richard Steiff Teddy* of 1902/03 which was produced in 1983 in the limited number of 10,000 pieces worldwide.

The special replica program for collectors has been expanded annually since 1980 by adding further items. Depending on the numbers produced, they disappear very quickly. In the beginning, some of the objects were made in large numbers. Sales were slow and collectors were disappointed because the animals were too common. Today, the collector very often does not even get a chance to see the replica due to the very low production numbers of some of the items. They are all sold before they even reach the regular toy market. An example of this phenomenon was the polar bear of 1909 who was the collectors' favorite in 1987. Many new collectors also are unaware of earlier replicas. The chart on page 157 lists years, names, item numbers, sizes and numbers made of all German replicas produced between 1980 and 1989. Almost all of those were also available in America.

A replica is not always an exact copy of the original. When comparing the replica *Bully* (1986) with the original of 1927, one notices that the replica was missing the ruff around the neck (typical for those days) and the collar tag with metal edge. The pattern used as basis for the replica must have been a *Bully* from the early 1930s. *Teddy Rose's* replica was stuffed with excelsior instead of the soft and light kapok stuffing of the original in 1925.

The trend to collect Steiff animals, originals or replicas is still growing. They are not only bought as pure investments, but mainly because of a collector's passion or as reminders of the "good old days."

Summary Steiff Replicas 1980-1989

Year	Name	Item No.	Size cm (in)	Replica of	Number of Items Issued	
1980	Steiff Original Teddy	0153/43	43 (17)	1903	6,000	CCB
1983	Richard Steiff Teddy	0150/32	32 (13)	1902/03	10,000	CB
1984	Felt Elephant	0080/08	8 (3)	1880	10,000	CB
	Tumbler Bear	0082/20	20 (8)	1894	9,000	CB
	Lion Leo, lying	0111/21	21 (8)	1956	—	—
	Lion Leo, lying	0111/35	35 (14)	1955	—	—
	Giengen Teddy Set	0162/00	—	1906	16,000	CB
1985	Penguin	0105/17	17 (7)	1928	8,000	CB
	Bear on Wheels	0085/12	12 (5)	1905	12,000	CB
	Dicky Bear	0172/32	34 (13)	1930	20,000	CCB
	Nikki Rabbit	0134/22	22 (9)	1952	3,500	—
	Nikki Rabbit	0134/28	28 (11)	1952	2,500	—
	Teddy Bear, golden	0165/38	38 (15)	1909	—	—
	Teddy Bear, golden	0165/51	51 (20)	1909	—	—
1986	Tabby Cat, lying	0104/10	10 (4)	1928	6,000	CB
	Bully Dog	0101/14	14 (6)	1927	6,000	CB
	Teddy Clown	0170/32	32 (13)	1926	10,000	CCB
1987	Polar Bear	0090/11	11 (4)	1909	3,900	CB
	Jackie Bear	0190/25	25 (10)	1953	10,000	CCB
	Betty Tennis Lady	9100/45	45 (18)	1913	3,000	CCB
	Gentleman in Frock Coat	9102/50	50 (20)	1914	3,000	CCB
1988	Duck	0081/14	14 (6)	1892	4,000	CB
	Dutch Rabbit	0095/17	17 (7)	1911	4,000	CB
	Teddy Bear, blonde	0166/25	25 (10)	1909	—	—
	Teddy Bear, blonde	0166/35	35 (14)	1909	—	—
	Teddy Bear, blonde	0166/43	43 (17)	1909	—	—
	Teddy Rose	0171/41	41 (16)	1925	10,000	CCB
	Farmer's Wife	9110/43	43 (17)	1912	3,000	CCB
	Farmer Joerg	9112/45	45 (18)	1915	3,000	CCB
1989	Pig w. Mechan. in Neck	0091/14	14 (6)	1909	4,000	CB
	Fox	0093/12	12 (5)	1910	4,000	CB
	Wiwag w. Teddy Bear	0132/24	24 (9)	1924	4,000	CB
	Donkey w. Mech. in Neck	0126/20	20 (8)	1931	4,000	CB
	Jumbo Elephant	0125/24	24 (9)	1932	4,000	CB
	Baby Bear on cart	0135/20	20 (8)	1939	4,000	CB
	Teddy Bear, black	0173/40	40 (16)	1907	4,000	CCB
	Jackie Bear	0190/35	35 (14)	1953	4,000	CCB
	Coloro Clown	9130/43	43 (17)	1911	3,000	CCB

C = with Certificate
CB = with Cardboard Box

Afterword

— Grandma Bear, where did we teddy bears come from?
— The questions you sometimes ask, Pezi! I can only remember that I was born a long, long time ago in Giengen. There was a giant pile of teddy bears and I was right in the middle of it. We were looked at very carefully and then a button was attached to our ears. That hurt a little. Then we were packed into cardboard boxes and the railroad took us into the world. I ended up in a toy store in Frankfurt and was bought by a woman. For quite some time I was lying inside my box until finally, underneath a tree with many candles, small arms were holding me tightly. I have wonderful memories of the many years with that human child.

One day, Uncle Robert came from America and he brought Robby along, a very big bear who had many stories to tell. He told me that teddy bears are in other countries, too. He told me of a friend of his in America who was born in the candy store in Brooklyn that belonged to the Mitchtoms. Pretty soon candy was no longer in demand, but bears still were. So the Mitchtoms founded a bear factory. Robby had even heard of teddy bears in Russia who had accompanied astronauts on their flight into space as their mascots. And for the Olympic Games, Mischa, the bear was designed.

Very famous bears with a button in their ears were sitting on President Theodore Roosevelt's table among glasses and plates, according to Robby. Everybody wanted to know their names. Nobody was familiar with it so they were given the President's nickname, Teddy.

Robby had already traveled a lot and had even seen English and French bears. Once he had a terrible fight with a teddy bear who claimed that his great-grandfather used to live even before 1860 in the home of the bear manufacturer Nicolas Schanne in Paris, on Bear Street (Rue aux ours). Robby did not want to believe that.
— And what IS the truth, Grandma Bear?
— Well, Pezi, if only we knew that. Almost everywhere, even in faraway countries, bears were made and we are related to many of them whose fathers are not quite as famous as ours. Many bears do not have a name because nobody ever wrote anything about them. After all these many years and the many tales that were handed down through generations of bears, even people do not know exactly anymore what really happened back then. But why is that so important for you to know? Every teddy bear is beautiful and wants to be loved. Unfortunately, some of us were thrown away because we were dirty or broken. Fortunately, this practically never happens anymore these days. It is something very special to be an old teddy bear. Thank goodness people have realized that just in time.

Look, Pezi, how beautiful it is here. Be happy that you have many more happy years ahead of you as a part of a collection.

Bibliography

Anka, Georgine/Gauder, Ursula: Die deutsche Puppenindustrie, Verlag Puppen & Spielzeug, Stuttgart 1978.
Fahl, J. Dr. Dipl.-Hdl.: Textilwaren im Verkauf, Winklers Verlag, Darmstadt 1959.
Hennig, Claire: Der Teddybär, in: Puppen & Spielzeug 3/84, Verlag Puppen & Spielzeug, Stuttgart 1984.
Pistorius, Rolf und Christel: Seltene Steiff-Tiere, in: Puppen & Spielzeug 2/88, Verlag Puppen & Spielzeug, Stuttgart 1988.
Pistorius, Rolf und Christel: Neu und trotzdem alt - Repliken und ihre historischen Vorbilder, in: Puppen & Spielzeug, Heft 6, Verlag Puppen & Spielzeug, Duisburg 1989.
Pistorius, Rolf und Christel: Neu und trotzdem alt - Die Aktie aus USA, in: Puppen & Spielzeug, Heft 8, Verlag Puppen & Spielzeug, Duisburg 1989.
Wallendor, Karl: Von der Nähmaschine zur Spielwarenfabrik, in: Brenztal-Bote vom 15.11.1930, Festausgabe, 50 Jahre Spielwarenfabrik, Giengen a.d.Brenz 1930.

Von der Nähmaschine zur Spielwarenfabrik, Festschrift zum 50jährigen Jubiläum der Fa. Margarete Steiff GmbH, Giengen a.d.Brenz 1930.
Die Spielwarenindustrie, Verhandlungen und Berichte des Unterausschusses fÜr allgemeine Wirtschaftsstruktur, 19. Band, Verlag E.S. Mittler & Sohn, Berlin 1930.
Die Entwicklung der Spielwarenfabrik, in: Brenztal-Bote vom 5.5.1955, Festausgabe zum 75jährigen Jubiläum der Fa. Margarete Steiff GmbH, Giengen a.d.Brenz 1955.
Die Wiege des Teddybären, Festschrift zum 75jährigen Jubiläum der Fa. Margarete Steiff GmbH, Giengen a.d.Brenz 1955.
Geschichte und Gegenwart einer Marke, Festschrift zum 100jährigen Jubiläum der Fa. Margarete Steiff GmbH, Giengen a.d.Brenz 1980.
Steiff-Katalog 1892, Reproduktion der Fa. Margarete Steiff GmbH, Giengen a.d.Brenz 1985.

Further sources were the Steiff main catalogs, supplementary catalogs and advertisement leaflets and brochures as well as Steiff advertisements between 1894 and 1989 taken from our private archives.

Index